New Book

DATE DUE

D1307326

Guide to the Arts of the Americas

GUIDE TO THE ARTS

PRE-COLUMBIAN ART
Consultant: Gillett Griffin

AMERICAN INDIAN ART
Consultant: Peter T. Furst

Edited, designed, and produced by MARSHALL LEE

OF THE AMERICAS

Harmer Johnson

RIZZOLI
NEW YORK

First published in the United States of America
in 1992 by RIZZOLI INTERNATIONAL PUBLICATIONS INC.
300 Park Avenue South, New York, NY 10010

An International Archive of Art Book

ACKNOWLEDGEMENTS

Gratitude in great measure is due to the many collectors, dealers, and institutions who contributed photographs and access to their works for reproduction in this book, particularly Spencer Throckmorton, New York and Sante Fe; W.E. Channing, Santa Fe; and André Emmerich, New York. The captions in the illustration sections include acknowledgement of the owners of individual works where appropriate. The illustrations in the text pages are reproduced by courtesy of the following: American Museum of Natural History, New York: 41 bottom; Bonnie and Rex Arrowsmith, Santa Fe: 145 bottom; Tyrone Campbell, Santa Fe: 141 bottom; Millard Holbrook, Santa Fe: 25 right top, 151 top; Museo Regional de Antropologia, Jalapa, Veracruz: 37 bottom; Museo Nacional de Antropologia Mexico City: 40 bottom; New York State Museum: 26 left top, 151 bottom; Peabody Museum, Yale University: 26 right bottom; The Art Museum, Princeton University: 12 left; Etnografiska Museet, Stockholm: 20 right bottom; George Shaw, Aspen: 27 left bottom.

Where no owner's name is given, the work is in a private collection. Note that the indicated locations of works are as of February 1992.

Library of Congress Cataloging-in-Publication Data

Johnson, Harmer. / Guide to the arts of the Americas / Harmer Johnson;
    edited, designed, and produced by Marshall Lee.
        p.   cm.
        Includes bibliographical references (p.   ) and index.
        Contents: Precolumbian art / consultant, Gillett Griffin—
    American art / consultant, Peter T. Furst.
        ISBN 0-8478-1597-8
        1. Indians—Art—Guidebooks. 2. Indians—Antiquities—Collectors
    and collecting—Guidebooks. 3. Indians—Museums—Guidebooks.
    4. Art—Forgeries—America. 5. Art thefts—America. 6. America—
    Antiquities—Guidebooks. 7. America—Guidebooks. I. Lee, Marshall, 1921—II. Title.
        E59.A7J64 1992
STATON 704'.0397—dc20   92-8449
                                                          CIP

Printed and bound in Italy

Contents

Preface

ON THE QUESTION OF COLLECTING

The more intense a controversy becomes, the more the advocates of each side tend to argue in oversimplified generalities and neglect significant distinctions. Thus the argument deteriorates until it is all but impossible to resolve rationally and fairly. The recent debate over the morality of collecting the art of non-Western cultures of the Western Hemisphere, and certain other ancient and/or tribal cultures, is a victim of this process. Worse yet, emotion has often replaced reason in arguments. Following is an attempt to find solutions based on mutual concern, balance, and reason.

On the one hand, there are those who believe that all such collecting is immoral, antithetical to scholarship, and/or illegal. Others feel that collecting some objects under some conditions is valid morally, culturally, and legally—in terms of legal philosophy if not statutes. Individuals on both sides differ somewhat in their positions. The general public probably accepts the anticollecting view, which is the one that is presented most sympathetically in the press. Political support then follows.

To a large extent the argument against collecting is influential because its proponents often promote it very aggressively. They also tend to express themselves intemperately, customarily referring to those in favor of collecting as "looters", "grave robbers", and "criminals", since many objects in museums and private collections were originally found in tomb sites by excavators who sold the articles in the art market, often flouting local laws. Such inflammatory epithets obscure the real issues and unfairly malign art professionals and collectors, who sincerely believe their views to be at least as legitimate as those of their opponents. (It may be argued that archaeologists also are "grave robbers" who take objects from tombs for their own professional purposes.)

What, then, are the issues, and what may fairly be said in favor of each side? The issues vary somewhat according to the cultures involved, but this discussion will be limited to the subjects of this book—Pre-Columbian and American Indian art. Nevertheless, our range is wide enough to encompass most, if not all, of the relevant principles.

There are three groups who oppose collecting: (1) scientists (archaeologists, ethnographers, anthropologists) who contend that the existence of a collecting market promotes the loss of some scientifically interesting information through the destructive excavations by nonscientists; (2) governments of countries in which ancient artifacts are to be found, which contend that such artifacts are the property of the government (the national patrimony claim); and (3) contemporary members of ancient cultures, who object to the acquisition by outsiders of their religious artifacts. The arguments are discussed below, with some proposals for resolving the controversies.

THE SCIENCE CLAIM

Certainly it is true that most private excavators of ancient objects are unconcerned about what their excavations may reveal of historical or scientific value, and they usually destroy the informative aspects of these sites. This is deplorable and regrettable. But the question remains, does this circumstance justify the abolition of collecting? The answer has two parts:

First, it should be possible to manage things so that the interests of both science and art are served. For example, instead of outlawing private excavations, let them be licensed by the government and supervised by qualified persons. This would allow the discovery of both marvelous works of art to be enjoyed by many *and* information of interest to scientists and historians. The practical realization of such a plan would be difficult and imperfect, but not impossible. It is logical to suppose that those who risk prison in illegal pursuit of salable objects would welcome being relieved of this hazard by paying a reasonable license fee and a small percentage of their income to the state, particularly if unrestricted activity resulted in more finds. A qualified supervisor (paid by the fees and the state's share of sales) would be present at the dig to ensure that the work is done properly and that any useful information is adequately recorded. In fact, this system would result in *more* information, since the number of sites excavated scientifically would be greatly increased.

Those who are familiar with conditions in the field would not expect such a licensing system to eliminate corruption or destructive exploration entirely. But illegal digging has been going on all over the world for thousands of years, and it is foolish to think that anything will stop it. How much better it would be to channel it as much as possible into socially useful ends. Indeed, because of the relatively small number of archaeologists and the limited time and money available to them, a very large number of ancient works of art would remain buried, perhaps forever (yielding neither art nor information), were it not for the economic incentive that collecting provides nonscientific excavators.

The second part of the answer involves balancing the value of knowledge and art. To the scientist, factual information is obviously of first importance, and surely the discovery of a cure for a terrible disease or a way to predict earthquakes would be worth the loss of many works of art. In practice, however, such discoveries are not likely in the excavations under con-

sideration. For the most part, the knowledge acquired in archaeological digging, if any, is only marginally interesting to the scientists and of such small value to others as to be negligible. The question is, then, is the possible loss of some information of small interest to the world at large, or even the occasional loss of some information of somewhat greater interest (the licensing system would reduce the possibility that information of real importance would be lost), worth depriving the world of the millions of aesthetically and spiritually enriching experiences provided by many fine works of art? Can we justify leaving a great work of art buried forever because bringing it to light might involve the possible loss of a small bit of knowledge about its origin?

Even if a work *is* brought out, it remains effectively lost to the world if it is kept in the cellar of a university archaeology department. There is no reason why, once the information it can yield has been scientifically recorded, it should not be sold (preferably to an art museum) and the proceeds used to finance further archaeological work.

Attention has been drawn to the distinction between art museums, some of whose holdings are enjoyed by the public (some works usually remain in storage), and private collectors. In principle it seems harder to justify the latter, but in practice the works they acquire tend eventually to be bought by or donated to museums. Thus, works of art pass through the hands of private collectors on their way to public exhibition; without the collectors these works might never become available. It is also common practice for collectors to lend works to museums for special exhibitions and to make their collections accessible to scholars.

THE PATRIMONY CLAIM

This is a complex and delicate subject, whose political, economic, and ethnic components are more significant than the ostensible ethical or

moral issues. Taken as a whole, the question cannot be dealt with successfully; it must be divided into its significant parts, with appropriate solutions found for each. There are five issues: (1) legitimacy of modern government claims to ancient cultures, (2) architectural monuments, (3) private property rights, (4) cultural importance distinctions, (5) international recognition of patrimony claims.

Government claims to ancient cultures

To the extent that such claims are made by governments on the American continents, they must be viewed in the light of the historical fact that these governments acquired their powers by conquest of the native peoples— who are the creators of the works claimed. While such governments have physical power over anything within their borders, it is hard to see how they can morally claim cultural patrimony for works taken by force from people they subjugated—and substantially destroyed.

Here it should be noted that moral claims by the people of the concerned cultures themselves have more validity than those of the governments to whose authority they are subjected. The moral rights of sovereign peoples, such as certain Indian tribes living in the United States, should be respected, but so should the legal rights of persons who have acquired tribal objects under some conditions. Also, distinctions must be made between objects that were integral to the culture and those that were made specifically for sale. In this area it is not good to generalize, other than to recognize the validity of cultural patrimony rights when properly claimed by sovereign peoples with respect to their own works.

Architectural monuments

Regardless of the legitimacy of governmental claims, there is no justification for removing from their original locations architectural features integral to their sites; these were meant to be experienced where they were built or placed.

Having expressed this principle, it is necessary to observe that such monuments may properly be removed to safer places if they are threatened by major environmental damage, vandalism, or other severe hazards. However, the responsible government should, if it is unable to prevent damage, keep the work in the vicinity of the original location, and on public view.

Private property rights

In the normal course of things, any object found on private property belongs to the property owner. Some governments claim as national property found objects of ancient origin. But may a government rightfully claim such ownership if it lacks moral rights on the basis of cultural patrimony?

Cultural importance distinctions

Disregarding questionable cultural patrimony claims by governments in the Americas, but granting the reasonable interest of nations in keeping important works of art within their borders and acquiring them as public property (while recognizing the private property rights of those who legitimately come into possession of such works), why not emulate Great Britain by allowing governments the option of acquiring an important work by purchase or, otherwise, letting the owner take or sell it anywhere? Granted that very poor countries would be at a disadvantage; they could establish a fund for such purchases by imposing a (reasonable) export tax on works taken abroad and/or using the income from licensed excavators.

International recognition of patrimony claims

The emotional impact of specious charges that collectors are looters and grave robbers, combined with the dubious claims of nonnative governments to "their" cultural patrimony, has created a climate of opinion in most of the world favorable to patrimony claims. Support of these claims by other governments is furthered by the acquiescence of politicians unwilling to arouse the ire of governments from which they want favors. Since government patrimony claims in the Western Hemisphere have no moral validity, and the pursuit of diplomatic favors is not a proper basis for the support of these claims, the international community should not provide such support. Specifically, the 1970 UNESCO Convention on Cultural Property should be reconsidered.

Indeed, are not works of art the patrimony of the world more than that of a state or even a culture? It can be argued that found works made by people long gone belong to all humanity, not to those who happen to live near where the works were found or whose culture is descended from that of the makers.

What rights should derive from the political boundaries within which the works of artists are made? Are the paintings of El Greco the

patrimony of Spain, where they were made, or of Greece, where the artist was born and grew up? Are Van Dyke's portraits of English lords the patrimony of England or the artist's native Belgium? The questions themselves reveal the absurdity of the concept of national patrimony. In the physical sense, works of art belong to whoever has legal possession of them according to the general rules of property. In the cultural and moral sense they belong to everyone.

Art is a category of property that differs fundamentally from any other, and the rules concerning it must be unique. While other property may be transferred totally from owner to owner, art always remains to some extent the property of the artist.

The artist, while living, may convey physical possession of a work to another, but not the moral rights to change or destroy it. When the artist dies, those moral rights may be vested in an agency or a relative, but only as a guardian. However, the cultural rights, which are an extension of the moral rights, belong to the world—to the universe, if you will. That is the true meaning of patrimony.

RELIGIOUS CLAIMS

There is a need to distinguish between the claims of peoples who are currently practicing religious observances that involve objects sacred to them and peoples whose *ancestors* may have regarded certain objects as sacred but who do not today invest these objects with religious meaning. For example, Zeus was sacred to the ancient Greeks but is not to Greeks today. Contemporary Aztecs, Maya, and Inca do not worship the gods of their ancient forebears (although vestiges of traditional rites and beliefs can sometimes be perceived in their practice of Christianity), so representations of them are not now sacred. Also, many objects

that are collected are *believed* by some to have had religious functions, but for the most part we do not really know if they did.

On the other hand, some contemporary peoples, notably the North American Indians, have living religions that involve sacred icons of various kinds, and in most cases these should be out of bounds for collectors. There are exceptions, since the ceremonial traditions of the tribes vary. Some objects used in religious observances are personal property, so there are cases where collecting is legitimate, but the principle of inviolability of truly sacred objects stands.

A NOTE ON TERMINOLOGY

The terminology used in each field of art history is quite specific and generally accepted by its scholars (there are occasional disagreements), even if some of it seems illogical or ungrammatical to others. Sometimes popular usages are adopted by scholars for nonscholarly publications simply to avoid confusion. Thus the term "Eskimo" is used in this book although "Inuit" is proper ("Inuit" is used here when the reference is prehistoric). "American Indian" is used to refer to the native peoples of North America above the Rio Grande (other than the Eskimos), although, strictly speaking, the natives of Mexico, Central America, and South America are also "American Indians" (and Mexico is technically part of North America). The term "Native Americans" is used by some to refer to the "Indians" (already a misnomer) of North America, but it is not used here since the term is equally applicable to the natives of the other Americas and to non-Indians born in the U.S. When the term "native Americans" is used in this book, it has a small "n" to indicate that it is descriptive rather than a proper name.

"West Mexico" in Pre-Columbian art terminology is not "western Mexico", of which it is only a part, but a specific cultural area referred to by that name. "Middle America" refers not to the political boundaries of Central America but to the cultural region scholars call "Mesoamerica" (see page 36).

The original name of the great abandoned city in Central Mexico called Teotihuácan is unknown. The present name is an Aztec word, so it is accented according to Aztec pronunciation.

When the names of Pre-Columbian or North American Indian peoples are preceded by "the" they are spelled without a plural "s" since they are being used as adjectives, even though the noun that would follow is only implied, i.e., "the Navajo" actually means "the Navajo people". The inhabitants of modern political states are referred to collectively as "the Mexicans", "the Canadians", etc.

Capitalizing the initial letters of words like "Pre-Columbian", "Historic", "Prehistoric", "Classic", "Basketmaker", and others that are not normally capitalized indicates that they are being used as proper names of specific historical periods or art styles. (When used to refer to an era rather than a style, "pre-Columbian", "prehistoric", etc., are spelled with a small initial.) If occasional inconsistencies in this system remain, the Editor takes full responsibility.

M.L.

On Collecting
AN INTRODUCTION

Pre-Columbian and American Indian art have traditionally been treated as separate subjects, and so they are in this book, but from the perspective of the natives of the American continents they are essentially one. One artificial distinction that we have created is geographical, with the U.S./Mexico border as the dividing line. The chronological distinction, too, is arbitrary, since the North American Indian cultures also predate the European invasion; that is, they are also pre-Columbian. However, most of these have continued to develop their arts to the present, whereas the native civilizations below the Rio Grande were effectively destroyed in the sixteenth century and the living descendants of their peoples do not create works in the ancient traditions. It is only this difference that justifies the division into two subjects.

We live in a world increasingly governed by specialization. Collectors today are often reluctant to acquire objects with only slight or no cultural affinity with their collections. This was not true in the past. In the eighteenth and nineteenth centuries, curio cabinets of great diversity were found in many homes. These contained both "natural curiosities"—seashells, fossils, narwhal tusks, stuffed birds and animals—and "artificial curiosities", the man-made artifacts brought back by explorers. The latter objects were considered to be on a fairly low aesthetic plane, and certainly not worthy of inclusion in art museums. They were collected as oddities and souvenirs of exotic trips. Now our approach to the creative work of non-Western peoples is more sophisticated. We collect these objects not as curios but in full appreciation of their equality with our own art.

OPPOSITE PAGE

Left: Maya, Tulum; 1000–1200 AD; terracotta; H 5" (12.7 cm).

Right: Zia; c.1900; terracotta; H 13" (33 cm).

SOURCES FOR COLLECTORS

For collectors of Pre-Columbian and American Indian art there are essentially two sources: the auction houses and the dealers. The former include Sotheby's and Harmer Rooke in New York, which hold several specialized sales each year. Until the 1970s as much as 80 percent of the lots sold at public auctions were purchased by dealers, but this has gradually changed as advertising and publicity have brought the private buyer into the auction houses. The buying pattern has altered accordingly, as private bidders, often willing to pay more than dealers—who must resell at a profit—now form a larger part of the audience.

The auction companies now thrive on strong media coverage of high prices and wildly successful sales. In contrast, the dealers, whose sales outstrip by far all the auction houses combined, maintain a low profile. Details of transactions are closely guarded, clients' names are rarely revealed, and sales are not noted in the press. For example, the highest auction price paid for a Pre-Columbian work at this writing was $429,000, for an Olmec serpentine mask sold in New York in May 1991. This level has been surpassed many times by dealers, but the general public will never be told the specifics.

Buying in auction is totally different from the way a collector buys from a dealer. Although the object offered in auction is on public view for several days prior to the sale, the length of time from the start of bidding to the drop of the gavel can be as brief as thirty seconds. A precise and cool mind is needed to cope with such a fast decision. The drama of a public auction is calculated to produce sales, with excited bidders extending themselves beyond their preset limits—something that can happen to dealers as easily as to collectors. There are buyers who thrive on this competitive and theatrical mode of acquisition, but many prefer the quieter, less harried relationship they have with their dealers. As in all fields of art and antiques, some collectors buy from both auction houses and dealers, while others feel more comfortable working with just one or the other.

Buying Pre-Columbian or American Indian art at the source, apart from the very real legal problems, is not necessarily the cheapest way to collect. Many visitors to Mexico or Arizona have returned with objects for which they paid more than the same items would have sold for in New York, Paris, or Milan.

FAKES AND FORGERIES

All areas of collecting are beset by forgeries. When genuine objects are plentiful and inexpensive, there is little incentive for the forger; the slight financial return cannot justify the effort. The problem of fakes was accentuated by the escalating prices of the 1970s and 1980s, but museum basements contain countless examples of early forgeries, many dating to the late nineteenth century. Some were undoubtedly sold as genuine to unsuspecting travelers, while others were offered as copies. Not everyone felt a need to possess the real thing; often a reproduction purchased from a local peddler was a satisfactory memento of the trip. In any case, forgeries have never been more plentiful than they are today, with the high prices of authentic works encouraging the forger to spend more time producing increasingly believable and challenging fakes.

Determination of authenticity is based on many factors, but one's first reaction is often the most accurate and can sometimes be experienced while still at a distance from the object. Does the work "feel" correct? Collectors and dealers often speak of a visceral knowledge that tells them if a work of art is fine or poor, a masterpiece or a forgery. This sense of quality and legitimacy, which does not necessarily spring from an academic background, is referred to as having an "eye" for the subject. Such ability seems to be almost genetic in a few, is slowly gained by others, and remains absent in many.

Collectors must use all their faculties, knowledge, and experience when considering an object. Is the style correct for the period when it is purported to have been made? Is the color of the clay correct? Are the patina and surface encrustation legitimate, or were they artificially applied? Is the weight consistent with known authentic examples? Many thoughts run through the mind when first viewing an object. Some are conscious, others not, but all combine to form an opinion.

Fakes are more cleverly and carefully produced now than in the past. Before archaeologists, museum curators, dealers, and collectors were exposed to the vast number of Pre-Columbian and American Indian objects now available, the forger was on safer ground. Anything that (1) came from Middle or South America, New Mexico, or Alaska, (2) looked to be of native manufacture, and (3) possessed somewhat alien features could be fobbed off as authentic. But now our knowledge of the cultures of the Americas is considerable and expanding. Today the successful forger must know perfectly the characteristics of the original work being copied, must use the correct materials, and must be exact in the style and iconography. As each fake is exposed, the maker tries to correct the error in the next piece. For this reason, many museum curators avoid public statements that describe in detail the mistakes they discover.

As technology advances, scientific tests are used more and more to judge authenticity. These are invaluable, but they need to be viewed with some caution, as will be shown. One important examination is the carbon14 test used to determine the age of wood and other organic materials. Carbon is a fundamental constituent of all living matter. When a plant or animal dies it ceases to take in radiocarbon, one of its naturally occurring isotopes, and the level begins to fall at a rate determined by the radioactivity decay law. If the number of atoms of radiocarbon remaining and the initial number can be determined, the time elapsed since death can be calculated.

The most-talked-about examination for ceramics is the thermoluminescence (TL) test. Crystalline materials that have been exposed to ionizing radiation emit thermoluminescent light when they are heated. When pottery is exposed to the test, its age is determined by measuring the time elapsed since it was last heated to a temperature of about 400°C or more, as it would have been when originally fired.

The TL test is useful if those conducting the experiment and interpreting the results are aware of the pitfalls. Ancient ceramics are usually found broken and often incomplete. A modern artisan can reassemble a pot from just a few shards and add a plaster filler where there are gaps in the original. There are countless ceramics on the market today that are partly authentic but have substantial areas of restoration. If a plug is drilled from such an object to do a TL test, the result may be misleading. If the plug came from an ancient shard, the verdict will be that the item is from the ancient era. If the sample came from a restored section, the test will indicate a modern copy. At that point, other considerations must come into play. If the object is a painted vase, ultraviolet light directed on the polychrome decoration will show restoration work. An x-ray will show where the breaks are and where the restorations might be. (Unfortunately, damage and repairs by themselves are

no guarantee of even partial authenticity, since forgers often will construct a pot, intentionally break it, and then reassemble the shards to give an impression of ancient damage.) In order to shield their painted designs from penetrating solvents that could determine whether the pot is legitimate, forgers now often seal the surface of their work with a layer of lacquer. However, a gentle flame directed on such a coating will create blisters, whereas heat on pure slip decoration will have no effect.

These scientific tests are, of course, of little use to the collector examining a work in a dealer's gallery or auction room; one can hardly bring a blowtorch to those august halls. The only tool that may realistically be used is a magnifying glass, which can reveal details the eye cannot detect. These might include painted root marks added by the forger to make the ceramic appear to have been buried, modern brush strokes to which particles of hair have adhered, machine-polished stone surfaces, and the marks of modern filing or soldering. A small amount of acetone applied to a painted surface will often reveal areas of repainting and falsification.

CONDITION, REPAIRS, RESTORATION

Collectors are constantly faced with the problem of determining to what degree a ceramic vessel or sculpture has been repaired and what extent of repair is acceptable. Some collectors like their objects to appear in perfect condition, even if composed of fragments, and insist that all cracks, joins, and repair lines be covered carefully by tinted plaster and pigments. Others want to see where the breaks are and to what extent the work is incomplete.

There are also contrasting views on what to do about an object which has parts missing, such as feet, fingers, ears, sections of a head-dress, etc. The standard curatorial approach is either to leave the sculpture incomplete or to restore the missing parts with a contrasting color so the new surfaces can be readily identified. Many collectors will restore to their original appearance only selected areas, perhaps facial features, while others will insist that all fragments and absent sections be made to look as if the piece is in a perfect state. There is a wide gap between an object honestly repaired and an overrestored work which consists largely of modern plaster. The extremes are clear enough, but there is a blurred area between them that presents a challenge to museums and collectors.

Tears and holes in damaged textiles can be rewoven (at considerable expense) and stains can often be removed, but a weaving can never regain its original appearance and value. Textiles should be cleaned only by professionals who specialize in this work and have a thorough understanding of the properties of dyes.

DISPLAY AND PROTECTION

Just as decisions about levels of restoration are of concern to collectors, so too is the way in which an object is displayed. Some collectors' homes resemble warehouses, with objects crammed into every nook and cranny, poorly lit and almost inaccessible for viewing. Other collectors display their prized possessions on marble columns or mounted on expensive stands and illuminate them with spotlights. Most fall somewhere between the two, avoiding the look of a crowded museum basement but keeping the presentation of the objects in reasonable relation to their importance.

While it is satisfying to have a fine work displayed to its best advantage, the most important concern is preservation. If possible, each object should be mounted in such a way as to minimize danger from falls, contact with other objects, exposure to excessive light or heat, radical changes in humidity, or handling by inexperienced visitors.

Obviously, it is preferable to have objects mounted by a professional, and in the case of very valuable and fragile pieces this is a necessity. But such work can be quite expensive, so the collector should acquire some skill in the matter. A simple way of informing yourself is to look carefully at museum and gallery installations. It may not be possible for you to construct every kind of mounting, but with some ingenuity a good solution can usually be found. Do not overlook the usefulness of lucite boxes as bases or enclosures. These come in all sizes and are not very expensive. Brass or steel wire in thicknesses suitable for forming rigid armatures is available in large hardware stores, though one must avoid using materials that are likely to abrade the surface of the objects. This is a particular problem with pottery and wood sculpture. Adhesive-backed felt pads are effective protection in many situations and are easily obtained. Hobby shops and display supply houses offer a variety of ready-made mountings.

Stanchions that mar the presentation of stone sculptures can be avoided by drilling a hole in the base of the object for insertion of a support. Many collectors use this technique, while others consider it abuse. Certainly, an amateur attempt can result in a seriously damaged or shattered work of art, so professional advice should always be sought.

Pre-Columbian gold items are often transformed from pendants to wearable brooches by the addition of soldered pin attachments. However, this drastic step affects both the integrity and the value of the work.

PRE-COLUMBIAN ART

A HISTORY OF COLLECTING

Widespread collecting of the native arts of North, Middle, and South America is a relatively recent phenomenon, but it had its beginning five hundred years ago, when Christopher Columbus arrived in the New World and the local "Indians" came to trade gold jewelry for his sailors' trinkets.

Columbus found only small amounts of gold on his first visit and the following two (in 1493 and 1495), but nevertheless, word reached Europe that wonderful treasures were waiting for explorers with the courage to sail for the New World. In 1519 Hernán Cortés was driven by a passion for gold to attack the Aztec capital of Tenochtitlan. Moctezuma, the ruler, believing Cortés to be a god, was persuaded to surrender all that the Spaniards wanted—the fine gold jewelry of the treasure house and the exquisite feathered regalia of the court. Francisco Pizarro reached the Incan kingdom of Peru in 1531 and, with 180 soldiers, pillaged the territories. Any object of gold or silver was taken, and the Incan ruler, Atahualpa, was put to death in a terrible act of betrayal.

Between 1492 and 1650, 181 tons of gold and 16,000 tons of silver were shipped to Europe from the Spanish possessions in the Americas. The explorers, who were driven by the excitement of gold to plunder the kingdoms of Mexico and Peru, could not exactly be classified as collectors; nevertheless, many precious objects that did miss the melting pots of Spain went into public and private collections through-out Western Europe. Jade and gold necklaces from the first expeditions were put in church collections (there are excellent examples in the Vatican); the great Aztec feather-and-gold shield of King Ahuizotl now resides in the Ethnographic Museum of Vienna; and the mask of the Aztec war god Tezcatlipoca—the face of a human skull covered with turquoise, jet, shell, and pyrite, given to Cortés by Moctezuma in 1521—is now in the British Museum. However, it was not until the late nineteenth and early twentieth century, when European and American museums and universities sent archaeologists into Middle and South America and many fine collections were assembled, that the general public began to be aware of the riches from these ancient cultures.

Collecting Pre-Columbian ceramic art was at first strongest in the United States, but there is an increasing European interest, and there are now many more collectors, dealers, and specialized museum exhibitions in Europe than before. On the other hand, Pre-Columbian stone sculpture, such as the face panels of Teotihuácan, the powerfully carved linear fig-

Teotihuácan; 200–300 AD; mask; H 55/8" (14.3 cm).

Tlatilco; "pretty lady"; terracotta;
H 31/8" (8 cm).

Olmec; c.1000–800 BC;
jade; H 4" (10.1 cm).

KINDS OF COLLECTIONS

The makeup of Pre-Columbian collections is as varied as the people who form them. Some collectors acquire objects from many cultures, others develop a taste for specific ones, while still others collect by material or subject. The culture of the Olmec, with its exquisite blue-green jades from La Venta and mysterious half-jaguar-half-human imagery, is among the most collected and valuable. Similarly sought after are the precious stone and shell carvings of the Mayan civilization and the delicately modeled terracotta figures from Jaina.

The West Coast Late Formative cultures of Colima, Nayarit, and Jalisco produced wonderful burnished ceramic figures and animals that are eagerly collected and have a visual appeal that does not require any special knowledge to be appreciated. When first discovered, these

Jaina; terracotta; H 73/4"
(19.6 cm).

Colima; terracotta; 131/4"
(33.7 cm).

handsome sculptures were often used by the locals for target practice. Fortunately, the present demand for these works means that they are no longer being destroyed.

Aztec stone sculpture, with its symbolism and powerful statement, is in high demand.

Miniatures, well suited to a small apartment and often less expensive than more monumental works, can form an entire collection. The most popular of these are the terracotta "pretty ladies" of the Preclassic period in the Valley of Mexico. Finely modeled and painted animals, birds, and fish, such as those seen on Moche ceramic vessels, are highly desirable.

Moche; stirrup spout vessel;
terracotta; H 11" (28 cm).

The gold and silver that attracted the explorers are no less desired today. Ancient jewelry has an international market and is considered more desirable if it can be worn. (However, because of security risks, the genuine Veraguas gold eagle pendant is left in a vault while a facsimile is worn to the dinner

Veraguas, Panama; "eagle"; gold,
H 27/8" (7.3 cm).

Maya; terracotta; H 7 3/4" (19.6 cm).

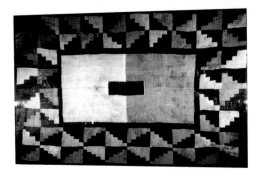

Nazca; *manta*; cotton; 60 x 93" (152.4 x 236.2 cm).

Carchi, Ecuador; terracotta; H 8 1/2" (21.5 cm).

party.) Peruvian textiles appeal to the modern sense of design and are likely to cost far less than a painting by even an unknown contemporary artist.

Collectors are now looking for objects from areas that in the past have been largely ignored or, at best, seen as poor relations to the "high" cultures of Mexico and Peru. Ecuadoran and Colombian ceramics, such as those of the Tairona, Manabi, and Carchi peoples, are finding a new market. Panamanian and Costa Rican material is more popular, as collectors realize that a fine volcanic stone *metate* or brilliantly painted Coclé pedestal bowl is no less wonderful than a Veracruz stone *hacha* or Mayan painted vase. There is a strong interest in the Taino culture of the Caribbean—not only for its aesthetic qualities but because it was the first New World culture seen by the Spanish explorers.

Taino; regurgitation spoon; bone; L 12" (30.5 cm).

Costa Rica; *metate*; stone; L 19 1/2" (49.5 cm).

FAKES AND FORGERIES

The faking of Pre-Columbian art is rampant and can be found in pottery, wood, stone, shell, gold, and silver objects, and copies of major textiles appear occasionally. Forgeries were plentiful by the early part of this century. Zapotec pottery funerary urns from Monte Albán were a favorite with the early copiers. Many were taken back to Europe, and auctions of the early 1930s at the Hotel Drouôt in Paris were laden with them. Large numbers have now been identified by today's more sophisticated experts as fakes, including some in the

British Museum and the National Museum of the American Indian in New York City. However, decades of grime, with a few additional chips and cracks from the wear and tear of handling, can make an object appear more convincing. Fake Zapotec urns continue to drift onto the market, and innocent buyers continue to acquire them.

Zapotec, Monte Albán; urn; terracotta; H 16" (40.6 cm).

Moche; terracotta; H 7 1/2"
(19 cm).

Erotic pottery from Peru is particularly salable, and the supply of genuine examples falls far short of the demand, so it is often faked. These pots, usually in Moche or Chimú style, can be made of perfectly genuine lower halves, with the tops elaborately remodeled. Authentic ancient molds are sometimes used to make modern copies. In these cases the results cannot be faulted on stylistic grounds, so other methods of judging authenticity are needed. TL testing is most useful.

The market is swamped with bogus Olmec and Mayan heads, figures, pendants, and plaques sculpted from vividly colored jades, serpentines, and other decorative stones, many from countries and mining sources far from those that supplied the genuine objects. The iconography is often incorrect, with alien head-dresses and jewelry, and make-believe glyphs are provided. The depiction of the human face is rarely accurate. Surfaces are artificially polished to an unnatural shine, and there is an absence of the patina that develops over centuries. Perforations for suspension or attachment show signs of metal drilling, and twentieth-century file marks are seen.

Terracotta figures can present another problem. Since they are almost invariably excavated in fragments, a site might contain a large number of heads, bodies, and limbs, all genuine but disconnected. Many figures are properly repaired in these circumstances, but sometimes a miscellany of unrelated parts are joined to make complete figures. While these are composed of authentic fragments from the same archaeological zone and period, the finished product is not legitimate.

The dry coastal desert of Peru provides excellent conditions for preservation of the ancient wood excavated from gravesites. Like the wood found in ancient Egyptian sites, this can survive in remarkably good condition for thousands of years. The carbon14 test tells us the age of the wood used to make a sculpture, but not, of course, whether the carving is ancient. A forger can carve a reproduction from a genuine fragment of Pre-Columbian wood and the scientific test will say that it is ancient, but the eye must determine if the style is consistent with works from that era.

Most ancient gold objects come from Costa Rica, Panama, Peru, and Colombia, and fakes originate from all four. As in other areas of deception, the specious gold works vary in quality and level of conviction. Many are obvious fakes, but others are brilliant works by master goldsmiths with an excellent knowledge of ancient styles and techniques. To convince a skeptical buyer that the gold pendant being offered is genuine, fakers often supply elaborate proof. There are many unscrupulous "experts" with impressive-sounding titles and credentials who, for a fee, will provide the sellers with certificates of authentication. When presented with such a document, invariably stamped with insignia that suggest governmental sanction, the unwary consumer is easily persuaded. Elaborate archaeological digs are occasionally planned for unsuspecting tourists. They are taken to a site where, even as they watch, a gold artifact is "unexpectedly" unearthed. The tourists gleefully purchase the treasure from the diggers and return home with a lifetime of exciting tales. They do not know that the gold pendant had been planted in the ground for their benefit and that it had been manufactured the previous week.

CONDITION, REPAIRS, RESTORATION

Most Pre-Columbian material is made of pottery, and questions about condition apply usually to that medium. Honest repairs and restoration will stabilize the condition and appearance of an object; dishonest work will result in embellished and fallacious forms. A badly worn Mayan vase with little painted design remaining can be restored to something close to its original state, but beware the unscrupulous restorer who adds new gods and glyphs with abandon.

Peruvian textiles are an important, and vulnerable, part of Pre-Columbian collecting. Their repair should be undertaken with care, as previously noted.

It is extremely difficult to repair gold and silver objects since it is necessary to apply heat, and this can seriously harm the ancient surface. There are very few qualified restorers in this field, and no action should be taken without competent professional advice.

THE MARKET

The Pre-Columbian collecting world is expanding, as more people are exposed to the wonders of the ancient Americas and realize that for a moderate sum they can acquire a 2,000-year-old treasure. Indeed, Pre-Columbian art has always been relatively affordable—providing an agreeable surprise to collectors approaching the subject for the first time. While collecting in most areas of art and antiques has become too expensive for the average person, the ancient arts of Middle and South America are still within reach.

There is, however, a popular misconception—equating the great age of an object with high monetary value—that affects inexperienced collectors in this field. The fact is that there is a vast amount of available Pre-Columbian art and artifacts, spanning 3,000 years of Middle and South American history, so the value of such objects relates much more to the quality and appeal of individual pieces than to their age. Nevertheless, while Pre-Columbian material in general is not rare, a small percentage of the objects *are* rare, and their value is correspondingly higher.

The explosive growth of Pre-Columbian collecting occurred in the period beginning about 1960, though a few adventurous souls were buying as early as the 1920s and 1930s. The enthusiasm for Pre-Columbian art in the late 1960s, when auction houses and dealers were able to sell material at all levels of quality, was dampened somewhat in the 1970s by legal issues raised by passage of the UNESCO Convention on Cultural Property. The uncertainties aroused by a few highly publicized cases created a generally negative mood among museums, collectors, and dealers, but the market rebounded when it became apparent that the practical impact of the Convention would be mainly in the area of major architectural features rather than the objects commonly collected.

Fortunately, Pre-Columbian art never became part of the wild investor syndrome. It was always reasonably priced and did not fall prey to the bouts of speculation that confused and upset other areas of the art market. The entry of European and Japanese buyers has strengthened the market tremendously, and auction audiences are now composed of many nationalities, not the least of which are buyers from Mexico and South America, where so many fine collections have been formed. The market is now truly worldwide.

AMERICAN INDIAN ART

A HISTORY OF COLLECTING

The collecting of American Indian art was certainly secondary to the other objectives of exploration, but the expeditions of Cook, Vancouver, Malaspina, and others did result in much material being taken back to Europe. The earliest example of Historic period (post-1492) art for which there is documentation is the mantle of Powhatan, the great Algonquin chief, which was brought to England from Virginia in the early seventeenth century by his daughter Pocahontas, who had married the Englishman John Rolfe. The hide cloak is now in the Ashmolean Museum, Oxford. Objects collected by Prince Maximilian of Wied are now in the museums of Berne, Berlin, and Stuttgart.

From the first days of exploration the Old World could afford the luxury of collecting, but it was not until the latter part of the nineteenth century that the American collector emerged. Until then, North America had preoccupations and needs related more to survival than to art collecting. Besides that, the native Americans were seen as a threat to the early settlers, and this prejudice did little to improve the public's perception of Indian culture.

Hopi; 1935; Malo kachina; H 18 3/4" (47.6 cm).

23

Nevertheless, significant groups of artifacts entered American museums in the early and mid-nineteenth century: for example, the Jarvis collection of Eastern Plains material, now in the Brooklyn Museum, and the objects assembled by the artist George Catlin, now in the National Museum, Washington, D.C. However, it was the images of early photographers such as Edward Curtis that brought the cultures of the North American Indian to the attention of white people, and the advent of railroads that enabled travelers to Indian lands to bring back artifacts as souvenirs. During the heyday of anthropological collecting, from 1875 to about 1930, institutions amassed large collections. With the advent of the Great Depression, money for collecting disappeared.

The establishing of government-licensed Navajo trading posts, begun in the 1860s, spurred interest in native arts. Tourists came home with textiles for themselves, and the Santa Fe Railroad enabled commercial shipments to the large cities. Entrepreneurs opened stores in many communities. In Carson City, Nevada, the Emporium Company promoted the basketry of local Washo weavers. A basket by the most famous of these, Datsolalee (died 1925), was sold there in 1897 for $1,500, a huge sum for those days.

Interest is especially strong in material made prior to 1850, which is considered the approximate date when Indian artisans had completely integrated native techniques and imported trade goods. The date marked the full flowering of American Indian cultures prior to disintegration. With the increased use of European materials, particularly the glass trade bead, the nature of American Indian art changed. From the introduction of the first large pony beads to the multicolored beadwork of the late nineteenth and early twentieth century, the appearance of Indian art was irreversibly altered.

An historical watershed came toward the end of the nineteenth century. The final destruction of the Indians' way of life and their forced settlement on ill-conceived reservations signaled a change in much of native American culture, particularly on the Plains. Enforced reservation existence did, ironically, produce Sioux, Cheyenne, and Arapaho ledger drawings (made on ruled ledger pages supplied by the U.S. Government), now eagerly sought by collectors, but many other material examples of Indian creativity were lost forever. Commercially tanned hides appeared, aniline dyes replaced vegetals, and trade beads became increasingly vivid.

The varying degrees of tribal collapse are visible in the changes in their cultures. Most of the peoples of the Southwest, whose unbroken tradition reaches back over two thousand years, were not subjected to the displacement and genocide inflicted elsewhere, and this relatively settled existence encouraged continued cultural expression.

KINDS OF COLLECTIONS

Pottery

Collectors are attracted to Southwest Prehistoric pottery—the dramatic black-on-white images on Anasazi bowls, *ollas* (wide-mouthed pots), and animal effigies; Mimbres vessels with their mysterious iconography; and the other forerunners of the late eighteenth- and nineteenth-century Historic revival.

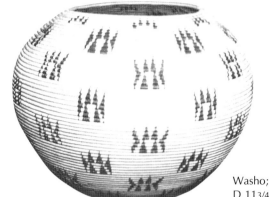

Washo; Datsolalee basket; D 11 3/4" (29.8 cm).

Sioux; c.1880–90; beaded buckskin; L 21" (53 cm).

The twentieth-century commercial development of ceramics, pioneered by Maria Martinez of San Ildefonso, created what is probably the largest single Indian art market. Today, there are countless potters of varying abilities and with mixed success, though all seem to find a place at one level or another in the market. Dynasties of potting families have established themselves: Martinez and Gonzales of San Ildefonso, Guttierez and Tafoya of Santa Clara, Chino and Lewis of Acoma, Nampeyo of Hopi.

San Ildefonso; Maria Martinez blackware vase; H 12 3/4" (32.3 cm).

was made), and *serapes*, but also Pueblo *mantas*, kilts, and sashes and Saltillo *serapes* from northern Mexico.

The Northwest Coast Chilkat blankets, the best-known of native weavings after the Navajo blanket, appear regularly in auction. Many have been bleached by exposure to strong light, so when examining a Chilkat the collector should look carefully at both sides.

Mimbres; terracotta; W 4 7/8" (12.3 cm) (miniature).

Jewelry

Navajo, Hopi, and Zuni silver and turquoise jewelry was made largely for Indian wearing until the 1930s, when traders realized the market potential. The craft grew rapidly, and artists began signing their work for the non-Indian market. The Navajo and Hopi designs were relatively simple and standard, while the Zuni developed a more complex channel-and-inlay mosaic technique with varied stones, shell, and coral. Contemporary jewelry makers have taken the craft a step further into abstraction and sculpture and the use of exotic materials alien to the Southwest. These have an appeal far beyond the American Indian jewelry market. The most famous makers, such as the late Charles Loloma of Hopi, have an international following. For the collector whose interest lies in the less commercial work, jewelry from the early part of the century remains the only silver and turquoise worth acquiring.

Textiles

Appreciation for all American Indian art has expanded rapidly since the mid-1970s, but in no area is this more apparent than textiles. The clarity of design and dramatic color statements of Indian weavings have an obvious appeal today. It is not by chance that many contemporary artists collect Navajo textiles and that galleries selling modern art exhibit them. All fine early textiles are sought, not only the eyedazzler weavings, Germantowns (named for the Pennsylvania town where aniline-dyed yarn

Navajo; c.1925; buckle; silver and turquoise; H 3 1/8" (7.9 cm).

Navajo; 1860–69; man's *serape*; 52 x 75 1/2" (132 x 191.8 cm).

Zuni; c.1925; bola slide; silver and stone mosaic.

Apache; H 28" (71 cm).

Baskets

The diversity of Indian basketry is immense, the most important areas of origin being the Southwest, California, and the Northwest Coast. Figurative depictions, such as dogs and humans in Apache baskets and butterflies and rattlesnakes in Mission and Washo baskets, are popular, as are the wonderfully feathered treasure baskets from the Pomo of Northern California. Tiny Pomo baskets, many no more than one-quarter of an inch in diameter, fetch huge prices. (In 1971, six Washo baskets by Datsola-

Pomo; miniature baskets with dime.

lee sold at auction in New York for a total of $26,150, and the audience had cheered at the unprecedented prices. Those same baskets would have sold in 1991 for between $250,000 and $350,000 each.) A category of baskets more recently collected is the plaited splintwork of the Northeast. Though not as elegant as the work from other areas, and therefore still underappreciated, this is a far older tradition than the more finely woven and elaborately designed baskets of the West.

Kachinas

For many years collectors have treasured kachina dolls, the small painted wood representations of spirit beings, usually associated with the Hopi. Fine early examples from the late nineteenth century have become extremely valuable and difficult to find. The carving tradition, however, continues unbroken. Contemporary kachinas by acknowledged masters of the craft are widely available and are as popular as the older, more traditional works.

Archaeological material

Many of the early collections were centered around stone artifacts: flint points, blades, and pendants. A favorite was the birdstone, an abstract avian form of uncertain origin and use. Bannerstones and other elegant gorgets, often sculpted from beautifully veined hardstones, find a ready market.

Most collectors and dealers of North American archaeological stone and pottery artifacts live in the Midwest, where so much of the ma-

Birdstone; L 3 7/8" (9.8 cm).

Hopewell; bannerstone; W 4 3/4" (12 cm).

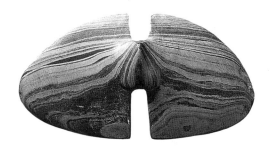

terial is found, still turned up by the plow or discovered on the surface. It is extremely important for collectors to have known find-spots for their artifacts. An arrowpoint without an identified locale is less valuable than one with a precise history.

There are many collectors' clubs whose members work passionately with all archaeological material, including pottery and shell. Specialized journals and magazines regularly advertise material for sale, and relic shows abound.

Area and subject

Some collectors acquire material from particular geographic or tribal areas, such as the Great Lakes, Northern Plains, or Northwest Coast. Others concentrate on subject matter. Warfare and weaponry intrigue buyers of tomahawks,

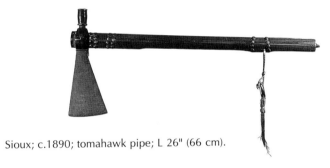

Sioux; c.1890; tomahawk pipe; L 26" (66 cm).

clubs, lances, gun cases, and bow cases. There are pipe enthusiasts whose holdings range from the complex argillite carvings of the Haida to the animal and bird effigies of the Woodlands and Mounds cultures. Material associated with the Ghost Dance, including painted shirts and dresses, wands, rattles, and

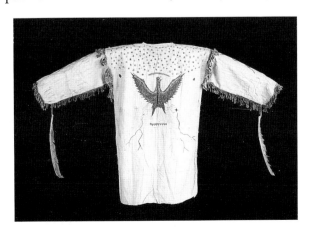

Ghost Dance shirt.

drums, have long fascinated collectors, for both its artistic qualities and the tragic and dramatic historical context in which it was created. (The Ghost Dance religion, founded by the Paiute messiah, Wovoka, held that a time would come when ghosts of Indian ancestors, buffalo, and wild horses returned to a new earth where only Indians would live. The 1890 massacre at Wounded Knee effectively ended all belief and hope.)

Objects depicting American flags and eagles, such as beaded and quilled pipe bags and vests, are popular. An exhibition composed of

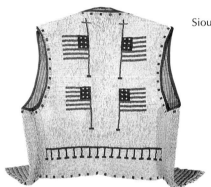

Sioux; c.1890; vest; beaded hide.

flag images was held at the Museum of Contemporary Crafts, New York, in 1976. That this was shown at a crafts museum makes a point about the nature of American Indian collecting. The visual appeal of the material is close to that of American folk art, and many dealers sell both. A Navajo pictorial textile showing American eagles and the Stars and Stripes is not out of place when exhibited next to a hooked rug or weather vane.

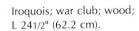

Iroquois; war club; wood; L 241/2" (62.2 cm).

Eskimo art

The summer surface thaw in Alaska signals the Eskimos' seasonal trek to dig for prehistoric ivories of the Old Bering Sea, Dorset, Thule, and Punuk cultures. Collectors are attracted to eighteenth- and nineteenth-century Eskimo ivory carvings of figures and animals, particularly when enhanced by a glorious dark or honey-colored patina.

Northwest Coast art

One of our earliest childhood associations with the North American Indian is the totem pole from the Northwest Coast. It is material culture from there that first filled the anthropology storerooms of the world's museums, and the sculpture that, at its finest, is the most expensive today. Early Northern-style masks of the Tlingit, Haida, and Tsimshian (at their simplest, suggestive of Asian origins), delicately carved

raven rattles, boxes, and bowls, command collector attention. The Southern style of the Kwakiutl, Nootka, and Salish, less elegant by today's standards, has not received quite the same adulation from collectors.

Contemporary arts and crafts

Contemporary arts and crafts are a vital and profitable aspect of the American Indian art business. This activity is most intense each summer in Santa Fe, particularly in mid-August, when as many as six auctions are held in less than a week. Thousands of shoppers wander from gallery to gallery. The frenetic

Tsimshian; 1885; mask; wood; H 12" (30.4 cm).

buying reaches its peak at Indian Market, when the Indians sell only their contemporary arts and crafts. For the serious collector and dealer a predawn rising is necessary to get the choice pieces.

Painting

Painting on paper is the most recent art form to be adopted by the Indians of the Southwest. Although the use of commercial watercolors began shortly after the turn of the century, it was the 1932 establishment of the Santa Fe Indian School, an experimental class designed to instruct young Indian students in the use of the new medium, that led to the acceptance of Indian painting as a new artistic expression. The works tend to be highly decorative and executed in a flat, opaque gouache technique. Recent work shows a dissatisfaction with restrictions imposed by the flat medium and a desire to experiment with new techniques and imagery.

FAKES AND FORGERIES

Forgeries appeared early in the collecting of American Indian art, and many late-nineteenth-century collections are now seen to contain some. These are usually of pottery and stone, such as birdstones, effigy pipes, and stone figures of Mounds culture type. These still appear on the market and can confuse the buyer when there is a genuine nineteenth-century label attached.

Flint knapping has become popular, and many seemingly superb examples of points, all recently manufactured, have come into the marketplace. It requires great experience to determine which are genuine and which are not, since antler and rock are used to make them.

Bone and ivory carvings in Northwest Coast style have been copied in large numbers, as have wood food bowls and rattles. Some were made in the United States, but many come from other countries, including Japan.

The rich brown patinas of early Eskimo carvings can be artificially created by staining and polishing, and many forgeries have appeared in auction rooms and galleries since the mid-1960s.

Great store is placed in the fact that the turquoise in a particular bracelet, ring, or necklace is from one of the important Arizona, Nevada, or New Mexico mines, such as Bisbee, Blue Gem, Morenci, or Cerillos. As this increases the price of a work considerably, buyers must trust the seller or their own eye when determining the source of the stone. Because of the worldwide interest in Southwest jewelry, much of the contemporary output comes from non-Indian makers. Since most of the Southwest turquoise mines have closed, the present artisans, Indian or otherwise, have had to turn to other sources, including the Middle East. As the demand for affordable turquoise increases, more items are set with dyed stones, poor- quality turquoise, reconstituted turquoise, or entirely different stones.

As with Pre-Columbian art, one of the most trying problems in detecting forgeries is determining whether all the elements of an object are correct. All might be authentic individually, but when combined they are not. Medicine bundles, at best an obscure subject for most collectors, are imaginatively "improved" by adding exotic fragments, or are constructed entirely of parts from unrelated bundles. Beaded and quilled hide shirts from the Plains are transformed by the addition of hair into "war-shirts". Scalp locks made from species other than Homo sapiens are regularly seen. Imperfect Hopi kachina dolls are given new headdresses and symbols. Plains and Pueblo hide shields and covers are repainted with more salable motifs such as Ghost Dance emblems, figures, and animals.

Basketry is probably never faked, but the buyer needs to be sure that an "American Indian" basket is not from Southeast Asia or South America. The latter appear in small auction rooms and stores, but most are easily detected by their stitch, coil, and color. It must be noted, however, that baskets from South Africa are similar in their technique, colors, and motifs to those of the Apache or Pima.

Weavings from Mexico are markedly different from Navajo textiles, in both construction and design. They are also less expensive, so they are occasionally offered as coming from north of the border.

Reproductions of Indian art and artifacts, clearly made as copies and often signed by the makers, can be so like the originals that they fool sophisticated collectors and dealers. The use of Indian techniques and correct materials makes the copies convincing, even though substitutes are sometimes used. To give leather the look of deer hide, furniture wax is applied. Painted turkey feathers can look like eagle, hawk, or owl feathers. Taco sauce can provide a false patina on brass, while a sprinkling of vacuum cleaner dust gives the look of age to beadwork.

In 1913 William "Buffalo Bill" Cody created a problem for future collectors when he organized a reenactment of the 1890 massacre at Wounded Knee for his Wild West Show. Because few authentic costumes were available, he had copies of Sioux regalia manufactured

Copy of Northern Plains pouch made for William "Buffalo Bill" Cody.

for the show. These were convincing to his audience, and are sometimes offered today as legitimate examples of nineteenth-century Plains beadwork. A similar danger comes from today's hobbyists, absorbed in the cultures of the North American Indian, who collect authentic material but also make their own exact copies to use in reenactments of historical events such as the defeat of Custer at the Little Big Horn and other famous battles.

The value of an object increases if it has an impressive provenance, or traceable history of ownership. The ultimate, and overused, provenance is "Sitting Bull". Hundreds of clubs and costume parts have been offered with this claim; many of these are from tribes that had no connection whatsoever with the Sioux leader.

CONDITION, REPAIRS, RESTORATION

An important consideration in tribal arts is patina, particularly in wood sculpture. This usually refers to African and Oceanic art but is relevant to certain American Indian material. A rich, dark patina on wood indicates considerable age and use and can substantially increase the value of an object. A Northwest Coast mask whose back is worn from generations of contact and handling will attract a buyer more than will a mask of comparable age that was acquired in the field before a usage patina could develop. This applies also to grease bowls encrusted with decades of oil, pipe stems, and Northeastern burl bowls and crooked knives. Since an excellent patina will increase value, the temptation to artificially create or enhance one is considerable.

American Indian art was often kept in homes under poor conditions, so it is usually found in an imperfect state. Though advanced conservation techniques can do much to cure damage, condition plays a major role in desirability and value.

Baskets are sometimes dry and brittle, and careless handling can cause damage. Overly dry and warped baskets can be revived, but restoring missing parts is virtually impossible. Hide pipe bags, moccasins, and shirts, originally as supple as cloth, are reduced to rigid slabs of leather by prolonged exposure to hot and dry climates. When they crack and split, rejuvenation is impossible. Such adverse environments and incorrect handling can result in damaged threads and consequent loss of beadwork, while organic materials may suffer the ravages of insects.

Condition plays an essential role in establishing the value of ceramics, regardless of the reknown of the potter. A vessel by Maria Martinez that is chipped or abraded, even if that area is small, will not be of interest to a serious collector and will not appreciate significantly. On the other hand, Mimbres black-on-white picture bowls, the most valuable works of Prehistoric pottery, are almost invariably found with a hole punched through the center of the body. These apparently intentional "kill holes" are often restored before a vessel is sold. This is acceptable to most collectors, but sometimes a bowl with a large hole that includes a substantial part of a painted design is reconstructed and repainted to appear perfect. The buyer must beware of a Mimbres bowl in seemingly pristine condition.

Repairs to Navajo weavings can be made with the limitations indicated earlier. Given the differences between the vegetal and aniline dyes used, it is important to avoid the bleeding of colors often seen on incorrectly treated rugs.

THE MARKET

In the past there was a marked regionalism in the buying habits of American Indian art collectors. For example, Europe has long been interested in early Eskimo and Northwest Coast art, but contemporary Northwest Coast Indian art—masks, rattles, and boxes—sold best in that part of the country. Modern Southwest jewelry, weaving, and ceramics were more salable in Scottsdale and Santa Fe than New York and London. This has changed as the world's involvement with American Indian art has increased. When Christie's, London, sold the James Hooper collection on November 9, 1976, with strong bidding in all areas, it was evident that the world market was far broader than had been believed. Now collectors and galleries abound almost everywhere. There are superb kachina collections in Europe and wonderful Navajo blankets in Japan.

The most identifiable of Navajo blankets, the so-called chief's pattern, has often been discovered in garages keeping automobile engines warm in winter months and in kennels providing a similar service to animals. In the 1960s an

Navajo; c.1870; "chief's blanket"; 64 1/4 x 74" (163 x 188 cm).

excellent blanket could be discovered in a store, even correctly identified, and bought for just a few hundred dollars. The chances of that happening today are slight. A world auction record for American Indian art was set by a c. 1850–1855 Navajo First Phase blanket ($522,500, Sotheby's, New York, November 28, 1989), and now anyone with a Navajo weaving that appears old hopes that he or she is holding a treasure. (More than likely, the "early chief's pattern blanket" will turn out to be a 1920s rug in the same style.)

Vast quantities of Indian rugs were woven in the first half of this century. Design, color, tightness and quality of the weave, size, and condition are all factors in determining their value. Some makers are more skilled than others, and this is reflected in the widely different prices.

The value of fine early Southwest ceramics has risen dramatically since 1985, and buyers of Historic pottery pay high prices for the best *ollas* and bowls of the Zuni, Acoma, Zia, Santo Domingo, Cochiti, and other pueblos.

Northwest Coast Haida sculptures of argillite, the soft black shale that hardens after carving and exposure to the air, used to be sold at prices according to their size. Model totem poles were offered at $100 an inch, often regardless of the quality of the carving. Now a fine work by one of the nineteenth-century masters, such as Charles Edenshaw, can command a price that is many times that of an only slightly inferior sculpture.

Wonderful finds in Prehistoric Eskimo sculpture have been made, sold in the field for staggeringly high prices to visiting dealers, and than resold for even more on the international market. However, the richest sites have been thoroughly searched, few major sculptures are now being excavated, and the market is flooded with large quantities of mediocre material. The salability of both ivory and wood sculpture decreased in the late 1980s; prices had risen too swiftly in too brief a time for the market to sustain itself.

There is a relatively small audience for contemporary Eskimo stone sculpture and prints. The market is dominated by collectors in Canada, where fluctuations in the stock market can directly impinge on the monetary value of the Eskimo art.

Haida; late 19th Cent.;
model totem pole; argillite;
H 10 1/2" (26.7 cm).

CONCLUSION

This Introduction can be no more than that—an introduction to the myriad aspects of collecting, a pursuit that is hobby for some, a way of life for others. The rich and diverse native cultures of North, Central, and South America provide an opportunity to collect fascinating, and sometimes thrilling, art and artifacts, whatever one's taste and means. In the following pages, the history and characteristics of these works are discussed and illustrated in such a way as to give beginning and advanced collectors a thorough—but by no means complete—survey of the kinds of objects available. The works illustrated are generally excellent examples of what may be found in galleries and auction rooms. Some extraordinary pieces are included to show the range of quality that exists, even though these works are quite rare and/or valuable. Such items have a star at the end of their captions.

During thousands of years of artistic creation, works of interest were produced by peoples in all parts of the American continents. Obviously, some produced more than others, and works from some places rarely appear in galleries and auction houses. To be as useful as possible to collectors, this book concentrates on the areas that provide works often seen in the international marketplace.

The illustrations are organized to give a comprehensive picture of the various styles of works, and to enable comparison of objects as a path to better understanding of their characteristics. The captions bring attention to aspects of quality and identification. In the Pre-Columbian section, the organization is according to cultures; the American Indian section is arranged by categories of objects.

Pre-Columbian Art

Lambayeque, Peru; mask; gold; W 9 1/4" (23.5 cm).

Map of
MESOAMERICA
and
CENTRAL AMERICA
showing some of the most prominent
pre-Conquest cultural locations

"I saw among them wonderful works of art and I marvelled at the subtle ingenuity of men in foreign lands. All of my life I have seen nothing that rejoiced my heart so much as these things. Indeed, I cannot express all that I thought." Thus wrote the great Renaissance artist of northern Europe, Albrecht Dürer, on seeing the things which Cortés had just sent back to his king during the conquest of Mexico.

For nearly five hundred years Dürer's joyous statement remained one of the few positive evaluations of the native artistic achievements of ancient America. Eurocentricity colored or clouded our view of art throughout the world. Europeans "discovered" America, Asia, and Africa—as if the peoples of other cultures and their achievements were inferior and waiting for European enlightenment.

Those who approach pre-Columbian art must be prepared to leave behind Western preconceptions and use their own eyes. They will be rewarded with the ingenuity that Dürer appreciated, as well as technical brilliance, a freshness of approach, and, often, a surprising sense of humor.

Looking south from the Rio Grande, we approach a geographically and chronologically complex series of cultures (see maps and charts). It is not feasible to discuss all of them, but we will look at the most artistically important ones, examining the styles and types of objects they produced.

The peoples of the Americas appear to have migrated across the land bridge (now the Bering Strait) that joined Siberia and Alaska during the last ice age—long before agriculture, animal husbandry, and the wheel were known in the Old World. From Asia the nomads brought shamanism and stone tools. Their descendants on the American continents invented for themselves agriculture, pottery, weaving, and stone architecture. In South America they discovered and perfected metallurgy, the domestication of animals, and the making of molds for pottery.

Although numbers of voyagers stumbled or drifted onto the American continents in the centuries before Columbus' arrival, they made no apparent contribution to the region's art, architecture, or technology. Ancient American art has a purity remarkably unmuddied by outside influences. It may be enjoyed if we open our eyes to another vision and a different approach to life.

35

MESOAMERICA

Ancient time in the pre-Columbian era of Mesoamerica (the area that includes southeastern Mexico, Belize, Guatemala, and adjoining areas of Honduras and El Salvador) is divided for convenience into six approximate periods: Early Formative (1500–900 BC), Middle Formative (900–600 BC), Late Formative (600 BC–100 AD), Early Classic (100–600 AD), Late Classic (600–900 AD), and Postclassic (900–1519 AD). (The Mexican West Coast cultures, which flourished about 100 BC–200 AD, occurred within the time span of the Mesoamerican cultures, but they are considered culturally separate and are not part of the same chronology.)

Chart showing the approximate periods of some of the most prominent pre-Columbian material cultures of Mesoamerica and Central America.

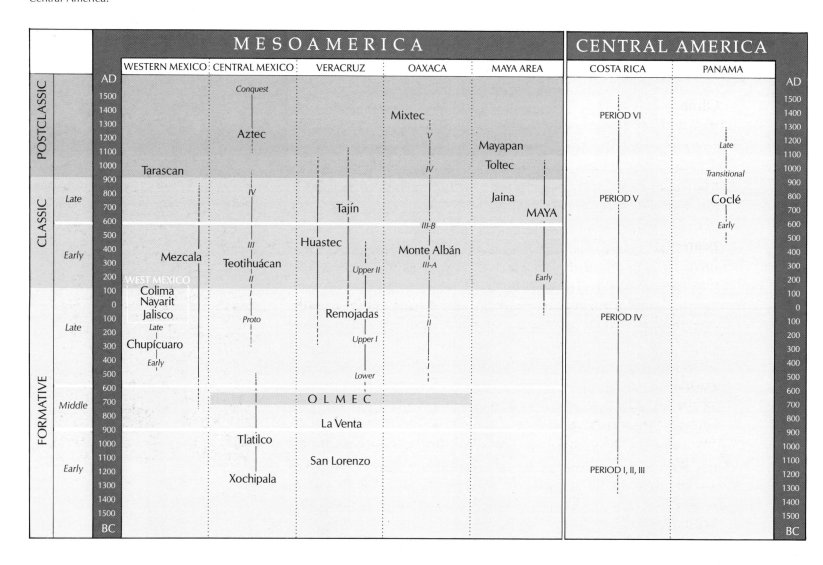

In the Early Formative era, the people in many villages in Mesoamerica made and buried small clay figures, along with bowls of food and important personal effects, with the dead under the floors of their houses, so that the ancestors might partake of the daily life of the family. Such figures are particularly plentiful in the states of Guerrero, Morelos, and Michoacán and vary widely in style from place to place. The most elaborate and elegant of them were discovered only in the 1940s, in the Tlatilco brickyards at the edge of Mexico City.

The working of hard stones by sawing with string and drilling with reeds, using abrasive sand and water, was probably developed earliest in the rocky state of Guerrero, near the town of Mezcala. These stones were worked into human and animal forms, masks, and models of temples. In nearby Xochipala, graceful bowls were scooped out of fine-grained stone. While the Mezcala people worked mainly in stone, the artisans of the Xochipala region also made superb clay figures, which in some cases can truly be called portraits. Their style is called Pre-Olmec.

Xochipala; terracotta; H 8 1/4" (21 cm).

Xochipala; bowl; stone; L 8" (20.3 cm).

Olmec

Olmec is Mexico's first great civilization and artistically possibly its greatest. Olmec iconography, and that of the Chavín culture in Peru, used potent animal symbols: royal power was represented by the jaguar, the harpy eagle, the cayman (alligator), and the serpent. Later, in coastal regions, the killer whale in Peru and the shark in Mexico were added to the list. The earliest depictions of these powerful creatures appeared first on the coast of Ecuador, and then they seem to have traveled south to Peru and north to Mexico, where they became the core of royal Olmec iconography.

The Olmec heartland is famous for its great ceremonial complexes, as well as colossal portrait heads of rulers, great thrones, and other powerful works carved of volcanic stone. Most of these works are now in museums in Mexico. The Early Formative Olmec ceramics of the Gulf Coast were buried in extremely acid soil and few have survived, but there are very fine ceramics from the highlands—from Las Bocas, Tlatilco, Tlapacoya, and Xochipala. The best of them equal any ceramic tradition in the ancient world. Large hollow figures—often of babies—seem to derive their technique from the Chorrera hollow figures of Ecuador but are artistically unique and brilliant. Smaller, solid Olmec figures were imbued with a vitality and character that are extraordinary. There are also

Olmec, San Lorenzo; c.1250 BC; H c.9' (2.74 m).

37

Olmec; terracotta; H 5⅝" (14.3 cm).

Olmec; bowl; blackware terracotta; D 5¼"
(13.3 cm).

Olmec; pectoral; jade; W 5¾" (14.6 cm).

marvelous Olmec ceramic vessels, some in the form of humans, birds, fish, or animals; others are gourd shapes, flat-walled containers, and bottles. Although these ancient wares of the Highland Olmec were low-fired (probably in the open), the use of kaolin slips, carving, and burnishing places them on the highest technical plane. The fine Olmec ceramic artists took great pleasure in contrasting highly polished with rough finishes, controlling fire-clouding, and elegantly modeling contour. Designs were deeply carved with masterful calligraphic strokes. These works speak to us eloquently today, as they surely did to their original owners.

At about 900 BC the focus of Olmec production changed rather dramatically and the Middle Formative era began. Stone monuments of the heartland become cluttered with iconography. The stela (a free-standing stone shaft with relief or incised markings) was introduced, and rock-cut reliefs appeared in the highlands. The powerful and beautiful early Olmec ceramic tradition was replaced by pottery of less distinction, lacking the dramatic iconography and rich finishes of the Early Formative. The vigor and strength of the early ceramic figures declined into slipshod workmanship.

During this period the Olmec discovered jadeite, one of the very hard and rare stones known as jade. Figures, masks, pectorals, necklaces, and earflares, as well as bloodletters and ritual paraphernalia, were beautifully fashioned of jade and distributed throughout the Olmec world and beyond. These works rose above the fine ceramics and even the austere and powerful early stone monuments in artistic importance. Jade became a symbol of rulership and power and to a large extent the bearer of late Olmec iconography.

The Middle Formative period closed at about 600 BC. The Olmec world slowly fell apart, to be replaced by numerous regional cultures during the Late Formative. This is a confusing period of which we know very little, yet it presaged the great Classic civilizations with which we associate ancient Mesoamerican art.

West Mexico   The art of West Mexico, which dates from about 100 BC to 200 AD, is especially approachable because it appears to be folk art, and therefore very human. However, it is not folk art—it is tomb furniture. The peoples of the present Mexican states of Colima, Jalisco, and Nayarit did not form dynastic kingdoms such as the Olmec pioneered in Mesoamerica. They clung to a village life and made ceramic images and containers to guard the honored dead and provide food and guidance to them in the afterworld. The ceramic objects were placed in deep vertical shaft tombs cut into soft volcanic rock. What distinguishes most of these objects is their aesthetic quality, imagination, and craftsmanship.

There seem to have been South American influences on West Mexican cultures. The only shaft tombs in Mesoamerica, in Colima and Jalisco, are similar to those found in Colombia and Ecuador. The stirrup spout, a complex ceramic form that was invented in Ecuador about 1500 BC, is found in Capacha-phase Colima circa 1450 BC and at Tlatilco, near Mexico City, at about 1200 BC. Whistling pots, pots in the form of stacked vessels, large hollow clay figures, and vessels in the form of animals and birds all seem to stem from the Chorrera culture of Ecuador and were adopted by the early cultures of West Mexico.

The pottery of Colima is perhaps the most engaging from West Mexico. Small solid figures were generally molded in a buff clay. They probably depict shamans in various guises—as warriors, drummers, women, clowns, and some touching maternities. Most have coffee-bean eyes. Many are whistles. It was believed that shamans spoke in a whistling language, so whistles were buried with the dead to enable them to call up a shaman to help them in the afterworld. Large ceramic vessels and hollow figures were generally given a burnished red slip, often with the addition of a cream slip and sometimes an accent of black. These hollow figures depict a great variety of human, animal, and vegetable subjects. Sometimes these constitute the entire vessel; sometimes they are incorporated into a larger abstract form. The most frequently seen animals are dogs. These are depicted in every condition, from fattened (for eating) to starved, sleeping, scratching fleas, and dancing in pairs. There are also large, elegant, lobed pots supported by tripods of parakeets, crayfish, or Atlantean dwarfs. In almost all cases, the care and craftsmanship on these vessels is consummate. Overall, Colima ceramics are unmatched for their combination of creativity and fine execution.

The Formative cultures, such as the Olmec and those of West Mexico, were the ones which experimented with stone techniques and sculpture, pottery, painting, and architecture. It was their followers—peoples of different ethnic backgrounds and languages—who rose to build the great civilizations which so impress and delight us with their remains.

Colima; whistle; terracotta; H 3" (7.6 cm).

Colima; terracotta; H 11 1/4" (28.6 cm).

39

Zapotec, Monte Albán; urn; terracotta; H 51/4" (13.3 cm).

Zapotec East of Guerrero, in the Valley of Oaxaca, the Zapotec people, stimulated by Olmec contact, built their centers on mountaintops. The principal center was Monte Albán. One of the most imposing ruins, it sculpts the top of a mountain 1,200 feet above the conjunction of three large valleys in the center of the modern state of Oaxaca. The Zapotec are credited with inventing one of the earliest true writing systems. They made early use of the corbel arch (probably invented in nearby Guerrero) and created some of the most impressive stone architecture. But their principal surviving sculpture is found in the form of clay urns, made to be placed in their stone-vaulted tombs. The potters used every clay sculpting technique possible: building by coil, applying sheets, balls, and twisted ropes, incising, carving, molding, and modeling to give vitality to these objects, which were placed in the tomb to exemplify the attributes and the special deities of the deceased.

Teotihuácan The Early Classic city and culture most familiar to the general public is Teotihuácan. Teotihuácan remains an enigma. In a wooded valley not far from the great Lake of Mexico, an area where little or nothing of political or cultural consequence had preceded it, a stupendous city was planned, laid out, and erected all at once, circa 150 AD. It was a city larger in extent than any other in the world of its time, with pyramids which still make us gasp. It was laid out on an approximately north-south axis with a central ceremonial causeway, anchored on the north by a Pyramid of the Moon and in the center by a complex known now as the *Ciudadela,* or citadel. Slightly to the northeast is the Pyramid of the Sun, one of the great wonders of the ancient world.

The city had, apparently, no central house of government, no dynasty of kings, no writing system (although both the Zapotec and the Maya, who had emissaries there, had writing), and great numbers of people of wealth apparently lived close together with tradesmen for centuries. The city may have been conceived and built in the common belief that the gods of Mesoamerica lived in that place, and there one could dwell among the gods.

The city was lavishly decorated with colorful stenciled frescoes on public buildings as well as private palaces. The few examples of monumental stone sculpture are locally made, and they tend to be crude and blocky. The famous masks of exotic hard stones, such as serpentine, jasper, and onyx, were usually made in places as far away as Puebla and Guerrero. The fa-

Teotihuácan; terracotta; H 71/2" (19 cm).

mous thin orange pottery came from the area of Cholula. Only flaked obsidian objects and thousands of clay figures and ceramics, including tripods and *incensarios*, were made in this international city. But objects from Teotihuácan and its style and motifs were exported even beyond the limits of Mesoamerica.

North of the Olmec heartland, on the Veracruz coast, the Maya-speaking Huastec forged their own cultures and civilization. Central Veracruz people built no stone cities in the Classic period; their genius was the working of clay into animated figures and large hollow effigies. These constitute some of the best ceramic sculptures made in ancient Mesoamerica. They are often lively, and there are examples of true portraiture. In one region, around the tiny village of Las Remojadas, the sculptors depicted people smiling and laughing, sometimes dancing, sometimes in pairs on swings. These smiles are not the "archaic smile" of sixth-century-BC Greece or the sixth-century-AD Buddhist sculpture of China, but genuine human expressions. Veracruz is possibly the earliest culture that intentionally depicted smiling and laughing in a large body of work. (It is disturbing to think, however, that these might be depictions of intended sacrificial victims, high on some ritual hallucinogenic or psychedelic substance, prepared to be launched into eternal paradise.)

   In northern Veracruz the Huastec built cities of stone with stone ball courts. The most important of these is El Tajín, which was considered the center of the Mesoamerican ball game. There are twelve courts at El Tajín, the central one bearing elaborate Late Classic reliefs, probably carved by order of the Totonac, who had moved in from the highlands and gained control of the Veracruz coast. A great number of stone effigies of ball game paraphernalia were made in this region. These include the *yugo*, or "yoke", worn at the hips as protection against the hurtling hard rubber ball (the actual protector was probably made of wood), the *palma* (a tall, thin piece attached to the top of the yoke), and the *hacha* (axe), which may originally have been a portable marking device for the game. It is not known what they meant, but they probably served as trophies of the ball game and were traded and emulated all around Mesoamerica. These stone objects range in design from simple to abstract to baroquely complex and were infused with symbolic meaning. In general, the simpler ones are earlier. The characteristic motif of the Tajín style is the interlace—proba-

Veracruz

Veracruz; terracotta; H 111/2" (29.2 cm).

Veracruz; yoke; stone;
L 153/4" (40 cm) W 121/2" (31.8 cm).

Veracruz; *hacha*; stone;
H 103/8" (26.3 cm).

Veracruz; *palma*; stone;
H 17" (43.2 cm).

bly a conventionalized cloud or dragon. It is found on early slate mirror backs and ball game furniture, as well as woven into the elaborate reliefs on Tajín ball courts.

The Maya   The greatest of the Classic period Mesoamerican civilizations was certainly that of the Maya. These people developed the most complex writing system, built the most elaborate and elegant architecture, and created sculpture and painting that rivaled any tradition of the ancient world.

The Maya were initially farmers who, sometime before the first century BC, went from living in tiny village groups to living under the aegis of dynastic rulers. These ruling dynasties maintained a continuous civilization, supported by their claims to divine ancestry and influence, for nearly a millennium. It was the warring drive for sacrificial blood and territorial dominance, combined with abuse of the delicately balanced forest land, that terminated the Late Classic period, with the abandonment of the Mayan cities and their ruling elite.

Architectural and sculptural styles, pottery types, and ceramic figures differ between the Early and Late Classic periods. Early Classic architecture is marked by large polychromed stucco deity masks stacked up on the facades of some buildings and the influence of *talud tablero*—the hallmark of official Teotihuácan style. The modern traveler is more aware of Late Classic styles, which were often superimposed over earlier buildings. Each region had its own typical style: Copán, a raised acropolis with richly decorated buildings made with deeply carved stelae (southeastern); Tikal, vertical skyscrapers (northern Petén); Palenque, hipped roof, surmounted by a tall roof comb (Usumacinta region); Río Bec, a palace flanked by artificial towers; Chenes, in which the principal doorway is the open mouth of a huge deity mask; and Puuc (northern Yucatán), which has so delighted and influenced modern architects.

Maya; stela; stone.

The principal Mayan stone carvings are the stelae, which recorded events in the history of the ruling family. These vary with the region. The stelae of Copán are carved deeply—nearly in the round; those of the Petén tend to be in shallow relief. Instead of stelae, Palenque used elegant limestone tablets embedded in the walls of its buildings to record its dynastic history.

Mayan buildings were often painted. At Palenque most of the buildings were red. One exception was the house of coronation, called by the ancient Maya "The White House". It had frescoes both inside and outside. Buildings in Yaxchilan, Uaxactun, Multunchic, and Tulum also contained narrative frescoes, but the greatest to have survived are at Bonampak and those painted by Mayan captives at Cacaxtla, in the state of Tlaxcala.

Jade, a symbol of wealth and power, was used for jewelry and costume adornment, but the elegant, careful workmanship of earlier pieces degenerated as jade sources were used up and the culture moved toward collapse. Bone and shell also were worked with extraordinary skill, although not many pieces have survived the steamy conditions of the tropics. The Maya must have been great masters of wood carving, but, with the exception of a few carved wooden lintels from Tikal, only two major wood sculptures have survived—both are figures which held mirrors. These were preserved in dry caves.

The most accessible Mayan art to survive is ceramics. In some sites, such as Palenque, El Lagartero, and Río Azul, large quantities of ceramic figures have been found. Outstanding is the island of Jaina, in the far west of the Mayan world (and therefore the entrance to the Underworld and an important necropolis), which contained thousands of figures in graves. Many were mold-made as whistles and rattles. Most depict humans or gods. Some reveal the Mayan sense of humor, and there is occasional portraiture.

Jaina; terracotta; H 9" (22.9 cm).

Another window into the ancient Mayan mind is through their painted and carved pottery, made to be placed with offerings of food in the tomb with the dead. Only in Greek, Mimbres, Moche, and Chinese Sung dynasty ceramics do we find such a rich pictorial tradition. The scenes deal mainly with the Underworld and the mythology of the gods. Here one discovers master painters, some of whom, in the Late Classic period, signed their work.

By 900 AD the Classic period had passed in Mesoamerica. Its great civilizations had fallen apart and its cities lay abandoned. The Mixtec had gained control of the Valley of Oaxaca; Monte Albán was deserted. The Totonac had supplanted the Huastec, pushing them north and west in Veracruz, finally leaving El Tajín deserted. A revolt by Otomí mercenaries, it is said, ended the great city of Teotihuácan, whose surviving inhabitants resettled around the shores of the Lake of Mexico.

The Postclassic period was a time of small warring states—it was the period of the Toltec. The hilltop site of Xochicalco was the last center of ancient Classic learning. Then

Maya; terracotta; H 71/4" (18.4 cm).

43

Tula became the capital of the new Toltec empire, which sent its warriors throughout Mexico. In Oaxaca, Mitla became the new Mixtec center, supplanting the Zapotec center of Monte Albán. Although the Maya had produced books painted on bark paper for about a thousand years, Mexican highland cultures, especially the Mixtec, now had their own books painted on deer hide, accordion folded, which chronicled dynastic histories. By 1000 AD metallurgy had arrived in Mexico, some 2,500 years after it had been developed in Peru. Gold and silver were more easily obtained now than jade, and gold jewelry was splendidly cast by the lost wax process. For a brief time in Mexico and Guatemala smelting furnaces provided a lead glaze for pottery, known as plumbate. Curiously, this was the only true glaze in all of the ancient Americas.

The Aztecs   The Aztecs, naked barbarians who had wandered into the Valley of Mexico in the thirteenth century as servants and mercenaries, learned and borrowed culture from the peoples living around the Lake of Mexico. They began to conquer their neighbors and expand, and in less than a century they dominated a considerable part of Mexico. They traded widely and established a zoo and a royal garden, which contained every plant that grew within their realm. But they demanded slaves and captives for blood sacrifice, as well as goods and commodities, and their subject peoples grew restive. In their dominant role, the Aztec were able to tap artists and artisans from all areas of their domain, and produced powerful stone sculptures, among other works. Gold and copper, for instance, were often worked in Michoacán, Guerrero, and Oaxaca and traded to Tenoctitlan, the island capital of the Aztec empire.

The Spanish conquest of 1519–1521, which was a total cultural shock, attempted to destroy all native culture and bring the native peoples to Christianity and European ways. This effort was, by and large, successful. The population, decimated by disease, was forced into a European mold, and the rich native invention was supplanted by an imitation of Hispanic European models.

Aztec; stone; H 15" (38 cm).

CENTRAL AMERICA   Central America tends to be ignored as a source of rich cultures, but its various countries produced a wealth of fine art in stone, gold, and ceramics. We have been all too impressed by the imposing pyramids, monumental sculpture, and art traditions of the major civilizations of Mesoamerica and tend to consider their neighboring cultures to the south provincial. It is true that the cultures of Central America were more tribal than dynastic and therefore lack monumental stone ceremonial architecture or stelae with glyphs. Our impressions are colored also by the dramatic confrontation of European and native American cultures that climaxed in Mexico and Peru—the countries which held the greatest riches for the Spaniards—and the words "Aztec" and "Inca" bring to mind a rush of romantic familiarity.

Modern political boundaries have little to do with ancient cultural areas. Honduras and El Salvador border Guatemala, whose ancient Mayan civilization spilled out into its neighbors' countries at Copán and Tazumal. Early Olmec monuments and the Mayan remains tie these areas to Mesoamerica. But Olmec and Mayan influences fade out the farther southeast one travels. The remains which are found reveal cultures of tribal orientation, yet artistic genius and invention were present here at a high level.

For those with open minds and eyes the artistic legacy of ancient Costa Rica and Panama is worth savoring. These two regions—particularly Costa Rica—have been regarded by some as areas without strong styles of their own—as being influenced by greater civilizations to the north and south. There was certainly influence from both directions, but both countries had distinctive cultures which were rich, original, and diverse.

Among the wonders of the Neolithic world are the perfect stone spheres found in Costa Rica, which come in sizes from three inches to twenty feet in circumference. These are found principally in the Diquís area, singly or in groups of up to forty-five. No one knows what function they served, but they reduce sculpture to its purest and most essential form—works which Brancusi or Noguchi might envy. Other great stone pieces are elaborate ceremonial *metates* (corn grinders), stools, and altars, generally found in the Atlantic watershed zone. Simpler ones were made in the Guanacaste region in the first five centuries of our era. There are also grave markers and volcanic stone figures from the Linea Vieja area.

Costa Rica is justly famous for its ancient jades. The actual jade sources seem to have been the Motagua Valley of Guatemala and anciently looted Mayan and Olmec tombs. Olmec incised celts and spoons and Mayan belts and belt dangles were generally sawed apart and the earlier carving was at least partly erased by the Costa Rican lapidaries who imposed their own deities and iconography upon the older works.

Costa Rica; *metate*; stone; L 20" (50.8 cm).

Coclé, Panama; gold; W 41/4" (10.8 cm).

45

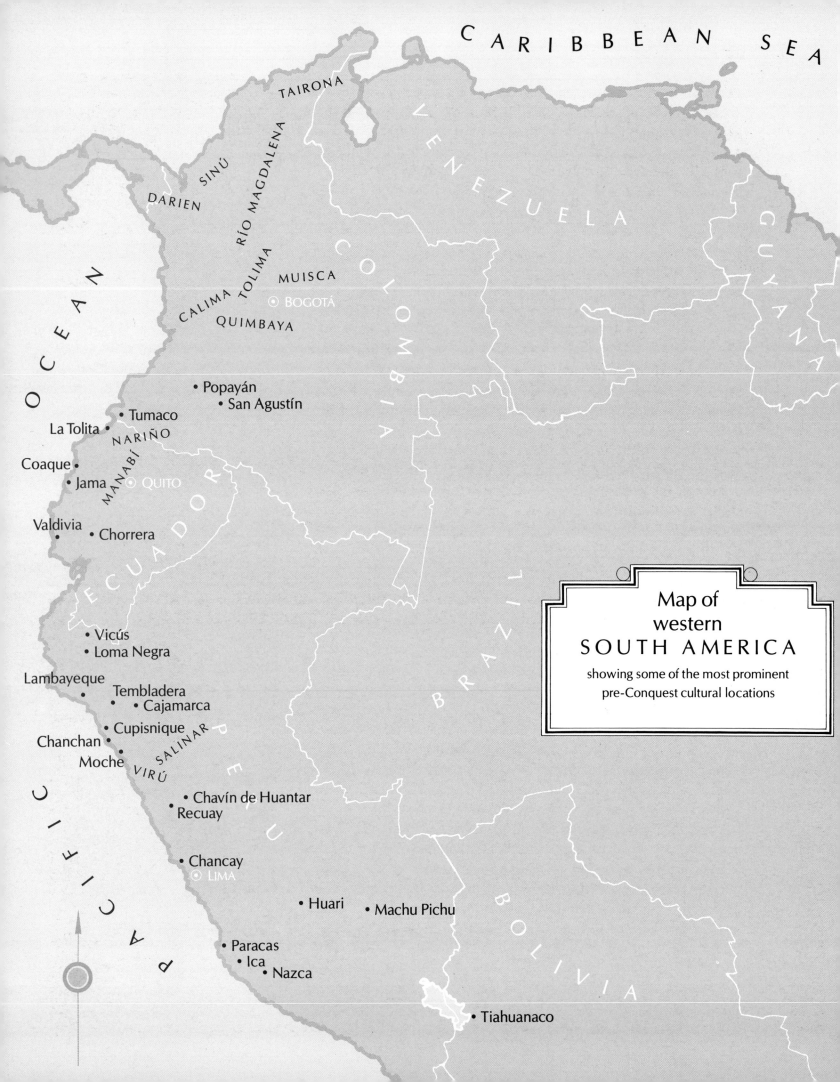

C A R I B B E A N   S E A

TAIRONA

V
E
N
E
Z
U
E
L
A

G
U
Y
A
N
A

SINÚ

DARIEN

RÍO MAGDALENA

TOLIMA

CALIMA

MUISCA

⊙ BOGOTÁ

QUIMBAYA

C
O
L
O
M
B
I
A

O
C
E
A
N

• Popayán

• San Agustín

• Tumaco

La Tolita •

NARIÑO

Coaque •

MANABÍ

• Jama

⊙ QUITO

Valdivia •

• Chorrera

E
C
U
A
D
O
R

B
R
A
Z
I
L

• Vicús

• Loma Negra

Lambayeque

Tembladera

• Cajamarca

• Cupisnique

Chanchan •

SALINAR

P
E
R
U

Moche

VIRÚ

• Chavín de Huantar

Recuay

• Chancay

⊙ LIMA

• Huari

• Machu Pichu

B
O
L
I
V
I
A

• Paracas

• Ica

• Nazca

P
A
C
I
F
I
C

• Tiahuanaco

Map of western SOUTH AMERICA

showing some of the most prominent pre-Conquest cultural locations

When gold-working technology arrived from South America through Panama, gold supplanted the harder-to-find jade. The Coclé gold objects are particularly beautiful, and their designs reflect the beautiful Coclé polychromed pottery of the time. The ceramics of Costa Rica and Panama, in fact, sometimes achieved an inventiveness and originality not found in late Classic wares of Mesoamerica. We are dazzled by the painted and carved scenes on Mayan cylinder vessels, but the actual vessel is usually a not-very-interesting ceramic form. In contrast, their variety of shapes and colors gives Central American ceramics a distinctiveness which has been generally undervalued.

Costa Rica, Nicoya; terracotta; H 13" (33 cm).

The oldest-known pottery shards in the Americas have been found in Brazil's Amazon basin. They are at least seven thousand years old, but few other traces remain of the civilization that produced them. The earliest fragments of ceramics from a preserved New World culture were found in Caribbean shell middens at Puerto Hormiga, near Cartagena, Colombia. They date back five thousand years and, like the Amazonian fragments, represent crude early attempts at making bowls.

SOUTH AMERICA
Colombia

Chart showing the approximate periods of some of the most prominent pre-Columbian material cultures of South America.

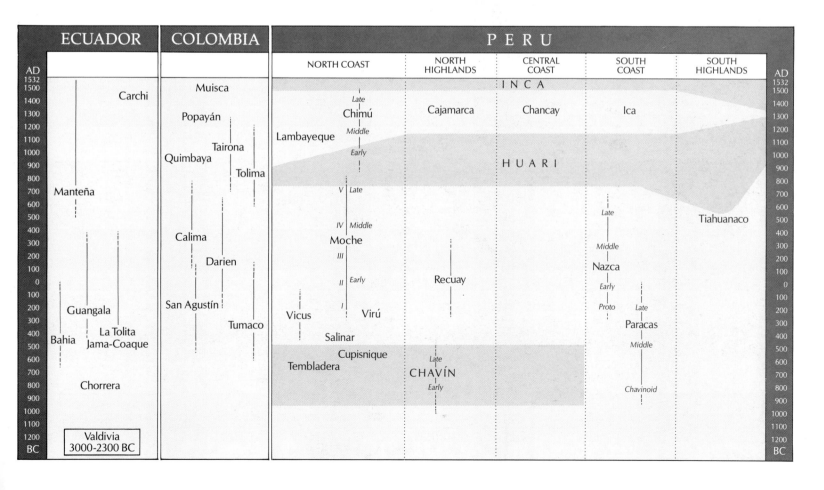

	ECUADOR	COLOMBIA	PERU				
AD / BC			NORTH COAST	NORTH HIGHLANDS	CENTRAL COAST	SOUTH COAST	SOUTH HIGHLANDS
AD 1532 / 1500	Carchi	Muisca	INCA				
1400				Late			
1300		Popayán	Chimú	Cajamarca	Chancay	Ica	
1200–1000		Tairona / Quimbaya	Lambayeque (Middle / Early)				
900–800		Tolima			HUARI		
700	Manteña		V Late				
600–500						Late	Tiahuanaco
400		Calima	IV Middle				
300		Darien	Moche (III)			Middle	
200–100			II Early	Recuay		Nazca (Early)	
0							
100 BC		San Agustín	I			Proto	
200	Guangala		Vicus / Virú			Late	
300		Tumaco				Paracas	
400	Bahia / La Tolita / Jama-Coaque		Salinar				
500						Middle	
600			Cupisnique	Late			
700			Tembladera	CHAVÍN			
800–900	Chorrera			Early		Chavinoid	
1000–1200 BC							

Valdivia 3000–2300 BC

The most sensational and beautiful ancient Colombian site has been made into a national park—San Agustín. There are over three hundred monumental stone carvings, mostly of men with ferocious feline attributes; some are said to be about two thousand years old. Near San Agustín is an area called Tierradentro, with a similar culture, but with great numbers of shaft tombs cut out of the local soft rock—possibly the inspiration for the shaft tombs of West Mexico.

But the greatest Colombian contribution to the art of the ancient Americas was their cast gold work. Gold was first worked in Peru, circa 1500 BC. It then spread to Ecuador and Colombia. The Peruvians had invented casting techniques, such as lost wax, but preferred to work sheet metal into objects—only rarely using casting. The Colombians perfected, and seemed to delight in, elaborate and complicated casting. Through it they created some of the great goldsmithing in Pre-Columbian times. Especially notable is the Quimbaya work.

Valdivia; stone; H 31/2" (8.9 cm).

Ecuador Ecuador seems to be the region that produced the first ceramic sculpture in all of the Americas. Indeed, it may have been the cradle of civilization of the New World. In 3200–2300 BC, at about the same time that the crude ceramics were made at Puerto Hormiga, Colombia, there were figures, as well as decorated pottery, at Valdivia on the Guayas coast of Ecuador. Both the pottery and the figures have style. The tiny figures, especially, stand as strong works of art which hold their own artistically.

Valdivia was followed by a series of impressive early cultures, some of which had a profound influence upon both the rich Peruvian coastal cultures and, more remarkably, the Guerrero and Olmec civilizations in Mexico. The culture following Valdivia, Machalilla, originated the complicated "stirrup spout", in which two pipes emerge from the body of a ceramic vessel to loop and join at the third, which, at right angles, becomes the spout of the assemblage. (The entire spout looks somewhat like a stirrup.) This invention, circa 1500 BC, traveled north to Mexico, where it soon died out, and south to Peru, where it became the principal ceramic form of the North Coast for two thousand years.

The next Ecuadoran culture, Chorrera (1200–500 BC), perfected the hollow standing figure, a concept that seems to have been borrowed by the Olmec, for whom it became their most important and sophisticated ceramic form. The later Jama-Coaque culture (300 BC–500 AD) seems to have invented the

Tolima; pectoral; gold; H 9" (22.9 cm).

Jama-Coaque, Ecuador; terracotta; H 13 1/4"
(33.7 cm).

Chavín; stirrup spout vessel; terracotta; H 9"
(22.9 cm).

Paracas; detail of burial textile.

clay mold for duplicating and mass-producing figures and vessels; this was adopted by Classic and Postclassic cultures in Mexico and Peru. Ecuador was home also to a number of fine ceramic traditions which have not become as well known as they deserve, as well as a fine gold-working tradition.

Peru The seeds of American civilization took root in the Amazon basin before it became an impenetrable jungle. Before 4000 BC this region was a savannah land with a moderate climate; by 3000 BC the jungle had taken over and people fled. But they remembered the reigning powers of the savannah-forest, those predators—the jaguar, the cayman, the harpy eagle, and the serpent. When the people migrated west to the Pacific, these were the basis of their deities. In the ocean they found many creatures—some, like the killer whale, joined their pantheon.

The earliest great civilization in Peru—the southern equivalent of Olmec—is Chavín, named for its principal site, Chavín de Huantar, on the eastern slopes of the Andes near the Amazon jungle. The Great Temple, constructed over many centuries, is honeycombed with secret passageways. Its beautiful stonework includes several extraordinary monumental relief carvings, which define the Chavín cosmos.

Chavín religion, with its Amazonian deities, spread its message and influence all over coastal Peru, from Vicús, near the Ecuadoran border to the north, to the Paracas Peninsula, south of Pisco. Stirrup spout vessels conveyed the Chavín religion and worldview with a power never equaled again in ancient Peruvian art. Like the Sung Chinese harking back to archaic Shang bronzes, later cultures in Peru archaized and used Chavín models in Moche and Huari-Tiahuanaco art nearly a thousand years later.

The Paracas Peninsula, a barren black-sand desert pushing westward into the Pacific, became a necropolis. The desiccated dead were wrapped as mummies in incredible lengths of richly tapestried cloth made from tunics, headbands, shirts, tents, and awnings. These embroidered *mantas,* woven during the period 500–100 BC, are among the most beautiful and virtuosic fabrics to have survived from ancient times in all the world.

The Nazca and Paracas peoples, living among dun-colored rocks and endless sand, craved color, and thus their fabrics and their ceramics were rich in subtle but vibrant hues. The Nazca peoples (100 BC–700 AD) produced elegant polychromed pottery, using forms and iconography quite different from those of their contemporaries to the north, the Moche. Most Nazca vessels have round bottoms, functional for nestling into the ubiquitous sand. Nazca pottery is attractive in shape and thin-walled. The polychromed designs were abstracted from nature or were mythological in subject. Little study has been done on the rich iconography as yet, but Nazca pottery holds a very special place in ancient American art.

Nazca; terracotta; L 91/4" (23.5 cm).

The Moche were of an entirely different artistic temperament. Their forms and much of their symbolism were inherited from the Chavín cultures. The Moche were able to put an extraordinary amount of information in naturalistic narrative form into the pots. The stirrup spout vessel became the official vehicle for expressing their mythology, customs, and daily life. The bodies of the pots were mold-made, then hand-finished. The wares were usually bichrome—a cream slip over the terracotta with dark red or brown accents or line drawings—in contrast with the polychromes of the Nazca potters. Moche potters often sculpted the bodies of their pots into naturalistic forms, such as a god, a personage, an animal or vegetable, or a whole scene, including landscape, figures, and architecture. Portraits of exceptional depth and elaborate fine-line scenes from their mythology were all in the Moche repertoire. This extraordinarily diverse decorated oeuvre has been seen by some art historians as the American equivalent of both the Greek vase-painting and Roman portrait traditions.

Moche; terracotta; H 10" (25.4 cm).

Like the civilizations of Mesoamerica, the Classic period civilizations of Peru became decadent and overextended and then collapsed. The Nazca and the Moche, as well as the highland civilizations, were overrun and subjugated by a southern culture known as Huari-Tiahuanaco, named for its two most prominent sites—Huari in south-central Peru and Tiahuanaco in Bolivia. The Huari-Tiahuanaco was a warlike and expansionist culture that imposed its art on the cultures that it conquered. Its religious iconography revived certain themes from the ancient Chavín religion. Its chief artistic glory was in its finely woven geometrical textiles, which remain some of the finest to have come out of the Andean area, although the use of finely faced stone in Huari-Tiahuanaco architecture anticipated the Incan architecture of half a millennium later. But this culture, too, died out, and was replaced by local civilizations that revived the cultures of their ancestors. The most powerful and important of these new cultures was the Chimú, or Chimor, empire of the Peruvian north coast. Their capital was a huge series of necropolis compounds called Chan Chan, loca-

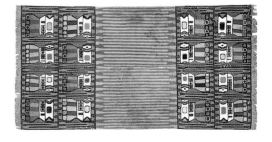

Huari, 500–800 AD; shirt; 78 x 39" (198.1 x 99 cm).

51

Chimú; blackware vessel; terracotta; H 9 1/4"
(23.5 cm).

Inca; shirt; 35 x 31" (89 x 78.7 cm).

ted only a few miles from Moche—the ancient center of the Moche kingdom.

Compared with earlier cultures, most Chimú art seems to us to be sloppy and even mass-produced. Chimú textiles are rare, but wooden objects tend to be crude and the ceramics dull, mold-made, and repetitive. Chimú metalwork was not as fine as that of their ancestors, the Moche. The gold was mined in Chan Chan by the colonial Spanish, who had also diverted the Rio Moche so that it would hydraulically destroy the immense Pyramid of the Sun—the largest pyramid in all of the Americas—and make it disgorge the golden contents of its tombs.

The Inca The Inca, like the Aztec, were late upstarts. They came from a tiny mountain valley high in the Andes, but their remarkable political organization and military prowess enabled them to overcome first their neighbors and then all surrounding cultures.

The greatest achievement of the Inca was their massive architecture. Their ability to move huge stones through seemingly impossible terrain, across river gorges and up vertical slopes, and to rock into place these megaliths without the use of a wheel leaves us in awe. But it is the harmony of their sculptural architecture with its dramatic surroundings that makes it one of the world's most unusual and satisfying building styles.

At their best, Incan pottery and textiles were more original than the Chimú or other regional styles which they borrowed. Most of the pottery was decorated with geometric designs. Though beautifully crafted, it often seems dull and repetitive. Some Incan textiles are better; the best are simple, bold, and distinctive. The Spanish melted down the gold and silver objects into ingots, so we have few examples.

What remains to us of these extraordinary and innovative civilizations challenges our preconceptions about "primitive" peoples and "primitive" cultures. The fragments which have survived stimulate us to wonder at the deep pools of creativity inherent in the human mind—pools which welled up independently on the American continents.

N.B.
Scientifically confirmed production dates for Pre-Columbian works are quite rare. The dates given in the following pages—usually as a span of several hundred years—should be understood to be approximations based on the general knowledge and opinions of various authorities in each subject.

MESOAMERICA

OLMEC

Olmec, Veracruz; c. 800 BC; man in "transformation" pose; polished gray hard stone with traces of cinnabar paint and an incised design; H 7" (17.8 cm); The Art Museum, Princeton University. This figure is one of the master-pieces of naturalistic Olmec sculpture. Despite its small size, it conveys monumentality and a spiritual tension that would surely be even greater if the eyes still had their inlays of shell or stone. The figure may once have been dressed with a kilt of perishable material, for the cinnabar that originally covered it stops at the lower body and resumes at the upper thighs. The toad design may represent the sitter's animal alter ego, or it may be a glyph that stands for the act of transformation.*

53

OLMEC

A. Olmec, Tabasco; c. 1000 BC; La Venta–style male figure; greenstone; H 7 1/8" (18.1 cm). Elongation of the head, accomplished by binding the infant's skull, realistically represented here and in other Olmec figures, was practiced not only by the Olmec but also by the Maya and, later, in North America, especially on the Northwest Coast.

B. Olmec, Veracruz; 1200–800 BC; votive axe representing the supernatural were-jaguar; stone; H 7 1/8" (18.1 cm). The were-jaguar is practically the defining symbol of Olmec art. The so-called flame eyebrows on this and similar representations may symbolize the feather crest of the harpy eagle, another prominent feature of the Olmec animal style.

C. Olmec, Veracruz or Tabasco; 1200–800 BC; child-like being; stone; H 4 7/8" (12.5 cm). This class of Olmec figure may represent forerunners of the *chaneques,* child-like rain bringers that still survive in the belief systems of some Mexican rural peoples.

D. Olmec, Rio Pesquero, Veracruz; c. 1000 BC; votive celt; veined and mottled gray-green jade-like hard stone; H 6 7/8" (17.8 cm). An astonishing number of incised and plain jade ceremonial axes and superbly carved jade masks have been taken from the Rio Pesquero area since the discovery of a large Olmec cache at this site in the early 1960s. Some of the masks may be seen in the museum of the University of Veracruz in Jalapa, the state capital.

A

B

C

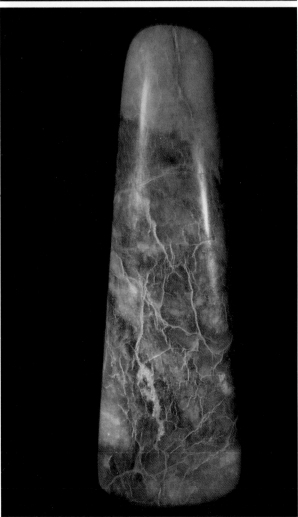

D

A. Olmec, Guerrero; 1000–800 BC; crouching animal with jaguar, harpy eagle, and crocodilian aspects; carved and engraved jade; L 4 3/8" (11.1 cm).

B. Olmec, Guerrero; c. 1000 BC; harpy eagle; carved and incised blue–green translucent jade; L 3 7/8" (9.8 cm). Long known as "spoons", these artifacts, most of which are in stylized bird form, are thought by some to have been tablets for hallucinogenic or psychedelic snuff used in visionary rites.

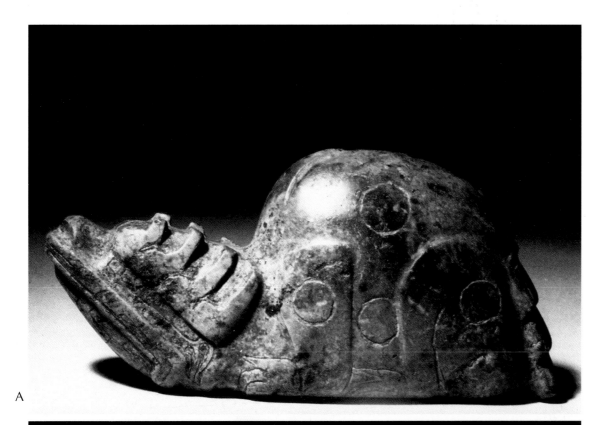

A

B

A

OLMEC

A. Olmec, Las Bocas (?); 1200–800 BC; bowl; kaolin-slipped terracotta with intentional firing marks; 5 1/4" (13.3 cm); The Art Museum, Princeton University. Like all other native American pottery-making cultures, past and present, the Olmec did not use the wheel, yet they produced some of the most exquisite vessel forms, solely by coiling.

B. Olmec, Tepantecuanitlan, Guerrero; 1200–800 BC; female figure; kaolin-slipped terracotta; H 4 1/2" (11.4 cm); The Art Museum, Princeton University.

B

OPPOSITE PAGE

Olmec, Tenenexpah, Veracruz; c. 1000 BC; female figure; terracotta with cream–colored polished kaolin slip and reddish turban; H 13 1/4" (33.6 cm). Like other nude Olmec figures, this one was probably originally clothed in appropriate garments.

57

OLMEC

A. Olmec, Las Bocas;
1200–800 BC; vase of masked
personage in acrobatic posture;
kaolin-slipped terracotta; H 8 1/2"
(21.6 cm). Several effigy vases in
the form of "acrobats" are known
from the Olmec period. "Acrobats" suggests entertainment, but
in fact yoga-like techniques are
used to induce altered states of
consciousness, and vaulting and
somersaulting are still employed
in transformation rites of
contemporary South American
Indians.

B. Olmec, Tlatilco or Las Bocas;
1200–800 BC; bottle; terracotta
with black slip and carved jaguar
paw design; H 7 1/2" (19.1 cm).
The four-pointed element within
the paw may stand for Venus as
Morning Star, a celestial phenomenon that was important in
Mesoamerican sky watching at
least since Olmec times and
probably earlier.

C. Olmec, Las Bocas;
1200–800 BC; figure of indeter-
minate sex; kaolin-slipped
terracotta with traces of cinnabar
paint; H 2 1/4" (5.7 cm); The Art
Museum, Princeton University.
This remarkable figure, just over
two inches high, again illustrates
the ability of Olmec artists to
achieve monumentality even in
the miniature. In style and
execution it clearly relates to the
much larger hollow figure on the
facing page.

B

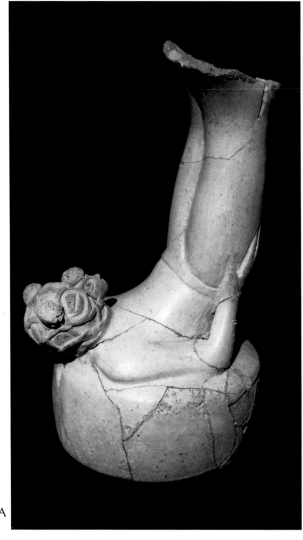

A

C

58

Olmec, provenance unknown;
1200–800 BC; baby; kaolin-
slipped hollow terracotta;
H 11 1/4" (28.6 cm). No matter
what their size—and these so-
called babies range from about
two inches to almost twenty—
these sculptures were modeled
with great attention to detail,
especially the face, hands, and
feet. They always lack specific
sexual characteristics and are
depicted with expressions and
gestures that suggest calling,
listening, or hailing.

TLATILCO

A. Tlatilco; 1100–900 BC; large hollow female figure; terracotta with red slip; H 141/2" (36.8 cm). Tlatilco, a large brick-clay pit formerly on the outskirts of Mexico City but long since swallowed up by urban sprawl, was the site of hundreds of burials, which yielded innumerable high-quality figures in the widespread Tlatilco style, as well as Olmec funerary offerings.

B. Tlatilco; 1100–900 BC; "pretty lady"; unslipped terracotta with white paint; H 31/8" (8 cm). The Tlatilco style is contemporary with, but distinct from, that of the Olmec, whose artists provided about ten percent of the offerings recovered from Tlatilco graves.

C. Tlatilco; 1100–900 BC; mask; terracotta; H 51/2" (14 cm). Tlatilco figures are generally female, but a small percentage are male, with features characteristic of shamans. Some of these miniature shamans wear masks, often grotesque, that cover only the front of the face; this one is a full-sized version of such a mask.

D. Tlatilco; 1100–900 BC; Janus-faced "pretty lady"; unslipped terracotta; H 41/4" (10.8 cm). Tlatilco figures are very varied, with some carrying children or dogs, others dancing or playing ball. Some are daubed with yellow, red, white, or purple, the colors of the sacred maize. Janus-faced or two-headed figures like this one may symbolize the principle of duality or personify the double ears of maize that are still important in Mexican Indian belief and ritual.

60

A

B

C

D

A

TLATILCO

A. Tlatilco; 1100–900 BC; jaguar effigy bowl; buff-colored terracotta with traces of cinnabar; D 6" (15.2 cm). Several carved animal effigy vessels of this style from Tlatilco are so similar in decorative details as to suggest they were created by the same potter.

B. Tlatilco; 1100–900 BC; fish effigy vase; terracotta with black slip and incising; H 8" (20.3 cm).

B

TLATILCO

A. Tlatilco style, Pacific slope of Guatemala; 1100–900 BC; life-death maskette pendant; terracotta with black slip and traces of cinnabar; H 2 1/16" (5.2 cm). A very similar but much larger life-death mask was found at Tlatilco; the same motif also occurs on the Gulf Coast and in other regions of ancient Mesoamerica.

B. Tlatilco; 1100–900 BC; shaman's mask; unslipped terracotta; H 6 1/4" (15.9 cm).

C. Tlatilco; 1100–900 BC; large-beaked baby bird; terracotta with black slip and traces of cinnabar; H 5" (12.7 cm).

D. Tlatilco; 1100–900 BC; Olmec-style *olla;* kaolin-slipped black terracotta; D 9" (22.8 cm).

E. Tlatilco; 1100–900 BC; bottle; terracotta with tan and black slip and grooved decoration; H 10" (25.4 cm). This is a characteristic Tlatilco form.

F. Tlatilco, Las Bocas; 1100–900 BC; vase representing a bottle on a cut-out ring base; terracotta with red slip; H 8 1/2" (21.6 cm).

A

B

C

D

E

A

XOCHIPALA

A. Xochipala; 1400–1200 BC; pendant; shell; H 4" (10.2 cm). Discovered only in the 1960s, the village culture site at Xochipala in Guerrero has yielded an enormous number of sophisticated artifacts, including shell ornaments with cut-out designs like this one, elegantly carved and polished steatite bowls (64B), and superbly modeled, often highly naturalistic, ceramic figures in a distinctive Early to Middle Formative style. Most of the figures are small and solid (63B, 64A) but there are also large hollow effigies (63C, 65). The early dates for this complex have been confirmed by thermoluminescence tests.

B. Xochipala; 1400–1200 BC; "pretty lady"; unslipped terracotta with traces of red paint; H 6 3/4" (17.2 cm).

C. Xochipala; 1400–1200 BC; hollow figure; unslipped terracotta; H 15" (38.1 cm). With its bulging cheek pouches and small animal ears, this extraordinary figure, one of the largest Xochipala clay sculptures known, apparently represents a "squirrel person", that is, a squirrel in its human manifestation. The squirrel plays an important role in the symbolism of some Mexican Indian peoples, including the Huichol, who call it the "companion of the Sun".*

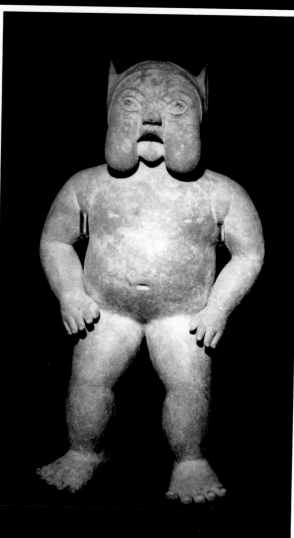

63

XOCHIPALA

A. Xochipala, Guerrero; 1400–1200 BC; seated woman; unslipped terracotta; H 4 1/2" (11.5 cm). While Tlatilco figures have been well known since the 1920s, the extraordinarily beautiful, naturalistic Xochipala figures began to be recognized as a separate, and older, tradition only in the 1960s.

B. Xochipala; 1400–1200 BC; tripod bowl; gray steatite with incised decoration and traces of cinnabar paint; D 8 1/8" (20.7 cm). The stone bowls from this site are among the most beautiful ever found in Mexico. The technology and decoration of some of these bowls is clearly Olmec, but the figures they accompany belong, rather, to a generalized Early to Middle Formative style of extraordinary beauty, expressiveness, and naturalism.

A

B

64

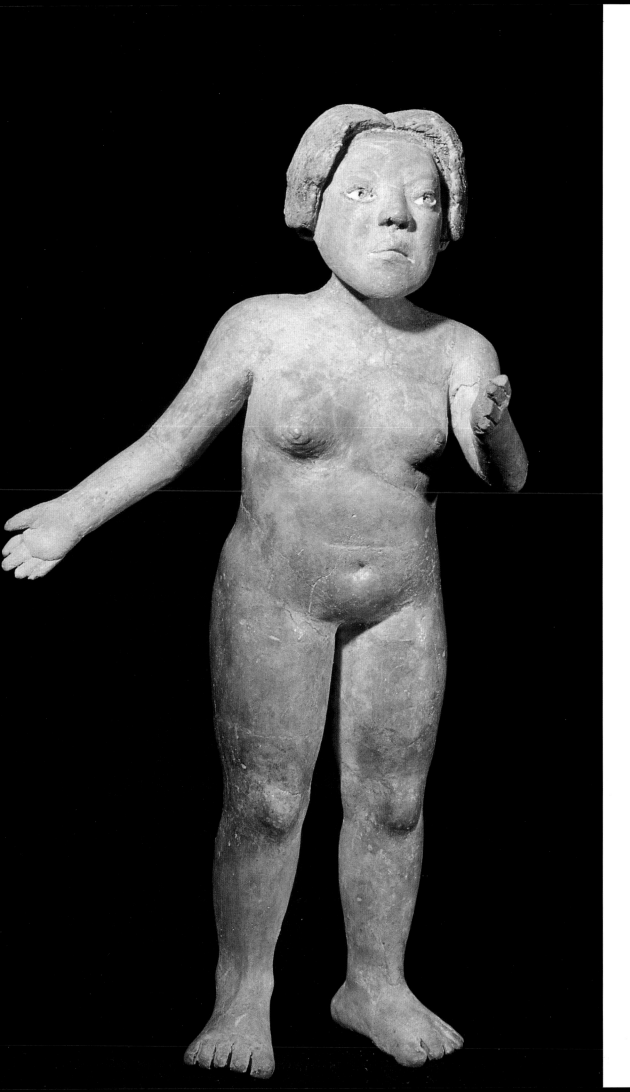

XOCHIPALA

Xochipala; 1400–1200 BC; woman; terracotta with traces of red paint and coloration in the eyes; H 9" (22.8 cm). Except for the feet, somewhat enlarged to permit her to stand without support, the proportions of this lovely figure conform closely to the human body. The hair, parted in the center and cut short, is beautifully detailed and, in sharp contrast with the Tlatilco figure style, the hands and feet are carefully and realistically modeled, with fingers and toes. Since many Xochipala figures are shown with clothing and other adornments, perhaps this woman once wore clothing of perishable materials.

XOCHIPALA

A. Xochipala, Guerrero; 1400–1200 BC; bowl; gray-green hard stone with engraved stylized animal in Olmec style with traces of cinnabar paint; D 7" (17.7 cm). This is a splendid example of a number of superbly carved and polished stone bowls, clearly of Olmec origin, found in Xochipala, accompanied by the most sophisticated early ceramic figures discovered in the Americas.

B. Xochipala; 1400–1200 BC; shaman; unslipped terracotta with traces of red paint; H 91/4" (23.5 cm). The costume, possibly representing feathers and thus associating the subject with birds and the sky world, and the two-horned headdress leave little doubt that this is a shaman.

C. Xochipala; 1400–1200 BC; ballplayer; unslipped terracotta with traces of red and white paint; H 41/2" (11.5 cm). In ancient Mesoamerica ball games functioned as sacred and divinatory rituals and reenactment of cosmic myths, rather than mere sports. There was not just one type of game or court but many; the Xochipalans evidently played a game involving a heavy ball and a triple wristguard, perhaps of wood covered with rubber or leather.

B

A

C

66

A

B

C

D

E

F

CHUPÍCUARO

A. Chipícuaro; 500–300 BC; female figure; unslipped, solid terracotta with traces of red and white; H 4 1/4" (10.8 cm). Chupícuaro is a village in Guanajuato where great numbers of small, solid figures like this one, larger hollow polychromed females, and pottery vessels in many shapes were found before the Solís Dam inundated the region in 1949. Subsequently, more funerary art in a similar style was found nearby and as far away as Michoacán.

B. Chupícuaro style, Querendaro, Michoacán; 500–300 BC; terracotta figures; tallest: H 5" (12.7 cm).

C. Chupícuaro; 500–300 BC; shaman; terracotta with light beige slip and traces of red; H 5 3/4" (14.6 cm). Single as well as double horns are widely associated with shamanism, and horned figures are assumed to be shamans.

D. Chupícuaro; 500–300 BC; female figure; hollow terracotta with red and white painted decoration; H 19 1/2" (49.5 cm). This is an unusually tall example of a well-known Chupícuaro type of standing figure, invariably female, with strong red and white, or black, red, and white, geometric designs applied over buff clay and polished to a high gloss after firing. In almost all cases there is little emphasis on the breasts but the belly protrudes slightly.

E. Chupícuaro; 300–100 BC; funerary mask; terracotta with red decoration on buff-colored slip H 6 1/2" (16.5 cm). With the eye openings over the half-closed filleted eyes, this mask might have been worn in life as well as death.

F. Chupícuaro; 500–300 BC; pedestal bowl; red slip with black and white decoration over buff terracotta; D 10" (25.4 cm).

67

CHUPÍCUARO

Chupícuaro; 500–300 BC; maternity effigy; highly polished terracotta with red slip and black and white geometric designs; H 9 1/2" (24.2 cm). Among the hollow polychromed female figures in this style, joined mothers and infants are rare, but those that exist are strikingly similar.

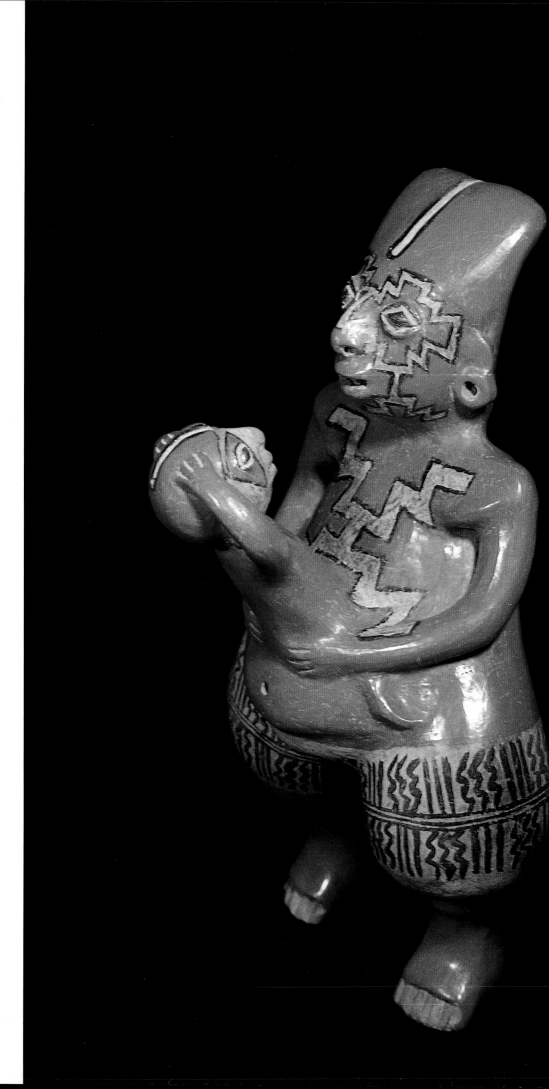

A

COLIMA

A. Colima; 100 BC–200 AD; shaman whistle figure; unslipped terracotta; H 51/4" (13.3 cm).

B. Colima; 100 BC–200 AD; figure of woman; unslipped terracotta; H 11" (27.9 cm). An unusually large figure in the highly abstracted "Colima flat" style. Great numbers of solid male and female, mostly standing, figures in this style have been found. They are generally between two and eight inches high, although some, like this one, are larger. A small percentage of "flats" have slips, such as 70B.

B

COLIMA

A. Colima; 100 BC–200 AD; shaman; terracotta with highly polished red slip; H 14 1/8" (36 cm); Lowe Art Museum, University of Miami. This extraordinary effigy represents the shaman as initiator and "father" of a young disciple, here shown hanging from his knees down the older man's front in a position suggesting birth. In his right hand the shaman holds an axe and in his left a small head, possibly representing the symbolic physical dismemberment and reassemblage of the initiation rite.*

B. Colima; 100 BC–200 AD; tomb attendant; terracotta with highly burnished brown slip; H 12" (30.5 cm). An excellent example of this class of relatively large but solid, rather than hollow, figures in Colima funerary art.

C. Colima; 100 BC–200 AD; personage wearing garment with elaborate engraved geometric design; terracotta with traces of polychrome; H 12 1/2" (31.8 cm). This type of solid figure is typical of those found at Autlán, a small early Colima site.

D. Colima; 100 BC–200 AD; shaman; terracotta with burnished red slip; H 12 1/4" (31.1 cm). Tomb attendants of this type wear prominent necklaces of either five (as here) or seven carved shell ornaments. Actual shells in this shape have been recovered from Colima sites.

70

A

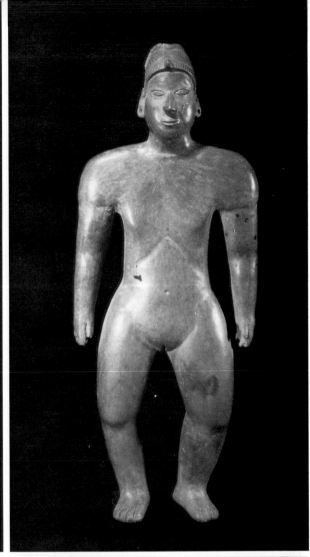

B

C

D

Colima; 100 BC–200 AD; shaman;
terracotta with red slip and incised ornamentation; H 14 1/2"
(36.8 cm). Once mis-identified as
"warriors", horned figures of this
type from Colima, sometimes
depicted in fighting stance, are
now generally recognized as
shamans. The meaning of the
pectoral protuberance, often
found on such figures, is not
known. It might represent a
pouch containing shamanic articles worn as a pendant.

COLIMA

Colima; 100 BC–200 AD; lidded cylinder vase; terracotta with burnished dark red slip on the vase and buff slip on the lid, with relief decoration; H 11" (28 cm), D 9 3/4" (24.8 cm). This funerary vase, unusual both in its large size and in that it retains its original lid, is embellished on four sides with relief representations of a man walking through an arch formed by a double-headed serpent. This may depict the deceased entering the Underworld. The imagery may also reflect the conception of the Sun God's traveling from west to east through an Underworld ringed by a giant double-headed serpent.

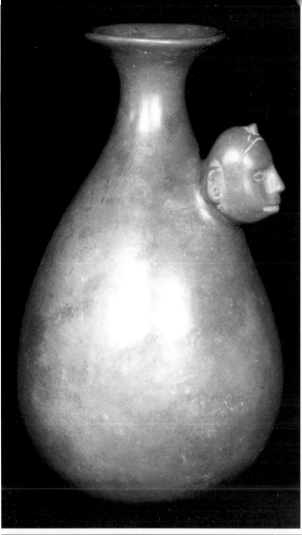

A

B

COLIMA

A. Colima; 100 BC–200 AD; vase with shaman head; terracotta with highly burnished red slip; H 141/4" (36.2 cm).

B. Colima; 100 BC–200 AD; bowl supported by acrobatic figure; terracotta with burnished red slip; H 101/2" (26.7 cm).

C. Colima; 100 BC–200 AD; vessel with three parrots standing on their tails supporting a gadrooned, globular bowl; terracotta with burnished red slip; D 13" (33 cm). These elegantly modeled pots were doubtless inspired by one of the many types of squash cultivated by the ancient Mexicans. Parrots were widely associated with the deified sun. Some vessels of this type have human or animal figures as supports.

C

COLIMA

A. Colima; 100 BC–200 AD; dog; terracotta with burnished orange slip; L 14" (35.6 cm). Naturalistically modeled dogs are the best-known of all Colima art. Most tombs contained at least one, and sometimes several. They appear in numerous positions, sizes, and conditions—from emaciated to, as here, fat. We can only guess at their purpose or significance.

B. Colima; 100 BC–200 AD; vessel with spout rising out of center of five-pointed star; terracotta with highly burnished red slip; H 4 3/4" (12 cm), W 7" (17.8 cm).

C. Colima; 100 BC–200 AD; spouted vessel with spines or spikes; terracotta with brown slip, with light buff overslip except on top, bottom, and spout; H 6 1/2" (16.5 cm). The spines or spikes on this and some other similarly adorned West Mexican ceramics almost certainly have a natural model in cactus or another spiny plant.

D. Colima; 100 BC–200 AD; *reclinatorio,* or headrest, in form of double bird; terracotta with orange slip; W 9" (22.8 cm). Found only in Colima, these curious artifacts reportedly supported the heads of the deceased, somewhat like the ceramic pillows of the Chinese. They are usually in the form of parrots and other birds.

E. Colima; 100 BC–200 AD; vessel in form of swallow-like bird; terracotta with burnished reddish-brown slip and traces of painted black line decoration; L 7 1/2" (19 cm).

F. Colima; 100 BC–200 AD; conch shell trumpet; terracotta with cream slip; L 9 1/2" (24.1 cm). The species of shell represented is the queen conch, a native of the Gulf of Mexico. The numerous shell trumpets found in West Coast burials are invariably of Caribbean rather than Pacific Ocean origin, giving evidence of early contact between widely separated peoples.

74

A

B

C

D

E

F

Nayarit, Ixtlán del Río style;
100 BC–200 AD; tomb guardian;
polychromed terracotta; H 26 3/4"
(68 cm). Despite a high degree of
stylization, this large, well-
modeled figure conveys a
natural, very human dignity.
Wearers of such a peaked cap
are believed to represent a Fire
Keeper or Guardian of the Fire.

75

NAYARIT

A. Nayarit, San Sebastián Red style; 100 BC–200 AD; standing nude woman; terracotta with polychrome decoration; H 21 1/4" (53.4 cm). Though named for the shaft tomb site at San Sebastián, Jalisco, this style of figure is found on both sides of the Jalisco-Nayarit border.

B. Nayarit; 100 BC–200 AD; house model; terracotta with cream slip and red-and-black decoration; H 11 3/4" (28.8 cm). With their lively inhabitants engaged in domestic as well as ceremonial pursuits, these house models, mostly from the Ixtlán del Río area, not only provide information about domestic architecture and activities but, because of their presence in tombs, tend to confirm that the ancients believed the deceased continued their daily life in the Otherworld.

C. Nayarit, Chinesco Type E; 100 BC–200 AD; seated woman; terracotta with cream slip and polychrome decoration; H 10 7/8" (27.6 cm). With their often puffy, closed or half-closed eyes, the sensitively modeled and well-finished figures in this Chinesco sub-style appear in trance or even death. Slits in the cheeks attest to a ritual dance in which the participants were linked by a cord passing through their cheeks. The name "Chinesco" derives from the Oriental-looking eyes of the figures in this style.

B

A

C

76

NAYARIT

A. Nayarit, Chinesco Type B; 100 BC–200 AD; female figure; terracotta with polychrome and negative decoration over red slip; H 11 1/2" (29.2 cm). Figures in this style (dubbed "Martian" for their oval heads) usually come in male-female pairs. They are characterized by very thin arms and legs, rings in the nose, eyes and mouth indicated by slits or paint, and hair indicated by engraved lines.

B. Nayarit, Chinesco style; 100 BC–200 AD; human effigy bowl; terracotta with red slip and black decoration; D 11" (28 cm).

C. Nayarit, Ixtlán del Río style; 100 BC–200 AD; female figure; polychromed terracotta; H 11" (27 cm).

A

B

C

D

E

F

D. Nayarit; 100 BC–200 AD; miniature bed figure; unslipped terracotta; L 4 1/2" (11.5 cm). Although these prone figures are usually called men or women, the protective arch over the head, similar to those on North American Indian infant carriers, suggests that these "beds" are actually cradles and that the figures are infants.

E. Nayarit, Ixtlán del Río style; 100 BC–200 AD; seated pair; polychromed terracotta; left: H 16 1/2" (41.9 cm) right: H 15 1/2" (39.4 cm).

F. Nayarit; 100 BC–200 AD; funerary procession; unslipped terracotta; L 9" (22.8 cm). Nayarit tomb art is famous for its lively representations of daily and post-mortem activities. The deceased is carried to his or her grave by family members preceded by three men carrying clubs or staffs and facing left. This recalls Hopi initiation ceremonies in which members of the Kwanitaka, armed with clubs, protect against witches that threaten from the left.

JALISCO

A. Jalisco; 100 BC–200 AD; seated male; buff-colored terracotta with traces of black and red paint; H 14 1/2" (36.8 cm). Crossed arms resting on up-drawn knees is a position typical of some Jalisco and Nayarit male figures, while females are usually seated on their legs.

B. Jalisco; 100 BC–200 AD; mother, or mother goddess, holding a child on her lap; highly burnished terracotta with brown slip and designs painted on the breasts and face; H 18" (45.7 cm).

A

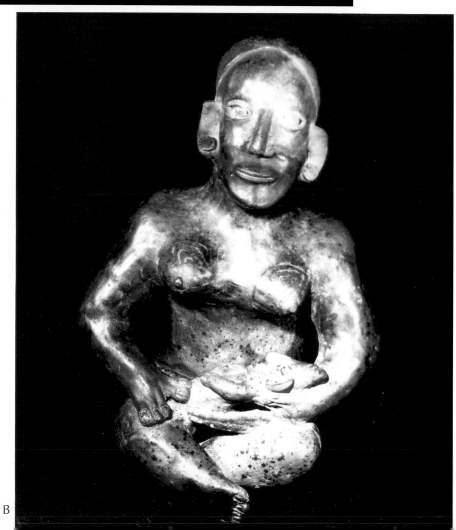

B

A

JALISCO

A. Jalisco; 100 BC–200 AD; male and female seated figures; buff-colored terracotta with traces of painted decoration; male: H 12" (30.5 cm); female: H 11 5/8" (29.5 cm). The heads of these dramatically stylized figural sculptures suggest the Guadalajara style, characterized by high foreheads and elongated features.

B. Jalisco, Teocaltiche; 100 BC–200 AD; funerary attendants; hollow polychromed buff terracotta with red, white, and black decoration; male: H 14" (35.6 cm); female: H 13" (33 cm). In this striking style the males always have a pair of mushroom-shaped "horns", identifying them as shamans associated with the sacred mushrooms or, possibly, personifications of the mushroom spirits. In some examples, the male pounds a drum, and both male and female are depicted as singing or chanting.

B

JALISCO

A. Jalisco, Ameca Gray type; 10 BC–200 AD; pregnant woman; terracotta with white slip and traces of color; H c. 16" (40.5 cm). These large, hollow figures are so standardized as to suggest that the personage represented is a goddess rather than a human being.

B. Jalisco, San Juanito style; 100 BC–200 AD; female funerary attendant; polychromed terracotta; H 21 1/2" (54.6 cm).

C. Jalisco, Ameca Gray type; 100 BC–200 AD; shaman holding an offering gourd bowl, with a female figure; terracotta with white slip; H 18" (45.7 cm). In a common variant on this theme, a singing or chanting shaman is seated, sometimes on the lap of the woman, who holds on to him from the back and faces left.

D. Jalisco; 100 BC–200 AD; four persons in a smoking ceremony; terracotta; H 11" (28 cm). Such scenes are invariably shamanistic, because shamans smoked the powerful *Nicotiana rustica* tobacco to feed the spirits and to induce altered states in which they sought advice from the spirits.

E. Jalisco; 100 BC–200 AD; effigy vase of man lying in fetal position; burnished terracotta with brown slip; H 6 5/8" (16.8 cm).

F. Jalisco; 100 BC–200 AD; dish; terracotta with red four-directional and sacred-center design on highly burnished cream slip; 6" (15.2 cm). This type of Jalisco ware relates to Late Chupícuaro ceramics, examples of which have been found in some West Mexican shaft tombs.

A

B

C

D

E

F

ZAPOTEC

Zapotec, Monte Albán III;
250–500 AD; figural funerary urn;
buff terracotta; H 8¾" (22.3 cm);
Munson-Williams Proctor
Institute, Utica, N.Y. These
complex effigies of gods and
goddesses with feathered head-
dresses and other attributes of
exalted status never contain
bones or ashes, and may have
functioned only as receptacles for
the soul or spirit power.

ZAPOTEC

A. Zapotec, Monte Albán II;
100 BC–250 AD; drinking or
libation cup in form of human
head with place glyph on
forehead; buff-colored terracotta;
H 6" (15.3 cm).

B. Zapotec, Monte Albán III;
250–500 AD; effigy urn of the god
Cosijo; gray terracotta; H 11 1/4"
(29.6 cm).

C. Zapotec, Monte Albán III;
250–500 AD; libation cup with
jaguar head effigy; gray terracotta; H 6 3/8" (16.2 cm).

B

A

C

A

B

C

TEOTIHUÁCAN

A. Teotihuácan III; 300–550 AD; lidded incense burner; polychromed buff-colored terracotta with mold-made appliqués; H 13" (33 cm). At Teotihuácan these elaborate works were apparently assembled by the family to symbolize different attributes of the deceased. After speeding the soul on its way in the smoke of the burning incense, the vessels were smashed and the pieces left in the tomb. Reassembling them is usually a matter of educated guesswork.

B. Teotihuácan III; 250–550 AD; mask; stone; H 77/8" (20 cm). Teotihuácan style funerary masks, originally inlaid with shell and obsidian eyes and probably shell teeth, were made not in the great city, but in the states of Guerrero and Puebla; indeed, very few have been found at Teotihuácan itself. Nevertheless, they epitomize the highest stylistic ideals of Teotihuácan.*

C. Teotihuácan style, Escuintla, Guatemala; c. 350 AD; male figure; polychromed terracotta; H 4 /2" (11.4 cm). This sumptuously clothed effigy was one of a group of six found on the Pacific coast of Guatemala but clearly made by a Teotihuácan sculptor. Teotihuácan figures are almost never so elaborately clothed, but instead were made to wear clothing of perishable materials.

TEOTIHUÁCAN

A. Teotihuácan; Late Formative, 200 BC–100 AD; mask; greenstone; H 7 1/2" (19 cm).

B. Teotihuácan III; 250–550 AD; cylindrical tripod vase; highly burnished terracotta with brown slip and incised design; H 5 5/8" (14.3 cm). This type of vessel, with its three squarish feet, is a characteristic Teotihuácan ceramic form, which varies mainly in the decoration on its surface.

C. Teotihuácan III; 300–400 AD; cylindrical tripod vase; buff-colored terracotta with incised low-relief stylized owl decoration; H 5 3/8" (13.7 cm).

D. Teotihuácan III; 250–550 AD; lidded tripod vessel; terracotta with burnished white kaolin slip and incised kneeling personage with bird headdress, holding a serpent staff; H 10 3/4" (27.3 cm).

E. Teotihuácan II; 100–200 AD; figure; stone; H 7 1/4" (18.4 cm). This figure was probably made in Guerrero. Many Mesoamerican cultures, from Olmec to Aztec, made small stone and clay figures to accompany the dead. The prominent drill hole in this example may be for the release of the spirit or one of the multiple souls that were believed to animate each individual.

F. Teotihuácan II; 100–250 AD; figure; stone; H 18 1/8" (46 cm). Teotihuácan stone sculptures as large and strongly modeled as this almost always come from the state of Puebla rather than Guerrero.

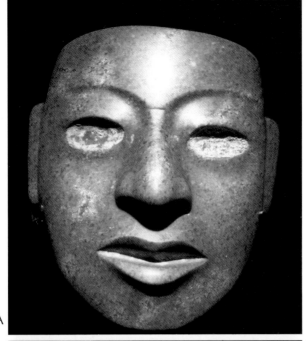

A

B

C

D

E

F

84

A

B

C

D

VERACRUZ

A. Huastec, Veracruz; Late Formative, 500–300 BC; ballplayer; unslipped buff-colored terracotta; H 10 1/2" (26.7 cm). Figures of this type usually show the ballplayer wearing a protective wrist guard, knee pad, and "yoke" around the waist.

B. Huastec, Veracruz; Late Formative, c. 500 BC–100 AD; aged woman; highly burnished buff-colored solid terracotta; H 4 1/2" (11.5 cm). Figures of this type may represent the old goddess the later Aztecs called Toci, Grandmother or Mother of the Gods.

C. Veracruz; Early Classic, 200–600 AD; effigy flute; unslipped buff-colored terracotta with appliqué head of the Old Fire God; L 13 1/2" (34.3 cm). The Old Fire God was an important motif in central Veracruz art during the Classic period; in Central Mexico he is the earliest recognizable deity to be depicted in stone sculpture.

D. Huastec, Veracruz; 1450–1519 AD; male personage; stone; H 26 1/4" (66.7 cm). Compared with Aztec stone sculptures, those of the Huastec, while always powerful, appear somewhat provincial. The Aztec style obviously found some of its inspiration in Huastec art.

85

VERACRUZ

Veracruz, Remojadas; Late Classic, 600–700 AD; smiling youth; mold-made, hand-finished, buff-colored terracotta with traces of pigment and a whistle in the headdress; H 20 1/2" (52.1 cm). The headband across the artificially deformed head is decorated with a Totonac version of the Mixtec and Aztec sign for energy or movement. These smiling male and female figures are very prominent in the Veracruz culture and are among the most well known images in Pre-Columbian art. Their significance remains a mystery.

A. Veracruz; Early Classic, 200–500 AD; head fragment of the Old Fire God; unslipped terracotta with burn marks at top rim; W 10" (25.4 cm). Complete seated figures of this important god, of which several large examples are known, have a large dish on the head for the burning of copal incense. Note that this head is near life-size.

B. Veracruz; Early Classic, 100–300 AD; yoke; fine-grained, highly polished diorite with incised serpent design and traces of cinnabar; L 16" (40.6.cm). Some scholars propose that these heavy stone yokes, which can weigh as much as sixty pounds, were actually worn in the ritual ball game to protect the player from the impact of the ball. However, remains of such yokes made of wood have also been found, suggesting that the stone yokes are trophies, replicating in permanent form more functional wooden belts. The form and the decorations also had symbolic meaning, perhaps signifying the uterine entrance into the Underworld, a region closely associated with the ball game. See 72 for an example of another use of the U-shaped symbol.

A

B

87

VERACRUZ

A. Totonac, Veracruz; Late Classic, 600–900 AD; *hacha*; basalt sculpture representing head of ballplayer wearing vulture headdress; H 8½" (21.6 cm). The Spanish term *hacha*, axe, for this type of sculpture refers to the axeblade-like thinness of many of these works. It is conjectured that figural *hachas* may have been used as markers in the ritual ball game.

B. Totonac, Veracruz; Late Classic, 600–900 AD; *hacha* in form of a monkey's head; basalt with shell teeth and eyes; H 6" (15.2 cm).

C. Veracruz, El Tajín; Late Classic, 600–800 AD; *palma;* basalt carved on both sides with Classic Veracruz double-outlined scroll motif; H 16½" (41.9 cm). These beautiful works got their name from a vague resemblance to palm leaves. Like the *hachas* (see 88A and 88B), they are associated with the ritual ball game. *Hachas*, perhaps of stone but more likely carved of wood, were worn on the front of a protective belt, but how the *palmas* were used is not known.

D. Veracruz, Remojadas; Late Classic, 600–900 AD; articulated figure; mold-made terracotta with movable arms and legs; H 13½" (34.3 cm). Articulated figures have been found in different parts of Mesoamerica, dating as far back as the early Olmec period.

A

B

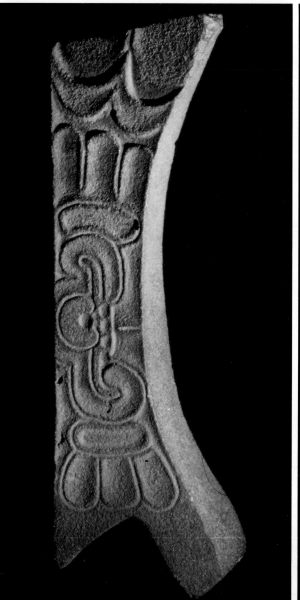

C

D

88

B

A

A. Veracruz; Late Classic, 600–900 AD; goddess; mold-made terracotta; H 9 1/4" (23.5 cm).

B. Veracruz, Remojadas; Early Classic, 100–300 AD; female figure, probably a goddess; buff-colored terracotta with white, light blue, and red pigment, and black tar to accent eyes and hair; H c. 14" (35.5 cm).

E

C

D

C. Veracruz; Late Classic, 600–900 AD; wheeled jaguar whistle figure; unslipped terracotta; L 7 1/8" (18.1 cm). Because the wheel was unknown in Mexico in pre-European times, wheeled animal figures, which have been found on the Gulf Coast, in Michoacán, and at Teotihuácan, present a puzzle. However, terracotta and metal wheeled animals were common in Asia from the third millennium BC, so the possibility of chance contacts cannot be ruled out.

D. Veracruz; Late Classic, 600–900 AD; whistle in the form of an anthropomorphic bat; mold-made terracotta; H 3 11/16" (9.4 cm). Whistle figures occur in enormous numbers in Veracruz art; archaeological examples found in the fields or graves are still used by shamans in curing ceremonies.

E. Veracruz; Late Classic, 500–700 AD; whistle figure representing a man self-administering an enema; unslipped terracotta; L 5" (12.7 cm). Rituals involving the rectal administering of intoxicating substances appear to have been widespread in pre-Conquest Mesoamerica.

VERACRUZ

A. Veracruz; Late Classic, 500–700 AD; man dressed in jaguar pelt and jaguar headdress; terracotta; H 37" (94 cm). Gulf Coast art is known for ceramic sculpture of large size and, despite a certain stiffness, great vitality. Donning a jaguar skin may represent a shaman's, noble's, or warrior's identity with, and transformation into, that powerful tropical cat.

B. Veracruz; Early Classic, 300–600 AD; priest or warrior painted with black tar (*chapopote*); terracotta; H c. 24" (61 cm).

C. Veracruz; Early Classic, 100–200 AD; nude man with filed teeth; terracotta with red paint and specular hematite on forehead and black tar to emphasize eyes; H 12" (30.5 cm); The Art Museum, Princeton University. This remarkably life-like and expressive figure was probably dressed and given real human hair.

OPPOSITE PAGE

MAYA

Maya, Jaina; Late Classic, 700–800 AD; whistle figure representing the Moon Goddess Ixchél; terracotta with traces of the distinctive Mayan blue on hair; H 73/4" (19.7 cm). The Late Classic Mayan cemetery on the island of Jaina has yielded thousands of lifelike figures that are considered the apogee of Mayan miniature terracotta sculpture.

B

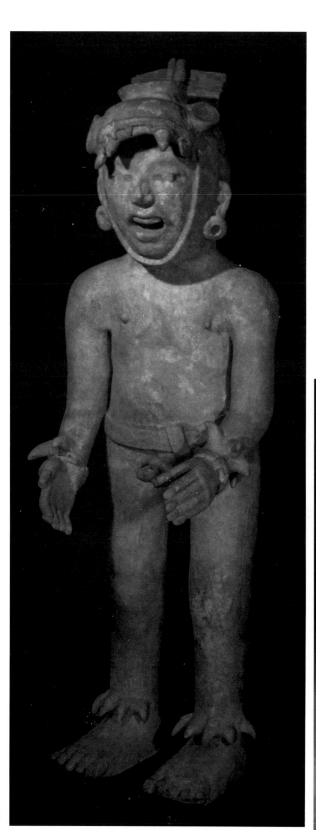

A

C

MAYA

A. Maya, Jaina; Late Classic, 600–800 AD; two figures; terracotta with traces of white, blue, and red paint; H 6 1/2" (16.5 cm).

B. Maya, Jaina; Late Classic, 600–800 AD; man bloodletting from his penis; unslipped terracotta with traces of Mayan blue and red pigment; H 5 1/2" (14 cm). Blood sacrifice from the sexual organ and other body parts was an essential part of Mayan and other ancient Mesoamerican religious ritual.*

C. Maya, Chiapas, Mexico; Late Classic, 600–700 AD; portrait head; stucco; H 8 7/8" (22.5 cm). The center tooth filed to a T shape is an identifying characteristic of the Mayan Sun God.

D. Maya, Jaina; Late Classic, 600–800 AD; rattle in the form of the Moon Goddess Ixchél; mold-made hollow terracotta; H 7" (17.6 cm). Mass production of molded figures is known from Late Classic times on the Gulf Coast, the Maya region, and Teotihuácan. At least ten examples of this figure from the same mold are known.

A

B

C

D

92

A

B

C

D

E

F

MAYA

A. and B. Maya, Jaina; Late Classic, 600–800 AD; two-sided whistle figure representing on one side a priest-shaman in a trance, one hand raised in a mudra-like gesture, and on the reverse the same man, with the same gesture, in his animal manifestation; mold-made polychromed terracotta; H 4" (10.2 cm).

C. Maya, Petén, Guatemala (?); Late Classic, 600–800 AD; pectoral carved with a Mayan ruler or deity in a feathered jaguar head-dress; jade; H 4" (10.2 cm).

D. Maya, Petén, Guatemala; Late Classic, 600–800 AD; pectoral depicting a young lord in a supernatural setting, with glyphs; shell; H 5" (12.7 cm).

E. Maya, Petén; Early Classic, 300–500 AD; tripod vase; terracotta with frescoed Teotihuácan-influenced jaguar design over a thin stucco base; H 7 1/4" (18.4 cm), D 8 1/2" (21.6 cm). During this period there were close trade and ideological connections between the Maya of the Petén and the great city-state of Teotihuácan.

F. Ulua Valley, Honduras; Late Classic, 800–900 AD; marble bowl carved with the complex scrolls and stylized animal faces characteristic of these relatively rare stone sculptures; D 7 1/4" (18.5 cm). Although the Ulua Valley is located on the southern fringes of the Mayan world, the Ulua style reveals little Mayan influence. Who actually produced these fine stone bowls and vases is not known.

93

MAYA

A. Maya, Petén, Guatemala; Late Classic, 600–800 AD; pictorial vase; terracotta; H 63/4" (17.2 cm). This is a beautiful example of Mayan figural vase painting, depicting a conversation between two supernatural animals in human position, the one at left a small deer and other possibly a rabbit. In Mayan cosmology the deer is associated with the sun and the rabbit with the moon.

B. Maya, Petén, Guatemala; Late Classic, 600–800 AD; cylinder vase; terracotta with a pair of catfish painted on a blood-red ground; H 69/16" (17.6 cm). In the *Popol Vuh,* the sacred book of the Quiche Maya, the Hero Twins reassemble themselves in the form of catfish after having been dismembered and their body parts scattered by the lords of the Underworld.

C. Maya, Guatemala; Late Classic, 600–800 AD; cylinder vase with raised relief of an old god in company with a spirit serpent and a flying bat deity; terracotta; H 6" (15.2 cm).

D. Maya, Petén, Guatemala; Late Classic, 600–800 AD; cylinder vase with codex-style depiction of a young lord seated beneath a sky band; terracotta; H 67/8" (17.5 cm). The term "codex style" comes from the similarity of the elegant painting on such vases to that of the Mayan books, or codices.

A

B

C

A. Maya; Early Classic, 300–500 AD; blackware tripod bowl in Teotihuácan style with incised cartouche, possibly a place glyph; terracotta with dark brown slip and trace of red; H 6¾" (16.5 cm), D 9" (22.8 cm). During this period, the great city-state of Teotihuácan in Central Mexico exerted considerable influence on parts of the Mayan world. Much of Mayan portable art and even some ceremonial architecture was made to conform with that of Teotihuácan.

B. Maya, Petén, Guatemala; Early Classic, c. 500 AD; mask; mosaic of green jade embellished with red and white shell and jet; H 5½" (14 cm).*

A

B

95

MEZCALA

A. Mezcala, Guerrero; 250 BC–250 AD; head; stone with eyes of inlaid shell; H 4 1/2" (11.5 cm).

B. Late Mezcala, Guerrero; Postclassic; mask in Sultepec style; stone; H 6 1/8" (15.4 cm). Masks in this style are relatively rare and, with the Olmecoid figure (E), demonstrate the broad stylistic diversity and the long span of the Mezcala stone–carving tradition.

C. Mezcala, Guerrero; 200 BC–200 AD; celt figure with folded arms; stone; H 13" (33 cm).

D. Mezcala, Guerrero; 200 BC–200 AD; figure; stone with eyes and teeth inlaid with shell; H 12 1/2" (30.5 cm).

E. Mezcala, Guerrero; c. 200 BC; Olmecoid figure; polished greenish stone; H 12" (30.5 cm).

F. Mezcala, Guerrero; c. 200 BC; celt figure; polished stone; H 11 1/4" (28.6 cm). A fine example of the purest Mezcala abstract style.

N.B.
Early Mezcala figures show a decided Olmec influence. Nevertheless, the beginning and duration of the Mezcala complex have until recently been a mystery. In 1987 an undisturbed Mezcala grave containing seven stone figures and masks was located. On the basis of radiocarbon assays of organic materials found there, archaeologists have postulated a range of 500 BC to 500 AD. Some scholars believe that further discoveries will place the beginnings of Mezcala culture hundreds of years earlier.

96

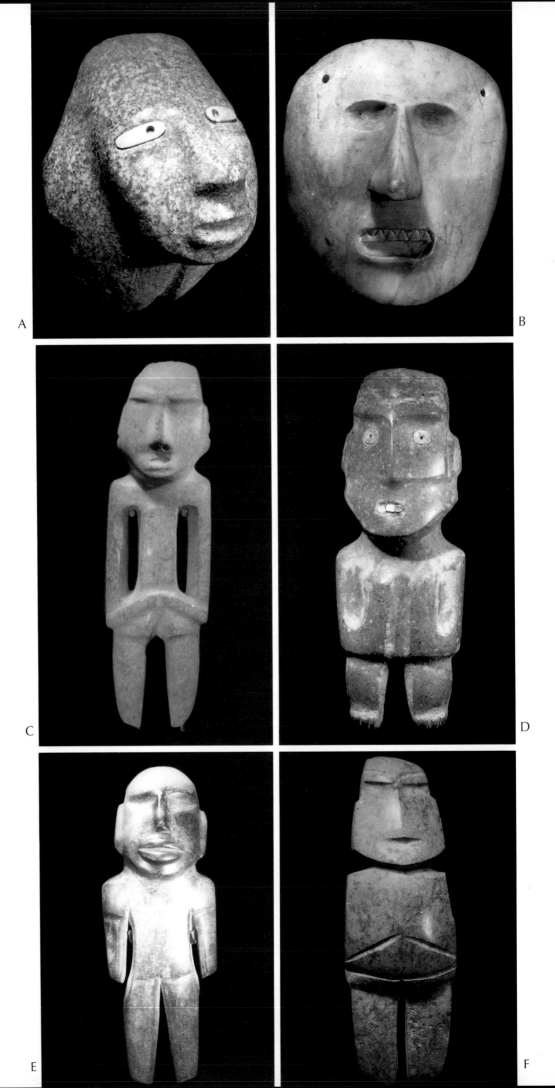

A

B

C

D

E

F

A

MEZCALA

A. Mezcala, Guerrero; 200 BC; seated figure; polished hard stone; H 4 1/4" (10.8 cm).

B. Mezcala, Guerrero; 250 BC–100 AD; temple model with stairway and seven columns on a three-level base; marble; H 7" (17.8 cm). These interesting artifacts may represent small temples constructed of wood or other perishable materials.

C. Mezcala, Guerrero; 250 BC–100 AD; four-columned temple model with two figures, probably representing deities; calcite; H 8 1/2" (21.6 cm). Figures on the roof of temple models are more often shown in prone position, making this one, with a vertical effigy, unusual.

B

C

TOLTEC

A. Toltec, Puebla; Postclassic, 1000–1200 AD; miniature toad effigy bowl; terracotta with plumbate glaze; L 3 1/2" (8.9 cm). Originating in southern Mexico, plumbate ceramics are characterized by lustrous surfaces with high iron content, fired at temperatures that were unusually high for Mesoamerica (up to 1740°F or 950°C). Their color is typically brown, gray, and, as here, olive-gray alternating with orange and reddish brown.

B. Toltec; Postclassic; c. 1000 AD; opossum effigy vessel; terracotta with plumbate glaze; H 6" (15.2 cm). As the only New World marsupial, the opossum was, and still is, a major figure in Mesoamerican mythology.

A

B

A

TOLTEC

A. Toltec, Tula, Hidalgo; c. 1000 AD; coyote effigy vase; terracotta with orange slip; H 7¼" (18.4 cm). Although Tula is more noted for stone sculpture than fine ceramics, this superb animal effigy vase, one of the finest ever to come from this site, is evidence that the great pottery tradition of Central Mexico did not die out with the Classic period.*

B. Tarascan, Michoacán; 1300–1500 AD; rabbit effigy smoking-pipe; unslipped terracotta with engraved decoration; L 7½" (19.1 cm). The Tarascans, noted for a wide variety of effigy tobacco pipes and high-quality polychrome pottery, were contemporaries of the Aztecs, who never succeeded in conquering them. The powerful native species of tobacco, *Nicotiana rustica,* was a sacred plant, smoked to feed and invoke the gods and spirits or to induce visionary trances. The rabbit was an important symbol, often associated with the moon.

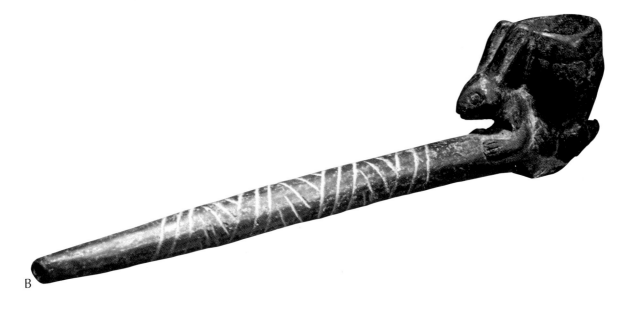

B

99

MIXTEC

A. Mixtec, Puebla or Oaxaca; 1300–1400 AD; monumental vase; terracotta with complex polychrome designs; D 18" (45.7 cm). The Mixtecs, contemporaries of the Aztecs, were renowned for their fine polychrome pottery as well as for turquoise-and-feather mosaics and gold jewelry. Vessels such as this may have been used to hold *pulque,* the fermented ceremonial drink made from the agave cactus that is still important in Mexico.

B. Mixtec, Puebla or Oaxaca; 1300–1500 AD; turkey effigy vase; terracotta with polychrome decoration; H 81/4" (21 cm). In Mexico, the wild turkey was a bird of the sun, eaten only on important ceremonial occasions. It occurs often in Pre-Columbian art, but some of the finest effigies of this magnificent bird are those made by the Mixtecs of Oaxaca or Puebla.

C. Mixtec, Oaxaca; 1300–1500 AD; ceremonial *pulque* drinking bowl; polychromed terracotta; H 47/8" (12.4 cm). Decorations include a three-dimensional jaguar head and painted symbols. On the pedestal is a red-and-white flint blade, an instrument with important mythological associations.

D. Mixtec, Oaxaca; 1200–1400 AD; jaguar effigy vase; polychromed terracotta; H 83/8" (22.3 cm).

A

B

C

D

Mixtec, Oaxaca; 1300–1500 AD; tripod vase with three-dimensional unidentified male deity with elaborate loincloth; polychromed terracotta; H 10 1/2" (26.7 cm). Based on the pictorial evidence in Mixtec manuscripts, Mixtec tripod vases like this one may have been used for the ceremonial cacao drink to confirm noble marriages and in other religious or state ceremonies.

101

AZTEC

A. Aztec, Tenochtitlan (Mexico City); 1450–1521 AD; seated man; basalt with shell inlays in the eyes; H 16" (41 cm).

B. Aztec, Tenochtitlan (Mexico City); 1450–1521 AD; corn goddess; stone; H 181/4" (46.4 cm), W 111/2" (29.2 cm).

C. Aztec, Tenochtitlan (Mexico City); c. 1500 AD; smoking–pipe in form of duck head; terracotta with red slip; L 51/2" (14 cm). Many pipes of the same design, representing ducks, have been found over the years in what was the Aztec capital, suggesting that pipes of this kind were used in a smoking ritual. All of the pipes found are either red or black.

D. Aztec, Guerrero; 1450–1521 AD; mask; obsidian; H 71/2" (19.1 cm). From Olmec times the lapidaries of Guerrero produced works of art in precious stones for clients in other parts of Mesoamerica. This beautifully polished mask formerly had shell inlays in eyes and mouth.

E. Aztec, Tenochtítlan (Mexico City); 1450–1521 AD; ear spool; gold-and-turquoise mosaic; D 23/8" (6 cm). Mixtec craftsmen in Oaxaca and in their own en-clave in the Aztec capital were responsible for much of the sump-tuous jewelry and feather-and-turquoise mosaic work, such as this piece, credited to the Aztecs.

F. Aztec, Central Mexico; 1450–1521 AD; floral ear spools; burnished black clay and gold foil overlay, with traces of cin-nabar; D 23/8" (6 cm).

G. Aztec, Cholula, Puebla; 1450–1521 AD; plate; polychromed terracotta with floral motifs in shades of red and black over a cream slip; D 81/4" (21 cm).

H. Aztec, Cholula; 1450–1521 AD; redware tripod bowl with turkey effigy rattle feet; terracotta with polished red slip, with unslipped supports; H 31/2" (8.9 cm), D 6" (15.2 cm).

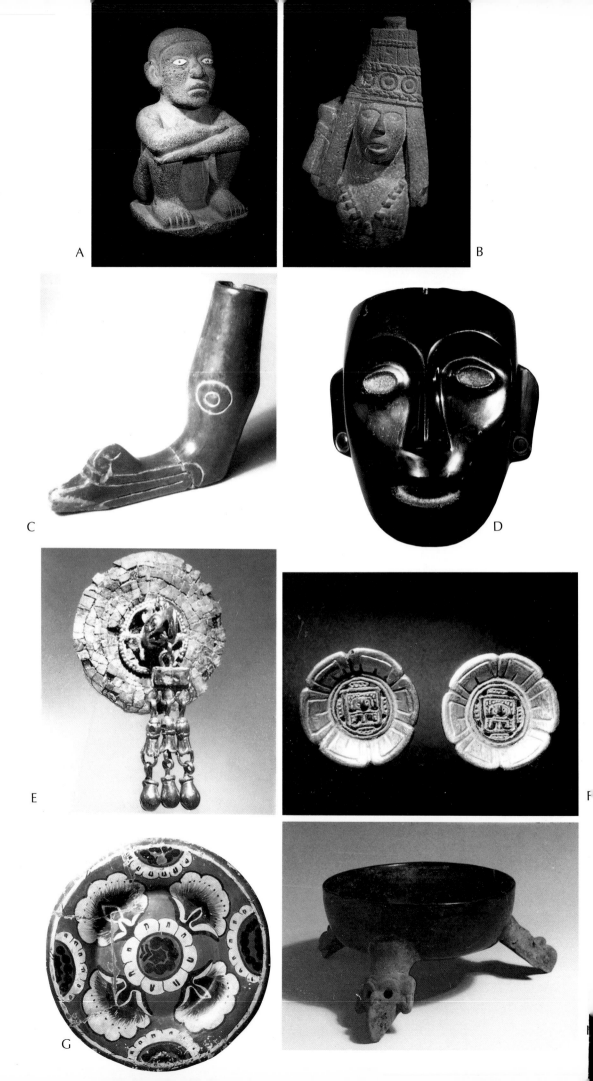

A

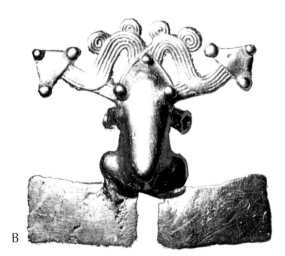

B

C

A. Veraguas, Panama; 800–1000 AD; "eagle"; gold; W 3 5/8" (9.2 cm). The Veraguas "eagle" is actually a king vulture, a prominent creature in Central and South American cosmology. Veraguas defines one of the two major traditions of Panamanian gold work, the other being Coclé. Most Veraguas gold was made by the casting technique known as lost wax. This involves pouring molten gold into molds made from originals sculpted in hardened wax. When the clay molds are fired, the wax melts and runs out—hence the term "lost wax".

B. Veraguas, Panama; 800–1000 AD; frog with a double-headed snake in its mouth; gold and copper alloy; W 2 1/2" (6.4 cm). The frogs depicted by the Pre-Columbian goldsmiths are tree frogs of the so-called arrow-poison variety, whose venom, one of the deadliest to occur in nature, was used for blowgun darts.

C. Coclé, Panama; 500–1000 AD; pendant in human form; gold; H c. 3" (7.6 cm). Most Pre-Columbian gold castings are not pure gold but gold and copper alloys that are properly known as *tumbaga*. Where copper predominates, a technique known as *mise en couleur* was used to bring the gold to the surface. Nevertheless, some pieces have a redder color than others because of their copper content.

PANAMA/COSTA RICA

A. Coclé, Panama; 500–1000 AD; pendant in the form of a were-jaguar; gold; H 5¼" (13.3 cm). The dominant element in these complex figures, which is repeated many times in Panamanian gold, is a man with the features of either a jaguar or an alligator, or both.

B. Coclé, Panama; 500–1000 AD; pedestal bowl with crossed bands in black, red, and purple; polychromed terracotta; H 7¼" (18.4 cm), D 10¾" (27.3 cm). This is a simple but striking example of the tall pedestal bowls typical of the Coclé ceramic tradition.

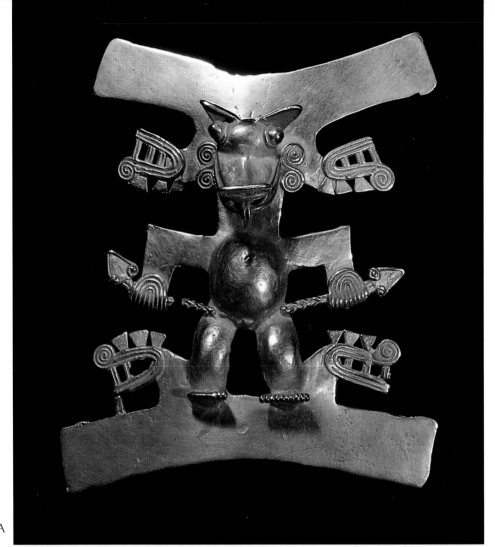

A

B

104

Costa Rica, Guanacaste, Nicoya; 1200–1400 AD; jaguar effigy jar; polychromed terracotta; H 16" (40.7 cm). This is a particularly elegant example of a type of vase considered typical of Nicoya polychrome. The feline head is modeled realistically, but the treatment of the front legs as arms and the rearing pose are rather human, presumably because of the widespread identification of jaguar with shaman. The massive haunches and hind legs are hollow, and contain clay pellets that make them into rattles; the tail forms the rear support.

PANAMA/COSTA RICA

A. Coclé, Panama; 500–1000 AD; pedestal vase with strongly painted stylized bird design in black, red, and purple on cream slip polychromed terracotta; D 12 1/4" (31.1 cm). The prominent crest feathers of the bird identify it as the harpy eagle, the largest of all eagles and, with the jaguar and the anaconda, the most prominent of animal allies and alter egos of shamans.

B. Coclé, Panama; 500–1000 AD; vessel depicting owl with wings painted in black and red, and head in polychromed low relief; terracotta; H 6 1/2" (16.5 cm).

C. Costa Rica, Atlantic Watershed; 200 BC–300 AD; effigy vessel in form of pregnant woman with incised body decoration; terracotta; H 15" (38.1 cm).

D. Costa Rica, Atlantic Watershed; Period IV, 1–500 AD; avian celt, probably representing harpy eagle; light blue-green jade; H 6 1/4" (15.9 cm). This is typical of a class of skillfully carved and highly polished Costa Rican jades in a color that was favored also by the Olmecs.

E. Costa Rica; c. 300 AD; animal effigy with painted and incised decoration; terracotta; L 7 1/2" (19 cm).

F. Costa Rica; Late Period IV, 1–500 AD; ceremonial mace head; stone; L 5" (12.7 cm). Formerly believed to be weapons, the stone mace heads carved in the form of birds, mammals, and even humans are now thought to have served symbolic and ceremonial functions.

A

B

C

D

E

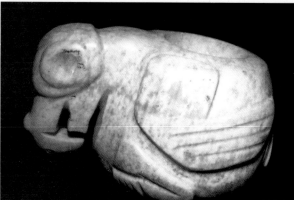

F

A

A. Costa Rica, Atlantic Watershed; Early Period VI, c. 1000 AD; ceremonial *metate* with circular flat plate supported by figures of long-tailed monkeys on a ring base; volcanic stone; H 9¾" (24.8 cm). Simple stone *metates* were, and still are, used in Mexico and Central America to grind maize and other foodstuffs, but these complex ceremonial sculptures probably functioned to prepare some sacred substance used in religious rites.

B. Costa Rica, Atlantic Watershed; Late Period V–Early VI, 700–1000 AD; male figure; volcanic stone; H 11½" (29.2 cm).

B

107

SOUTH AMERICA

COLOMBIA

A. Quimbaya; 1200–1400 AD; seated figures; unslipped solid terracotta with gold nose rings; left to right: H 7 1/8" (18.1 cm), 11" (28 cm), 5 1/4" (13.4 cm). The holes in the bodies and heads of these frequently seen, highly stylized human effigies suggest adornments of feathers, human hair, cloth, gold, or shell.

B. Tairona; 1200–1550 AD; black-ware vessel in form of crested, long-snouted animal; terracotta with black slip; L 12" (13.5 cm).

A

OPPOSITE PAGE

Tairona, Sierra Nevada de Santa Marta; 1000–1550 AD; Fine Brownware effigy vessel; terracotta with dark brown slip; H 8 1/8" (20.6 cm). The Tairona personified the sun as jaguar and the moon as puma, or mountain lion, and Venus, who was first a man and then transformed into a woman, as both Evening and Morning Star. Tairona imagery is closely connected with human, animal, and plant fertility, and with balance in the natural environment and the universe. Shamans are considered also jaguars, and jaguar transformation is evident in many ceramics. Of Tairona pottery, generally of high quality, none is better made, more richly decorated, and iconographically more complex than that in the Fine Brownware tradition.

B

COLOMBIA

A. Colombia, Middle Río Magdalena; probably 800–1500 AD; burial urn with a human couple seated on the lid; terracotta; H 23" (58.4 cm).

B. Nariño; 750–1250 AD; amphora; terracotta with black paint on cream resist; H 341/4" (87 cm).

C. Nariño; 850–1500 AD; mask of an aged coca chewer; terracotta; H 81/2" (21.6 cm). The chewing of coca with lime is an ancient custom in Andean cultures. Modern science has refined coca into the potent drug cocaine, but Indian peoples derive vital social, religious, and nutritional benefits from the much milder natural leaves of "Mama Coca".

D. Calima; 500 BC–300 AD; vessel in the form of a seated male; terracotta; H 41/2" (11.4 cm). Pottery in the Calima tradition conveys, regardless of size, a certain power and monumentality.

A

B

C

D

A

B

C

D

E

COLOMBIA

A. Tairona, Sierra Nevada de Santa Marta; 1000–1550 AD; Fine Brownware ocarina; terracotta; H 3" (7.6 cm). Though small in size, these iconographically complex and profusely decorated wind instruments are often masterpieces of ceramic sculpture.

B. Tairona, Sierra Nevada de Santa Marta; 1000–1500 AD; Fine Brownware animal effigy bowl with incised decoration; terracotta; L 123/4" (32.4 cm).

C. Sinú; 1000–1500 AD; ear ornaments; cast gold and *tumbaga* (gold-copper alloy); W 37/8" (9.9 cm); Museo del Oro, Ba Colombia, Bogotá. The ancie inhabitants of the Sinú basin were famed for their finely wrought gold jewelry. These ornaments were cast in "false filigree" from wax originals.

D. Tairona, Sierra Nevada de Santa Marta; 1000–1550 AD; pendant representing a masked supernatural; cast gold alloy; H 51/4" (13.3 cm). Very similar anthropomorphic pendants have been found in Venezuela, so Tairona pieces are occasionally identified as Venezuelan.

E. Sinú; 500–1000 AD; Darien style; pectoral representing a masked supernatural with paired mushrooms on the head, holding a bar with four perched birds; cast gold; H 33/4" (9.5 cm); Natural History Museum of Los Angeles County, California. These complex effigies were once called "telephone gods", for the resemblance of the dome-shaped head ornaments to the bells of old-fashioned telephones. The ornaments are now recognized as representing mushrooms, with the slender stems being characteristic of the sacred genus *Psilocybe*. There was an evolution of these pendants from early examples such as this, in which the mushrooms are quite naturalistic, to later, more conventionalized examples, in which the mushrooms are tipped forward, so that they appear like a pair of breasts, while retaining the stem in back.

111

COLOMBIA

A. Quimbaya; 400–700 AD; pectoral with a seated female holding a pair of mushrooms; cast gold; H 7 11/16" (19.5 cm). This splendid example, unusual in that the double-spiral ornaments such figures usually hold are replaced by a pair of mushrooms, belongs to a class of realistically modeled Quimbaya figures, vases, lime flasks, and other objects of great beauty and superb workmanship, some weighing as much as two or more pounds.*

B. Quimbaya; 500–1000 AD; pendant; cast gold; W 5" (12.7 cm).

A

B

ECUADOR

A. Valdivia; 2600–2400 BC; female figure; stone; H 3 1/2" (8.9 cm).

B. Valdivia; c. 2400 BC; female figure fragment; terracotta with red slip; H 3 3/4" (9.5 cm). Discovered only in the early 1970s, the Valdivia ceramic complex, consisting almost entirely of simple, charming little nude female statuettes with carefully dressed hair, is one of the oldest in the New World. This figure preceded by fourteen centuries the "pretty ladies" of Tlatilco.

C. Manabí; 700–300 BC; ceremonial jaguar effigy mortar; stone; L 5 1/4" (14 cm).

ECUADOR

A. Jama–Coaque, Manabí; 400 BC-500 AD; maternity figure; buff terracotta with traces of blue paint; H 5" (17.7 cm). The great variety, inventiveness, and elegance of this relatively early culture of Ecuador has until recently been overlooked by students of South American ceramics.

B. Jama–Coaque, Manabí; 400 BC-500 AD; seated male; hollow buff terracotta with polychrome decoration; H 11¼" (26 cm).

C. Jama–Coaque, Manabí; 400 BC-500 AD; woman wearing elaborate headdress; buff terra-cotta with firing marks; H 16½" (42 cm).

B

A

C

114

A

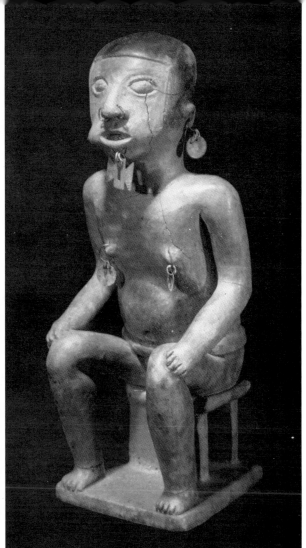

B

ECUADOR

A. Carchi; 1000–1500 AD; seated female coca chewer; terracotta with black resist decoration on reddish-brown slip; H 7 1/8" (18.1 cm). A large number of seated male and female Carchi figures with wads of coca leaves in one cheek have been found in the northern highlands of Ecuador and adjacent Colombia, which were once a single culture area.

B. Carchi; 1000–1500 AD; seated male coca chewer; burnished buff terracotta with black for hair and with copper ear, nose, chin, and body pendants; H 9 1/2" (24.1 cm).

C. Manabi, Manteño; 500–850 AD; blackware vase with head of small animal in relief; terracotta with black slip on body and unslipped relief; H 8 1/4" (21 cm).

D. Carchi; 1000–1500 AD; ceremonial twin-bowl vessel with monkey on center pole; burnished terracotta with black resist decoration; H 5 3/4" (14.6 cm).

C

D

115

CHAVÍN

A. Late Chavín, Tembladera, Jequetepeque Valley; blackware stirrup vessel in the form of a bowl with fruit; terracotta with black slip; H 10" (25.4 cm).

B. Late Chavín; 500–300 BC; grayware bottle; terracotta with gray slip; H 9 1/2" (24.2 cm). Like the Olmec in Mexico, the Chavín potters frequently contrasted highly burnished areas with roughened surfaces.

C. Late Chavín, Tembladera, Jequetepeque Valley; 700–400 BC; maternity figure; tan terracotta with incised and impressed design; H 6 1/4" (15.9 cm). A number of seated and standing male and female figures in the same style are known, but maternity scenes are relatively rare.

B

A

C

CHAVÍN

Chavín, Tembladera, Jequetepeque Valley; 700–400 BC; stirrup vessel with jaguar and San Pedro cactus in high relief; terracotta with highly burnished slip; H 13" (33 cm). This is a striking example of a series of very similar sculpted vessels depicting a close relationship between the jaguar and the mescaline-containing San Pedro cactus.

CHAVÍN

A. Chavín, Tembladera, Jequetepeque Valley; 700–400 BC; stirrup vessel with lively human figure apparently adjusting his hair; partly burnished and partly roughened gray terracotta; H 7 3/4" (19.7 cm).

B. Middle Chavín, Jequetepeque Valley; 700–400 BC; jaguar, harpy eagle, and anaconda stirrup vessel; H 11 1/2" (29.2 cm). By giving the harpy eagle the head of a jaguar and having it perch on a coiled anaconda, this tour-de-force of Chavín ceramic sculpture joins the three principal animal allies and alter egos of shamans into a single image.*

C. Salinar; 500–300 BC; stirrup vessel in the form of a horned owl; burnished and unburnished and roughened red clay body decorated with white and black; H 7 7/8" (20 cm). Salinar is transitional between Chavín and Early Moche. It maintained the spout form and the contrast between roughened and burnished surfaces characteristic of Chavín, but added polychrome decoration.

D. Paracas; 1000–600 BC; stirrup vessel with Chavín influence; polychromed terracotta; H 9 1/2" (24.1 cm).

A

B

C

PARACAS

A. Early Paracas, Ica Valley; 700–500 BC; spouted jaguar vessel with strap handle; dark brown terracotta incised and painted with red, yellow, and white; L 61/4" (15.9 cm). Unlike the contemporaneous Chavín culture, whose vessels were generally monochrome, Paracas emphasized color more than form, frequently employing enamel-like resin-based pigments which tended to decompose in time with the disintegration of the organic binder.

B. Middle Paracas, Ica Valley (?); 500–300 BC; spouted vessel with incised and polychromed feline mask; brown terracotta with red, yellow, and white resin paint; H 51/2" (14 cm).

A

B

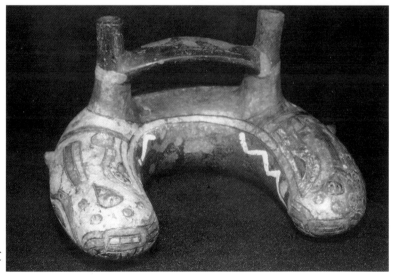
C

D

C. Middle Paracas; 500–300 BC; spouted and strap-handled vessel representing twinned fish; terracotta with buff base slip and resin-painted green, red, black, and white decoration; W 67/8" (17.5 cm).

D. Paracas; c. 500 BC; poncho; plain weave polychrome cotton textile; 31 x 31" (78.7 x 78.7 cm). Each of the four borders of this beautifully preserved ancient weaving is decorated with typically Paracas- and Early Nazca-style flying men wearing gold mouth masks with long protruding tongues terminating in serpents' heads. Each figure holds a pair of staffs and wears a large serpent as his ceremonial belt. Six similar flying figures decorate the center.

MOCHE

A. Moche III; 200–400 AD; stirrup portrait vessel of man with facial tattooing and white headdress with red chinstrap; terracotta with slips and painting; H 11" (28 cm). Rivaling Roman portraiture in its naturalism, one of the great portrait traditions of the world is that of the Moche of north coastal Peru.

B. Moche III; 200–400 AD; curing-scene stirrup vessel; polychromed terracotta; H 9" (22.8 cm).

C. Moche III; 200–400 AD; stirrup vessel in form of shaman as bird beating drum; terracotta with slips and paint; H 9 1/4" (23.5 cm). Bird symbolism in shamanism and shamans transforming themselves into birds are well documented among Indian peoples in South America. A shaman beating a drum is not uncommon in Moche art—what makes this work stand out is the motif of bird transformation.

D. Moche III; 200–400 AD; portrait drinking cup representing youth wearing netted cap; terracotta with slip and paint; H 7 3/8" (18.7 cm). This beautiful portrait vessel is unusual in that the face is left unslipped while the painted headband or cap is covered with a cream slip, painted, and burnished.

A

B

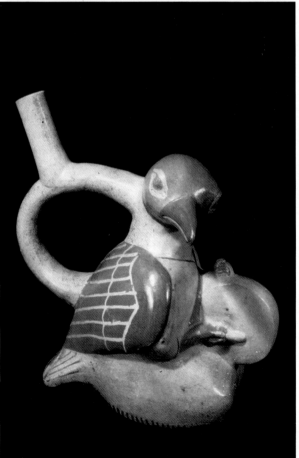
C

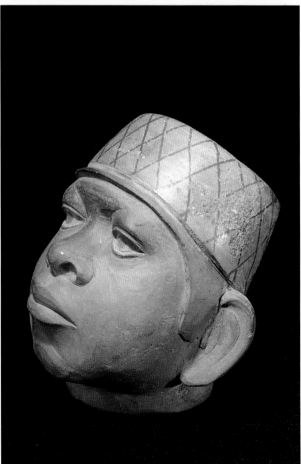
D

A

B

C

D

E

F

MOCHE

A. Early Moche, Loma Negra, Vicús; 300 BC–300 AD; crescent-shaped ceremonial knife with bat handle; patinated copper; W 45/8" (11.8 cm).

B. Salinar, Vicús; 500–300 BC; vessel of seated monkey holding conch shell; terracotta with burnished reddish-brown and cream slip; H 63/4" (17.2 cm); The Art Museum, Princeton University.

C. Early Moche; 200 BC–100 AD; figural vessel; polished brown and cream slip over red-brown terracotta; H 10" (25.4 cm). Although the dominant Moche ceramic form was, from the start, the stirrup pot, vessels in the form of a single human figure were produced during early Moche times.

D. Moche III; 200–400 AD; jaguar stirrup vase; cream-slipped terracotta with reddish-brown decoration; H 9" (22.8 cm).

E. Moche, Vicús; 100–500 AD; bottle with phallus spout; reddish-brown terracotta with traces of resist decoration; H 103/4" (27.3 cm). Resist decoration was achieved by the application of some organic material, such as resin, to parts of the surface of a vessel before firing; the area so covered "resists" the firing process and does not change color, resulting in negative patterns.

F. Moche III; 200–400 AD; toad effigy stirrup vessel; terracotta with reddish-brown slip and white paint; H 71/2" (19.1 cm). The toad was a popular subject throughout the Moche period. The species represented here is the large tropical toad, which played, and still plays, a prominent role in myth and ritual.

RECUAY

A. Recuay, Río Virú; 1–300 AD; double-bodied whistling vessel with opossum effigy; terracotta with cream slip and black resist decoration; H 6⅞" (17.5 cm). Contemporaneous with Early Moche, Recuay pottery is valued for its highly developed resist decoration, thin walls, and delicate modeling. The ingenious whistling pot is found from Mexico and Guatemala to Peru; here the whistle is concealed in the opossum. The whistles are activated when air is forced through them by blowing or filling and rocking the vessel.

B. Recuay; 1–300 AD; whistling pot in form of man leading llama and blowing panpipe; terracotta with white slip and polychrome paint; H 9¼" (23.5 cm).

NAZCA

C. Nazca; 300–600 AD; cactus spirit jar; terracotta with polychrome decoration; H 16" (40.6 cm). The cactus plants sprouting from the shoulders identify this exuberantly decorated jar as the anthropomorphized San Pedro cactus spirit. The crowding of color and design on the body of the vessel, contrasting with the simplicity of such earlier Nazca ceramics as D, is characteristic of the Late Nacza style.

D. Nazca; 100 BC–100 AD; figural vase; terracotta with cream slip and black-and-red decoration; H 8" (20.3 cm).

E. Nazca; 300–600 AD; bird effigy vessel; terracotta with cream slip and black-and-red decoration; L 5¼" (13.4 cm).

A

B

C

D

E

NAZCA

A. Nazca, Ica–Chincha; 1300-1500 AD; mantle; textile with feather mosaic; 29 x 46" (73.7 x 116.8 cm). Geometric figures such as this trio have analogies in hillside pictographs and petroglyphs. The extraordinary thing about the ancient feather work from Peru is that the natural colors and brilliance of the plumage has remained constant through the centuries.

B. Early Huari; 800–1000 AD; double-spouted vessel with "trophy" head; burnished terracotta with polychrome decoration; H 5 3/4" (14.6 cm). This type of jar with its pair of long, slender spouts is reminiscent of Nazca, but the angular treatment of the design elements clearly marks it as early Huari.

TIAHUANACO

A. Early Huari; 500–800 AD; shell mosaic; shell and stone inlay on polished spiny oyster shell base; H c. 4" (10 cm). Some of the finest shell mosaic work in the ancient Americas was produced by both the Tiahuanaco culture of highland Bolivia and the contemporaneous Huari, several hundred miles to the south.

B. Tiahuanaco, highland Bolivia; 600–800 AD; cap; cotton and llama wool; H 45/8" (11.7 cm), D 7" (17.8 cm).

C. Tiahuanaco, Titicaca basin, highland Bolivia; 600–800 AD; condor effigy pendant; polished spiny oyster shell with three-dimensional condor head of oyster shell mosaic with turquoise inlays; H 43/4" (12 cm).

D. Tiahuanaco style, Atacama Desert, northern Chile; 600–800 AD; snuff tablet; wood with turquoise inlays; L 73/8" (18.7 cm). In the bone-dry Atacama Desert were found large numbers of well-preserved objects of perishable materials, including many hundreds of decorated tablets like this one, beautifully carved from a hard tropical wood and bearing the unmistakable imprint of the Tiahuanaco art style.

B

A

D

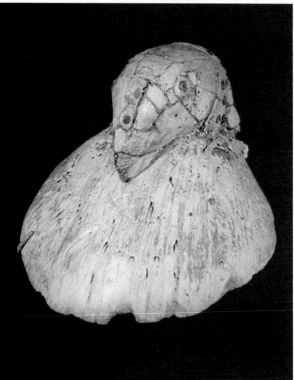

C

A

C

B

D

E

CHIMÚ

A. Chimú; 900–1450 AD; poncho panel with seated monkey; woven cotton; 28 x 21" (71.1 x 53.3 cm).

B. Chimú; 800–1100 AD; double-bodied blackware stirrup whistling pot; terracotta with polished black slip; H 9 1/2" (24.4 cm). Production of these ingenious sound-producing ceramics was common during the span of the Chimú kingdom and continued through the Inca period into the Spanish colonial era. Many Chimú stirrup-spouted vessels have, as here, a monkey or some other animal at the point where spout and handle meet.

C. Chimú; 800–1200 AD; blackware stirrup vase with a copulating couple; terracotta with polished black slip; H 7 1/4" (18.5 cm).

D. Chimú, 1000–1450 AD; beaker; beaten and repoussé gold; H 7" (17.8 cm).

E. Chimú; 1300–1530 AD; mask; beaten and embossed sheet gold; W 8 1/2" (21.5 cm). Like the wooden masks, face masks such as this one, of beaten and embossed sheet gold, silver, or *tumbaga* (alloy of gold with copper and other metals), were affixed to mummy bundles.

125

CHANCAY

A. Chancay; 1100–1200 AD; double-chambered whistling pot; low-fired terracotta with buff-white unburnished slip with gray-black decoration; H 9 3/8" (23.8 cm). This is typical of Chancay ceramics, which, in contrast to Chancay weaving, are generally not distinguished by a high degree of craftsmanship but have a folk-art charm.

B. Chancay; 1300–1532 AD; mummy bundle mask; cinnabar and white pigment over wood, with human hair, woven tapestry headdress and cape; H 8" (20.3 cm).

C. Chancay; 1300–1532 AD; painted textile; woven cotton, brown mineral paint; 46 1/2 x 46" (118.1 x 116.8 cm). The birds and the whirling symbol at upper left, possibly the sun, suggest that this burial cloth may depict a shaman's trance experience.

D. Chancay; 1100–1532 AD; anthropomorphic jar; terracotta with brown paint; H 20 1/4" (51.4 cm).

A

B

C

D

A

INCA

A. Inca/Ica; 1400–1530 AD; shirt; llama wool and cotton; 38 x 42" (96.5 x 106.7 cm).

B. Inca; 1500–1560 AD; *kero*; lacquer-painted wood; H 8" (20.3 cm). The goblets called *kero* were made not only of wood but of silver, gold, and terracotta. Some surviving *keros* of wood with polychrome painting are apparently pre-Hispanic, but judging from the mixture of European and indigenous motifs, many date to the early colonial period.

B

INCA

A. and B. Inca; 1470–1532 AD; alpaca and llama votive figures; top: black basalt; bottom: white marble; top: L 4" (10.2 cm), bottom: L 4 3/4" (11.5 cm). Small effigies of alpacas and llamas were deposited on mountainsides as sacrificial offerings to ensure the fertility of the land and the animals. They generally have round holes in the animals' back, probably to hold some sacred or medicinal substance.

C. Inca; 1460–1532 AD; baby llama; solid cast silver; H 2 5/16" (5.9 cm). Like the stone llamas, small effigies of precious metal were presented to the mountain gods as petitions for the increase of herds and the fertility of the crops.

D. Inca; 1470–1532 AD; *kero*-form goblet; silver with gold base; H 6 3/8" (16.2 cm). Similar in style to Chimú ceremonial drinking cups, this one was probably made by a Chimú silversmith for an Inca client.

E. Inca, Cuzco; 1470–1532 AD; male figure; cast silver; H 2 1/2" (6.4 cm). These charming little male and female figures evidently were not always nude, a few having been found wrapped in sumptuous miniature weavings and other adornments.

A

B

C

D

E

128

American Indian Art

Tlingit; c.1880; rattle; wood; L 14" (35.6 cm).

Makah

Klikitat

Yakima

Coeur D'Alene

Plains Cree

Blackfoot

Piegan

Assiniboin

Mandan

Chinook

Nez Percé

Hidatsa

Tillamook

Tenino

Flathead

Arikara

Crow

Coos

Bannock

Hunkpapa

Yanktor Siou

Karok

Teton

Klamath

Yurok

Yana

Shoshone

Oglala

Dakota Sioux

Hupa

Lakota Sioux

Yuki

Shoshone

Pomo

Cheyenne

Por

Maidu

Northern Paiute

Oma

Arapaho

Washo

Western Shoshone

Pawnee

Miwok

Kansa

Mono

Tulare

Southern Paiute

Ute

Cheyenne

Yokut

Panamint

Chemehuevi

Hopi

Navajo

Jicarilla Apache

Chumash

MISSION INDIANS*

Mojave

Tano

Keresan

PUEBLOS*

Yavapai

Zuni

Kiov

Tipai

Yuma

Maricopa

Pima

Eastern Apache

Western Apache

Tano

Mescalero Apache

Comanche

Papago

Casas Grandes

*MISSION INDIANS

Serrano
Luiseño
Gabrielino
Cahuilla
Diegueño
Fernandeño
Juaneño
Cupeño

*PUEBLOS

Jemez   Sandia
Taos   Laguna
Picurís   Chochiti
San Juan   Santo Domingo
Nambé   Santa Clara
Tesuque   San Ildefonso
Santa Ana   Acoma
San Felipe   Zia

Naskapi

Montagnais

Cree

Micmac

Malecite

Ojibwa
(Chippewa)

Ottawa

Ojibwa
(Chippewa)

Abnaki

Passamaquoddy

Menominee

Mohawk

Mohegan

Penobscot

akota

Algonquin

Oneida

Massachuset

Ojibwa
(Chippewa)

Huron

Onondaga

Santee Dakota

Winnebago

Cayuga

Seneca
Iroquois

Wampanoag

Brule

Potawotami

Algonquin

Pequot

Sauk

Iowa

Delaware

Fox
(Mesquakie)

Illinois

Erie

Susquehannock

Oto

Nanticoke

Missouri

Miami

Osage

Shawnee

Tutelo

Algonquin

Tuscarora

ichita

Caddo

Cherokee

Catawba

Chickasaw

Yuchi

Osage

Choctaw

Creek

Cusabo

Natchez

Biloxi

Atakapa

Timucua

Chitimacha

akawa

Seminole

Colusa

Map of
the continental
UNITED STATES
and southern CANADA

showing the approximate locations
of American Indian tribes in the
mid-nineteenth century.

NB. At any date during this period the locations
of certain tribes are subject to variation due to
their nomadic nature or the forced removal of
tribes or parts of them.

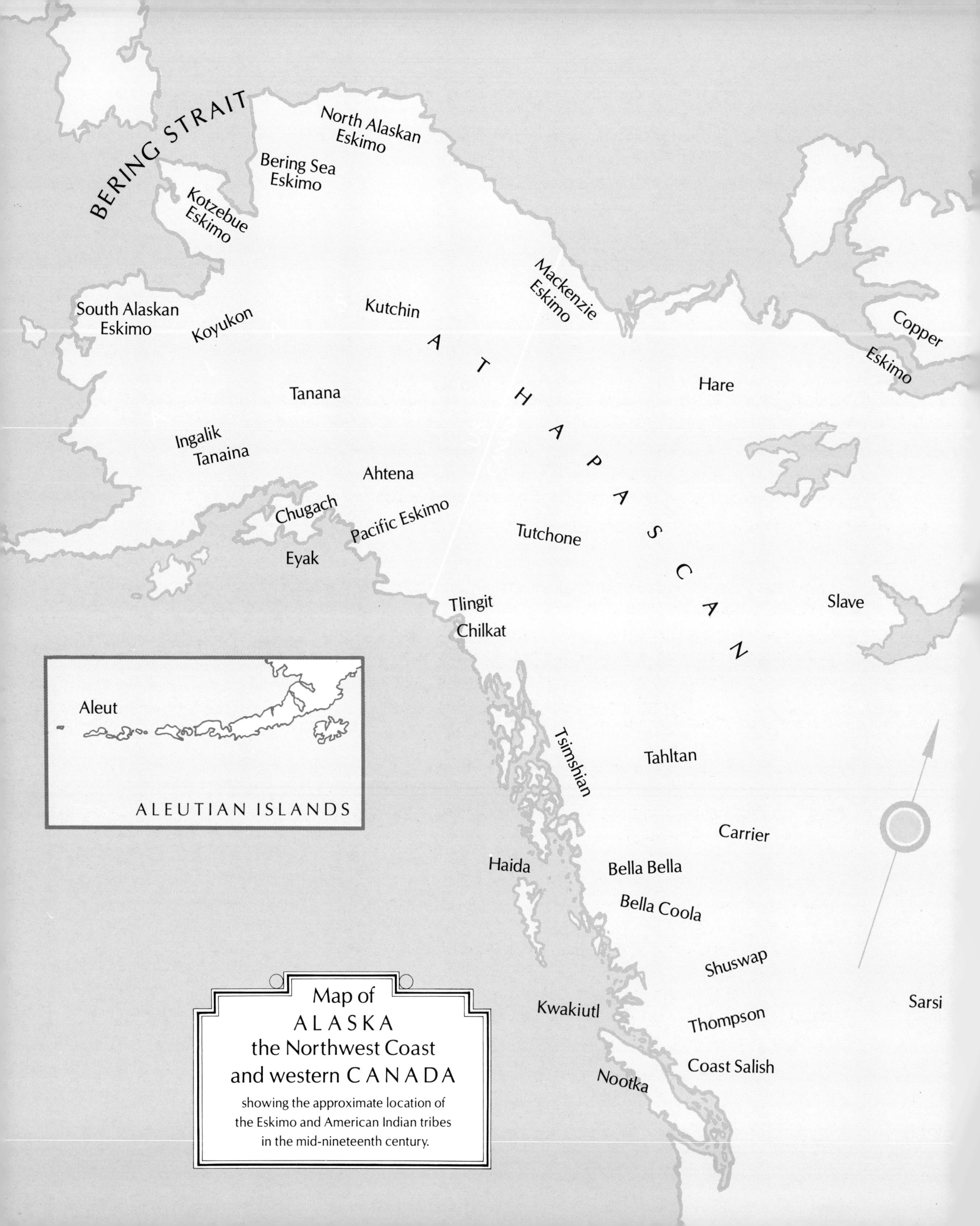

BERING STRAIT

North Alaskan
Eskimo

Bering Sea
Eskimo

Kotzebue
Eskimo

Mackenzie
Eskimo

Copper
Eskimo

South Alaskan
Eskimo

Koyukon

Kutchin

Hare

A T H A P A S C A N

Tanana

Ingalik
Tanaina

Ahtena

Chugach

Pacific Eskimo

Tutchone

Eyak

Slave

Tlingit
Chilkat

Aleut

ALEUTIAN ISLANDS

Tsimshian

Tahltan

Carrier

Haida

Bella Bella

Bella Coola

Shuswap

Map of
ALASKA
the Northwest Coast
and western CANADA

showing the approximate location of
the Eskimo and American Indian tribes
in the mid-nineteenth century.

Kwakiutl

Thompson

Sarsi

Coast Salish

Nootka

Widespread acceptance of American Indian art as *art* is relatively recent. Still, it is now so well established that only the most committed Eurocentrist would still dispute it.

The road has not been easy. For a long time the field suffered from a bias that held Old World art, especially the European tradition, to be inherently superior to the arts of the Americas, Africa, or Oceania. Objects from these areas were held to be anthropological artifacts whose proper place was the natural history museum. At best, they were viewed as "folk arts" or crafts—the works of people who may have had talent and skill but had no formal training in the European sense, and were straightjacketed by a rigid adherence to tradition that precluded individual creativity and even personal identity. The "primitive artist", it was assumed, was anonymous.

This is not true. Individual creativity was in fact recognized in tribal and other ancient societies, and work was judged according to well-established aesthetic criteria. It is wrong to assume that because *we* did not know the names of the artist, no one else did either.

The years since the 1960s have brought changes in this wrongheadedness. Use of the term "primitive art" to distinguish the arts of so-called tribal peoples from the "high" arts of Europe or Asia has mercifully gone out of fashion. Even used as a category, without pejorative implications, the term made the error of lumping together the arts of very diverse peoples. Unfortunately, no substitute terminology that conveys splendid art traditions and has no undesirable connotations has yet emerged (hence such accurate but unwieldy professional titles as "Curator of Native American, Pre-Columbian, African, and Oceanic Art").

In this reassessment collectors have played an important, even a crucial, role. Long before fine arts museums awakened to the fact that American Indian art had aesthetic as well as anthropological value, long before any institutions of higher education became persuaded that the study of American Indian (and Pre-Columbian) art was necessary for a well-rounded education in art history, many private collectors understood that what the best American Indian and Eskimo artists had produced was truly art. Indeed, it was these collectors, private and public, who sometimes kept an art form alive by providing it with a market when its former social and religious context had disappeared. The truth is that, far from "plundering" the pueblos of Acoma and Zuni of their treasured ceramics, the new tourist market supported the great Pueblo pottery tradition at a time when manufactured metalware was rapidly replacing handmade pottery for domestic use.

Far more than European or American societies, the indigenous cultures of North America provided many individuals—especially women—with the possibility of exercising their artistic talents in ways that were appreciated beyond the immediate family. This point about American Indian women as artists is fundamental. Certain of the arts were predominantly the province of Indian men. But a large percentage of the works we define as art are the creation of women. And, as art historian and ethnologist Marsha Bol has written about the Lakota Sioux: "Central to the feminine occupation were the artistic endeavors of quillwork, beadwork, and painting. . . . Art and its production stood on its own as a key ingredient in the definition of a Lakota woman. Doing art well was a sign of a woman successful in her society."

The contrast between this and the position of women as artists in Europe and the United States, at least until very recently, is glaring. Excelling at artistic work was, for a Lakota woman, necessary for making a good marriage, and she was expected to continue to create art all her life. On the other hand, the typical Euramerican woman artist of the nineteenth and early twentieth century not only rarely achieved recognition in the male-dominated art world but was expected to renounce all such hopes at marriage.

A guiding principle in understanding American Indian art is that the beautification of everyday objects served both spiritual *and* social purposes. The intent was never just decorative. Art was communication, and the communication had to be understood by the society as well as by the spirit beings on whom well-being depended. "Pleasing the spirits" is not just a romantic figure of speech: it was the major reason for making things beautiful. The purpose of art, the Navajo say, is to beautify the world. But the way the Navajo, and other native Americans, understand beauty is quite different from what we mean by it. The world in balance—that is beauty. People in balance with their natural and spiritual environment and with one another is beauty. In the American Indian worldview, there is no such thing as an "inanimate" object: everything—plant, animal, rock, tree, and tool—is alive and sentient. And that

134 AMERICAN INDIAN ART

Eskimo; c.1900; mask; wood; H 28" (71 cm).

applies as well to a design and the object bearing that design or shaped into a form. This is not to suggest that there are not also practical and social considerations, or that it is impossible to appreciate beauty of form, design, color, and artisanship in American Indian art without knowing about the religion, mythology, ritual, history, or social life of its creators. But some familiarity with the historical, mythological, or spiritual context of American Indian art enhances the pleasure of looking at or collecting it.

BASKETRY

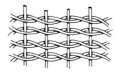

wicker

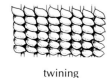

twining

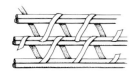

coiling

Basket weaving techniques

Non-Indians have long responded to the beauty of native American basketry. As Mason observed in his classic work, *American Indian Basketry* (1904), even at the beginning of the century fine American Indian baskets were something of a national craze: "In every state of the Union will be found rich collections, both in public and private museums. People of wealth vie with one another in owning them."

The oldest basketry in the New World has been radio-carbon-dated to about eleven thousand years ago. Probably it is even older; the earliest people to come from northeastern Asia, ten thousand to forty thousand years ago, almost certainly had made baskets.

There are only a few basic basket-weaving techniques, but North American weavers perfected many adaptations, variations, and embellishments. The basic technologies are coiling, plaiting, and twining. In the Northeast the predominant techniques were plaiting (usually ash splint) and twining (sweetgrass). In the nineteenth century many of the ash splint baskets were embellished with potato-stamp designs.

The Cherokee of North Carolina made plain and twill-plaited baskets of cane, oak, ash, and honeysuckle. But the most skilled Southeastern basket weavers were the Chitimacha of Louisiana, who used the twill-plaiting technique to weave fine polychrome baskets with geometric designs of natural and black- and red-dyed river cane.

Although plaiting and coiling were practiced throughout the Pacific Northwest, twining predominated there. The close-twined baskets of the Aleutian islanders are typically so tightly woven of very fine strands of wild grasses, so soft and pliable, that they almost rival textiles. The Eskimo made baskets both with stitched coiling and twining. The Alaskan Tlingit perfected a whole range of twining techniques for their much-admired basketry, which included hats, baby carriers, trays, shaman's baskets, large cylindrical storage containers with and without lids, trinket baskets, and so forth. Spruce root, cedar bark, bear grass, and fern furnished the basic materials, with roots, barks, and grasses used for false-embroidery decoration in reds, yellows, black, purple, green-blue, brown, and white. Small pebbles, lead shot, and bezoar stones from the stomachs of birds were used for the ingenious Tlingit rattle-lid baskets.

Tlingit; 1880–1900; rattle-lid basket; H 5" (12.7 cm).

In the Southwest, California, and the Great Basin all the major basket-weaving techniques were perfected centuries ago. But while the Southwest also had pottery, California did not, and so it was there that basketry was highly developed, baskets having to serve all the purposes for which the Pueblo peoples used earthenware.

California Indians used virtually every technique known throughout the continent, and some that existed nowhere else. The Pomo and some of their neighbors used a complicated technique of lattice twining that resulted in baskets so watertight they could hold liquid for days without losing a drop. No basketry is more admired by collectors than the Pomo feathered "treasure" baskets. Some were made for sale; others were sold only when need arose or an irresistible sum was offered. But within the Pomo culture the feathered baskets had important meanings. They were given to girls at birth and puberty, to brides as wedding gifts, and to women at other significant times in their lives. The women treasured them, and when they died, those they valued most were cremated with them.

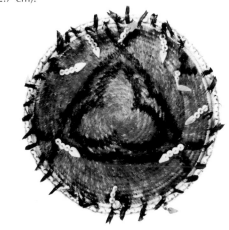

Pomo; feathered basket; D 5 1/4" (13.3 cm).

TEXTILES

Textile weaving differs from basketry in two crucial respects. First, with the exception of felting, true weavings are made of vegetal or animal fibers spun into continuous thread. Second, except for cloth produced by finger weaving, textiles require a mechanical device, such as the upright loom of the Pueblos (and, more recently, the Navajo) or the widespread backstrap or belt loom.

The principal weaving area in North America is the Southwest. From textile fragments that have survived we know that the Hopewell and other prehistoric Eastern Woodlands cultures were master weavers. But it is only in the Southwest that weaving has continued without interruption from at least two thousand years ago to the present.

Cotton and the loom were introduced into the Southwest from Mexico between 100 and 600 AD. However, during the early Basketmaker period (100 BC–700 AD), when there was little

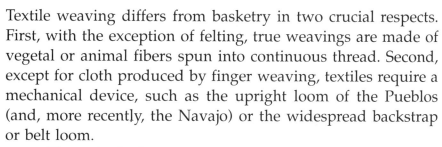

137

or no pottery making, the Anasazi, ancestors of the modern Pueblos, did finger weaving with wild plant fibers, the hair of dogs, mountain sheep, bears, and bison, and even feathers. The spindle whorl existed by 500 AD, but thread was made also by hand twisting and rolling on the thigh. Great care and artistry were lavished on decorated belts and sashes and on yucca fiber aprons and apron bands woven in the tapestry technique. Plain, twill, and tapestry weaving were all perfected during this early time. Weft-wrap, lace, and fine gauzes were common. Indeed, by the beginning of the prehistoric Pueblo period, 650–700 AD, weaving in the Southwest was on a par with that of the advanced civilizations of Mesoamerica.

Unlike pottery and basketry, which for the most part have been women's arts, weaving among the Pueblos was done by the men, often within the *kiva,* the ceremonial chamber. Exceptions were Zuni, where weaving was done by both sexes and the Navajo, among whom weaving was from the start a women's art. These ancient specializations changed only in the nineteenth century, when, under Anglo-American influence, weaving in the pueblos passed into the hands of women, a process that was virtually complete by 1900.

Spanish domination did not destroy the well-developed Indian textile arts. The production of utilitarian weavings actually increased because the Spanish settlers, unable or unwilling to weave for themselves, exploited the skilled Pueblo weavers. The Indians were forced to pay tribute not only in foodstuffs but in textiles produced on their indigenous looms. After 1639, the Spanish installed foreign treadle looms in Santa Fe to be worked with forced Indian labor. The Spanish also introduced knitting and crocheting with needles and soon impressed the Indians into producing great quantities of apparel with these new techniques. Sheep were introduced into the Southwest as early as 1600. By 1650 the Pueblo weavers were using both cotton and wool on the upright loom, which the Indians never discarded in favor of the European treadle loom. Nor did they replace the spindle whorl with the European spinning wheel.

Among historical Pueblo textiles are the several kinds of women's *mantas,* or shawls, some used importantly in wedding ceremonies.

The Navajo learned weaving from the Pueblos in the seventeenth century. Whether the early Navajo weavers were men, like their Pueblo teachers, or women is not known. Certainly since the beginning of the nineteenth century it has

Acoma (?); c.1860; woman's *manta*; 48 x 56" (122 x 142.2 cm).

Navajo; eyedazzler rug; 70 1/4 x 52 1/2" (178.4 x 133.3 cm).

been Navajo women who have been the masters of weaving in the Southwest.

At first the Navajo made use mainly of the natural colors of wool for blankets that followed the characteristic striped patterns of Prehistoric and early Historic Pueblo weavings. Northern Mexican wearing blankets and *serapes* also inspired Navajo designs.

The Classic period of Navajo weaving is generally considered to begin in the middle of the nineteenth century, but one could as easily count it from the very beginning of the century, because blanket fragments discovered in a rock shelter where Navajo men, women, and children were massacred by Spaniards in 1804 are virtually indistinguishable from mid-nineteenth-century weavings.

From the 1860s on, Navajo women were weaving fine wearing blankets not only for family use but for sale and trade. These gave way eventually to commercial clothing, but high-quality weavings were still made at the turn of the century. One innovation that resulted from the availability of bright aniline dyes was the "eyedazzler" weaving with zigzag and other busy patterns in bold, contrasting colors. Some eyedazzlers were poorly woven and garish in color, but there are also fine weavings of this type found in many private and public collections.

About 1880 to 1900 Navajo weavings first appeared enclosed by a solid border. This idea, completely foreign to the Navajo, was introduced by traders to satisfy the taste of white customers, who were used to Oriental rugs. The traders also asked Navajo weavers to copy the designs of Oriental rugs from catalogs they distributed. However, the weavers rarely copied the patterns without redesigning them according to their own taste.

An inevitable consequence of increasing commercialization was a decline in quality, but some early traders encouraged the weavers to hold fast to their high standards. Unfortunately, other traders ordered rugs by the pound, which made the use of heavy, coarse yarns more profitable than finely spun ones. In time, white customers became more sophisticated and traders increasingly insisted on higher standards, but poor workmanship and garish colors continued to flood the market.

It is not always easy to assign a Navajo rug to a specific area, but some distinctive regional traditions are Crystal, Ganado, Tees Nos Pos, and Two Grey Hills. A major revival of traditional soft vegetal colors and borderless horizontal patterns

Navajo; c.1940; Oriental style rug; 58 x 391/2" (147.5 x 100.5 cm).

began around 1920 and continues to the present. Its guiding spirit was Mary Cabot Wheelwright, a Bostonian patron of American Indian arts who later founded the Museum of Navajo Ceremonial Art in Santa Fe, now the Wheelwright Museum of American Indian Art. Miss Wheelwright, who owned an arts and crafts shop in Boston, distributed photographs of old Navajo textiles and guaranteed to purchase all weavings made in traditional styles and with natural colors. While Miss Wheelwright's Boston customers snapped up the fine new products, the Gallup wholesalers continued to prefer bordered Oriental-style rugs. Nevertheless, beautiful traditional rugs are still made at Crystal, Pine Springs, Burnt Water, and Wide Ruins.

Natural objects were occasionally depicted on Navajo blankets as early as the 1860s, but no true pictorial rugs older than the 1890s are known. Although many Navajo considered the use of their holy people in weavings to be sacrilegious, among the earliest pictorial motifs to appear are the spirit beings called *yeis*. More controversial still was the use of sandpaintings by a few weavers. These are complicated depictions in colored sands, charcoal, and other powdered materials of the heroes and events of the sacred origin mythology. They are used in curing rituals and are always destroyed when they have served their purpose. However, to avoid offending, no woven sandpainting precisely replicates its sacred prototype, any more than do the sandpaintings on board intended for the art market. Some element, however small, is left out, some color substituted for another. Sandpainting rugs are thought to be a recent innovation, but there is one that dates to 1896. Hosteen Klah (meaning Left-Handed), one of the best-known weavers of sandpainting tapestries, was a renowned medicine man and singer-sandpainter. He was held in considerable respect, but nevertheless, there was criticism from other Navajos when, in 1919, he began to transfer the sacred subject matter of the ephemeral ritual painting to the permanent woven tapestry. Even today, to avoid disapproval, a weaver of a sandpainting rug will take it directly to the trading post without letting the neighbors see it.

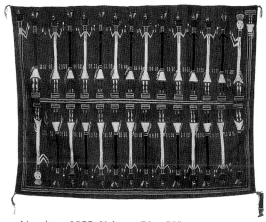

Navajo; c.1955; Yei rug; 76 x 59"
(193 x 150 cm).

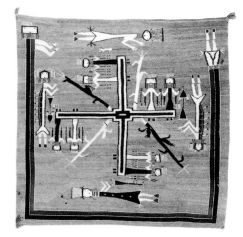

Navajo; sandpainting rug; 57 x 581/2"
(144.8 x 148.6 cm).

As with textiles, the place in native North America where the ancient ceramic arts survived and flourished without interruption to the present day is the Southwest. European influence

POTTERY

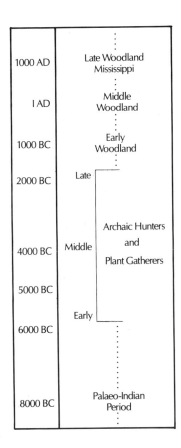

1000 AD	Late Woodland Mississippi	
I AD	Middle Woodland	
1000 BC	Early Woodland	
2000 BC	Late	
		Archaic Hunters and Plant Gatherers
4000 BC	Middle	
5000 BC		
	Early	
6000 BC		
8000 BC	Palaeo-Indian Period	

Chart showing the approximate periods of some prominent prehistoric Eastern cultures of North America.

Mississippian, Florida; c.1450; steatite; H 61/4" (16.5 cm).

failed to alter the basic technology: instead of adopting the wheel, Pueblo potters have continued to make practically all their earthenware by coiling. Outside the Southwest, pottery of high quality was produced in prehistoric times in many parts of the Eastern Woodlands, a vast area with many cultures that extended from the Mississippi Valley to the Atlantic and Gulf coasts, but the ceramic work ended when the Indian peoples were forcibly removed from their lands to make way for white settlement.

In the East, the oldest pottery comes from Late Archaic sites dating to the second millennium BC and the early Burial Mound period. The cultural focus of the Eastern Woodlands was Adena, named for a group of burial mounds in Ohio. Adena pottery is a considerable improvement on the coarse, grass, fiber-tempered ware of the Late Archaic, but it is still relatively simple, without much decoration. Beginning about 300 BC, the great Hopewell complex appeared and created numerous assemblies of earthworks and burial mounds, some containing hundreds of richly furnished graves, far larger and more complicated than those of Adena.

Hopewell lasted to the middle of the sixth century AD. Burials of this period were rich in fine ceramics and other funerary gifts, whose discovery sparked a veritable antique rush in the nineteenth and early twentieth century. These tombs yielded an enormous number of beautiful objects of fired clay, carved stone, and exotic materials—some imported over long distances—such as copper, shell, mica, meteoric iron, obsidian, and quartz. Hopewellian ceramics are of very high quality. At one Gulf Coast Hopewell site, Weeden Island, the funeral pottery had seemingly deliberate "kill-holes", some made before firing, others after.

There was a great flowering in the variety of ceramic forms, artisanship, and decoration during the Mississippian period, which had its climax between 1200 and 1500 AD. In addition to great numbers of effigy pots in human and animal form, Mississippian sites in Alabama, Kentucky, Arkansas, Tennessee, Ohio, Georgia, Florida, and Louisiana have yielded some of the finest engraved or painted prehistoric pottery in North America.

The Southwestern ceramic tradition began later than the Woodland. On the other hand, it has continued uninterrupted from about 300 BC, when fully developed ceramic techniques were introduced from cultures below the Rio Grande, to the present.

Quapah; 1650–1750; terracotta; H 11" (27.9 cm).

	MOGOLLON	HOHOKAM	ANASAZI
AD 1700			Historic Pueblo
1500			Regressive Pueblo
1300		Classic Stage	Great Pueblo
1100	V	Sedentary Stage	
900	IV	Colonial Stage	Developmental Pueblo
700	III		
500	II		Modified Basketmaker
300			
100		Pioneer Stage	Basketmaker
0	I		
100			
300			
500			
700 BC			
		San Pedro	

Chart showing the approximate periods of some prominent prehistoric Southwestern cultures of North America.

Mimbres; terracotta; D 11" (27.9 cm).

Pre-Columbian Southwestern pottery has three traditions—Mogollon, Anasazi, and Hohokam. Mogollan is named for the mountain range that extends southeast from central Arizona into Mexico. The Anasazi (Navajo for "the ancient ones") tradition developed on the high plateau north of the Mogollon Mountains. The Hohokam ("those who have gone" in the Pima language) were probably immigrants from northwestern Mexico who brought with them ceramic technology. Mogollon pottery was coiled and finished by scraping and polishing with a smooth pebble. Slips were common, but native American potters did not use true all-over glaze, which requires very high temperatures. In form, technique, and decoration, the earliest Mogollon ceramics were based on Mexican prototypes, but baskets and gourds also served as models. As in later times, when pottery had become more advanced, basketry patterns and decoration inspired many of the geometric designs on the black-on-white or polychrome ware for which the ancient Southwest is famous.

By far the most famous and admired of Mogollon pottery is Mimbres, a style that developed out of earlier red-on-white decoration with strong Anasazi influences. Mimbres, which first appeared about 1000 AD, is characterized by delicate and elegant fine-line geometric and life-form decoration, mainly in black paint on white.

At the beginning of the twentieth century, Mimbres was virtually unknown. Today there are thousands of Mimbres ceramics in public and private collections. Best known are the open bowls, but the complex runs the gamut of vessel shapes and uses. There is a great variety of what we today perceive as abstract or geometric designs but which may have conveyed specific meanings to the ancients. Most interesting are the numerous pictorial representations: mythological events, spirit beings, composite creatures, magic rituals, everyday activities, and a great variety of animal life, from insects and fishes to mammals and birds—many of them recognizable, despite stylization, by species. Most of these bowls have the same kind of apparently ritual kill-hole as do the funerary ceramics of the earlier and distant Weedon Island culture.

Anasazi pottery, unlike Mogollon, was from the start decorated with painted designs. Fiber temper had already been abandoned by the end of later Basketmaker and the beginning of the Pueblo tradition. Pueblo I pottery was still heavily influenced by Mogollon, but soon there were such typical Anasazi innovations as firing in a reducing atmosphere, that is, firing without oxygen, which made vivid black, white, and gray patterns possible.

After 1100 AD Anasazi pottery became really diversified. Many new forms were developed, including the famous Mesa Verde handled mug. Polychrome ware also appeared, with red, black, and yellow being used for decoration, something that could have come about only with a change in firing techniques.

Mesa Verde; 1100–1200 AD; terracotta; H 6" (15.2 cm).

The Historic period begins with the coming of the Spanish. The traditional arts continued undisturbed, but responded to the new market. It was during the successive Spanish, Mexican, and Anglo-American periods that Pueblo pottery expanded to include nontraditional forms and motifs, such as naturalistic birds, animals, and flowers, even as the women continued to make the old ceremonial and utilitarian wares for themselves.

Some later innovations, like the matte black on polished black perfected in the early 1920s by the Tewa potters Maria and Julian Martinez of San Ildefonso, became highly successful. And there were notable revivals of older styles, like that pioneered in the late nineteenth century by the Tewa-Hopi potter Leah Nampeyo of Hano, who, with some other First Mesa potters, helped restore Hopi ceramics to high quality by adapting the designs of ancient Sikyatki bowls.

Little, if anything, of the ceramic arts of the Pueblo Southwest would have survived in the absence of interest from white collectors and encouragement from a few archaeologists and museum curators. In the 1930s, Maria and Julian Martinez counted themselves lucky if they sold a dozen pots and bowls for $30. Fifty years later just one piece could bring thirty or forty times that sum. Some Pueblo potters still make vessels for their own ceremonial use, but most production is, as it has been since the turn of the century, for the white market.

San Ildefonso; blackware *olla* by Maria and Julian Martinez; H 7" (17.8 cm).

JEWELRY

If basketry is as old as humankind, so, surely, is the urge to adorn the body. But the function of jewelry has been more than that, for in many traditional cultures it is worn not just to beautify but as protection—to keep harmful spirits from slipping into the body through its various orifices. That holds true for native Americans no less than for other peoples.

Indians had jewelry made from both indigenous and imported materials. Even in the second millennium BC shells were traded from the Gulf of Mexico up to Minnesota.

145

Here again the Southwest stands out. One finds there a great variety of materials and techniques and skilled modern Indian jewelers who build on centuries of experience. For example, turquoise, the sky-blue and green native stone, was as esteemed in the ancient Southwest and Mexico as it is today, although indigenous natural turquoise has long since been mined out in New Mexico and Arizona.

In ancient times the Hohokam had the taste and necessary skills to work turquoise, as did the Mogollon and the Anasazi to some degree. The Pueblos continued the ancient skills, including cutting turquoise and other materials into small, thin, polished rectangular pieces and arranging them into complex mosaics, an art especially well developed at Zuni and Santo Domingo.

Combining turquoise with silver is a much more recent innovation that originated with the Navajo but soon came to be practiced throughout the Southwest. The Navajo first learned to work copper, brass, and iron from the Spanish and later were taught silverworking by itinerant Mexican *plateros*, or silversmiths. The pupils soon outstripped their teachers. The first dies for stamping Navajo silver work were those the Mexicans used for decorating leather, but the Navajo quickly started making their own. Bracelets with stamped designs were made in great numbers in the last quarter of the nineteenth century. Embossing and repoussage were also popular techniques. Casting was done as early as the 1870s.

Around 1880 Navajo silversmiths taught themselves to set turquoise nuggets in silver. This new style was quickly taken up by the Zunis, who had been working brass and copper into bracelets, bow guard mountings, buttons, and rings as early as 1830. Zuni smiths soon developed their own specializations, turning from the rather massive stones typical of their earlier work to ever more delicate polished settings. Zuni work differs from Navajo in that the latter has traditionally used turquoise to decorate silver, while in the Zuni it is the stones, typically arranged in clusters, that predominate. Hopi silverworking began in the last decade of the nineteenth century, when Lanyade, a Zuni who learned the craft from the Navajos, in turn passed it on to a First Mesa Hopi named Sikyatala. Hopi jewelers followed the Navajo and Zuni style until an entirely new, distinctively Hopi, style emerged in 1947 with the training, under the G.I. Bill of Rights, of a new generation of Hopi silversmiths.

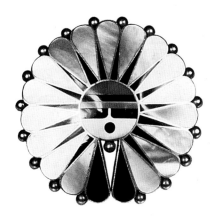

Zuni; 1986; silver, shell, and stone mosaic brooch; 2" (5.1 cm).

Navajo; "squash blossom" necklace; silver.

QUILL AND BEAD EMBROIDERY

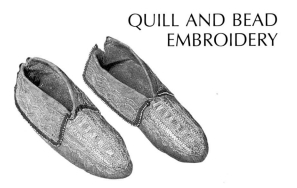

Iroquois; 18th Cent.; quillwork.

Ojibwa; 1880–90; bandolier bag; beaded cloth; L 38" (96.5 cm).

Sioux; 1875–85; saddlebag; beaded hide; W 19 1/2" (49.5 cm).

Crow; c.1880; beadwork.

Adornment of deer, elk, and other skins with dyed porcupine quills and glass beads, or a combination of the two, is a hallmark of the women's arts of the Plains, Prairies, and Woodlands. The natural range of the porcupine was the northern and eastern Woodlands, so it was presumably the peoples of this area who pioneered this uniquely native American art form.

The quills, which in their natural state are white, shading into brown toward the tip, were first sorted, washed, and softened with spittle before being dyed. The longest are only about three or four inches; they were elongated by tying or splicing with such skill that the connections were virtually invisible. Sometimes bird quills, natural or dyed, were used.

In the Northeast, another material used for embroidery on birchbark and cloth was dyed moosehair. This art was highly developed in the late eighteenth and early nineteenth century by the Huron and other eastern Woodlands tribes.

Imported colored beads were first introduced into the Great Lakes area by traders in the eighteenth century. Gradually their use replaced quillwork, although the latter never completely died out. In time, beads spread into the Plains and Prairie. At first, many Indians preferred "pony beads", small Venetian beads of colored glass. Even smaller ones, called seed beads, that had been used by the Iroquois reached the Ojibwa about the beginning of the nineteenth century, and from about 1850 they were the predominant type in Plains Indian embroidery. On the Plains, the adoption of seed beads brought a change in embroidery style, for while pony beads were usually sparingly applied, the large quantities of seed beads available resulted in allover bead embroidery.

The Sioux preferred fine-line renderings of triangles, terraces, rectangles, crosses, and hourglasses in blue, yellow, green, and white against a white background, while Crow women created massive blocks of rectangles, elongated triangles, and diamonds in dark blue, green, yellow, light blue, and lavender. Sioux beadwork is identifiable by the "lazy stitch", which results in a ridged pattern. Ojibwa women used the "couched" or "spot" stitch, in which the beads are put into position on sinew or thread, the first thread then being overlaid, or couched down, by a second, usually after each two beads. This holds the beads down firmly and gives the finished work a mosaic effect. Like quillwork, early bead embroidery did not stitch completely through the skin.

The semirealistic and realistic floral designs of the Ojibwa and some of their neighbors are often attributed to European influence. European prototypes probably account for some increased naturalism, but flowers and plants were part of the design inventory of Woodlands people long before European contact.

PAINTING

The more-or-less-representational paintings of hunting and warfare with which some Plains Indian men embellished their bison robes excited the admiration of the artists George Catlin and Carl Bodmer. A more widespread use of brush and paint among the Plains Indians was strictly a female art, the beautification of the parfleche—the ingenious envelope-like rawhide container—with polychrome geometric designs. The investment of shields and drums with spirit power through painted designs was general throughout North America.

In the 1920s a new art form arose in the Southwest, the painting of Pueblo life with water-based colors on paper or board. However, two-dimensional art has a long history among the Pueblos, who painted on the walls of kivas at least as early as 1100 AD.

SCULPTURE

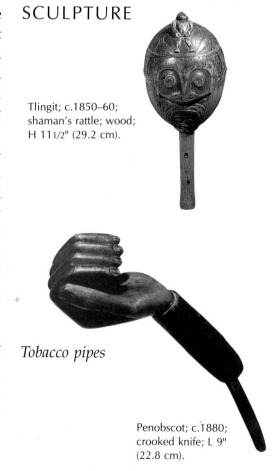

American Indian sculpture ranges in size from exquisite thumbnail miniatures carved from fossil ivory by ancient Inuit artists of the Bering Sea coast to the giant cedarwood totem poles of southern Alaska and British Columbia, some more than sixty feet high. Between these extremes are innumerable shaped objects of every size made from virtually every imaginable raw material.

Virtually all native American societies made three-dimensional images that could properly be described as sculptures, using a broad definition of the term—that is, a creative work in the round. Greek and Roman marble statuary is surely sculpture, but so are American Indian tobacco pipes and pipestems, totem poles, kachina dolls, ivory charms, figures, masks, shaman's rattles, flute stops, effigy bowls, ceremonial spoons, crooked knives, war clubs, and many other such works.

Tlingit; c.1850–60; shaman's rattle; wood; H 11 1/2" (29.2 cm).

Tobacco pipes

It is not surprising that for over two thousand years some of the greatest technical ingenuity and artistic talent of indian carvers went into making tobacco pipes. Tobacco was sacred, a gift of the gods, to be used only for ritual and ceremonial pur-

Penobscot; c.1880; crooked knife; L 9" (22.8 cm).

149

poses. It was consumed in many ways, but among the peoples of North America it was most commonly smoked, because the smoke carried prayers to the spirits and gave them sustenance.

The earliest pipes, simple tubes of stone or clay, date to the Late Archaic, evidence that tobacco was integral to North American Indian culture by 2000 BC. Early Woodlands people elaborated the tubes into human and animal forms. In the Middle Woodland period, 500 BC–500 AD, the art of pipe sculpture had already reached astonishing heights, with a great range of animals and birds—panther, beaver, bear, coyote, owl, falcon, raven, and cardinal—as well as human figures, as subjects. However, as faithful to the natural model as these miniature sculptures might appear, they were not just representations of the natural world; as the authors of the splendid catalog *Ancient Art of the American Woodlands Indians* (1985) have noted, "The kinds of animals that appear on Middle Woodland effigy pipes are those who often acted as spirit guardians or spirit protectors of individuals." Later, in the Mississippian period, some effigy pipes grew so large and heavy they could not have been passed, like the pipes of Plains Indians, from hand to hand, but presumably rested on a support or on the ground.

The peoples of the Eastern Woodlands, the Great Lakes, and the Plains and Prairies inherited the tradition of the effigy pipe, though not in the same way. The Iroquois sculpted relatively simple effigy pipes of clay and stone. The Great Lakes region produced the finest, most complex pipe sculptures of black and gray steatite, or soapstone. Often the effigy, animal or human, faced the smoker, perhaps a sign that the depicted subject was the owner's spirit helper or guardian. It was here also that the use of lead or pewter inlay began; indeed, there are a few early-nineteenth-century effigy pipes that were entirely cast and carved of metal.

The best-known material from which Plains Indian pipes were carved was the red pipestone that became known as catlinite, after the artist-ethnographer George Catlin, who visited the sacred source of the stone in southwestern Minnesota in the 1830s. The Sioux revered catlinite as the congealed blood of all the buffalo and all the Indians who had ever died. In addition to catlinite pipes of the simple T shape, Indian artists sculpted pipestone in a great variety of life forms—fish, bears, horses, cranes, and other creatures. The subject matter was inspired by myth and tradition, but these elegant sculptures

Plains; 1890; pipe; catlinite; L 8 3/4"
(22.2 cm).

Sioux; 1890; pipe; catlinite and lead; L 4 3/4"
(12 cm).

were produced less for ritual smoking than to demonstrate the artist's skill and gain income from sales to whites.

Masks have great antiquity in North America. Typically made of perishable materials, only a few ancient ones have survived. These are mainly from the far north, where conditions are more favorable for preservation. In the American Museum of Natural History there is a beautifully preserved mask comprising nine pieces of richly engraved walrus ivory, which was excavated at a prehistoric Inuit village in Alaska and dated to 350 AD. There are many other finds suggesting that a shamanic mask tradition must have been established nearly two thousand years ago in this region.

Masks

Northwest Coast masks, like those of other peoples, manifested a belief in transformation. What the mask portrayed is what the wearer became. Masks were worn in ceremonies that reenacted myths and reaffirmed the social and natural order. They represented animals and spirits significant to families, clans, or shamans.

All Northwest Coast masks share certain stylistic conventions, but there are enough differences to distinguish the masks of one group from those of another. Their dramatic effect was sometimes heightened through articulation. By pulling on strings, the dancer could make a hinged beak open and close in rhythm with speech or song or expose other spirits beneath the outer layer.

Tlingit; 1880; mask; wood; H 9 1/4" (23.5 cm).

The suppression of native religion by the whites nearly killed off the art traditions of the Northwest Coast. However, fine carvers working in the old style have emerged. Masks are carved not only for sale but to be used in reconstructed religious ceremonies.

The ancient masking tradition of the Iroquois, like that of the Pueblos, never succumbed to white pressure. Iroquois medicine societies still dance with basswood spirit masks. Most "False Face" masks depict humanlike spirits with long hair, sometimes distorted features, and staring eyes, but some represent animals and other beings. Another kind of mask, the so-called Husk Face, is woven or braided from corn husks. These represent spirit people and symbolize the gift of corn, beans, and squash that the ancient Iroquois received from another people.

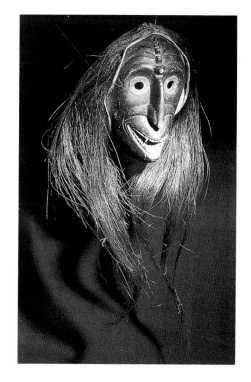

Iroquois; 1920; mask; basswood, horsehair; H 9 1/4" (23.5 cm).

151

Kachina dolls   The representations of kachina spirits that Hopis and Zunis carve from cottonwood root are not dolls in the conventional sense. "Effigy" is a better term for these popular sculptures.

Although some enforce discipline, kachinas are mostly benevolent spirits that bring rain, assure the growth of food plants, and reinforce the native cultures. Kachinas are manifested in three forms: they are spirit beings; men personify them in ceremonies; and they are embodied in "kachina dolls". These effigy dolls are presented on such occasions as the Farewell Dance of the Kachinas to children and women to familiarize them with the costumes of the different spirit beings and to transmit some of their benevolent power. The Zuni and the Hopi share a number of kachinas. Their dolls are easily told apart, however. The Hopi paint the costumes, jewelry, and other accoutrements; the Zuni use pieces of leather, cloth, wool, metal, turquoise, and other materials instead of paint. Also, the arms of Zuni dolls are often movable, while those of the Hopi are not.

The kachina cult is certainly pre-Columbian, but the proliferation of kachina effigies did not occur until the last quarter of the nineteenth century. Perhaps this was because anthropologists and tourists had begun buying Pueblo Indian artifacts. The Indians may also have felt a need for cultural preservation at a time when the U.S. Government was forcibly removing children from their parents and the old way of life.

The salutary effect of collector interest on the survival of this indigenous art is self-evident, as it is in the case of Pueblo pottery, even if a growing appreciation of American Indian art is not necessarily accompanied by a proper regard for the cultures and rights of those who created it.

Zuni; 1880s; Snake Dance kachina; H 103/4"
(27.3 cm).

Hopi; 1950; Snake Dance kachina; H 91/2"
(24.1 cm).

Penobscot (Maine); c.1780; container; birch bark with incised double scroll and plant decoration; H 9½" (24.1 cm). Birchbark basketry and this technique of decoration are both ancient and widely distributed from Siberia across sub-Arctic North America. The double scroll derives from unfurling spring vegetation and hence symbolizes new life.

BASKETRY
East

A. Mohegan (Connecticut); 1960–70; basket; ash splint decorated with potato-stamp design; L 151/2" (39.4 cm).

B. Algonquin (Northeastern Woodlands); 1780–1820; box; birch bark decorated with incised scrolls; H 11" (28 cm).

C. Penobscot (Maine); c.1820; basket; birch bark with incised designs of plants, houses, and geometric forms; L 51/2" (14 cm).

B

A

C

D

E

D. Cherokee (North Carolina); c.1880; basket; plaited dyed and natural river cane; H 17" (43.2 cm). Cherokee basket makers are renowned for their skill and taste in weaving long, thin, narrow splints of river cane into beautiful, complex geometric designs. In the 1930s white oak splints began to replace the much finer traditional river cane strips, leading to simpler, bolder patterns.

E. Cherokee (North Carolina); 1910–20; wicker basket; white oak and honeysuckle vine; D 13" (33 cm). Cherokee wickerwork is often used for utilitarian basketry such as laundry hampers, but here the weaver has made a utilitarian container into a work of art.

BASKETRY
Northwest Coast

Tlingit (Alaska); c.1880; hat;
basketry of twined spruce root
with bear design in native dyes;
H 9 1/2" (24 cm); The Art
Museum, Princeton University.

155

BASKETRY
Northwest Coast

A. Aleut (western Aleutians); 1860–80; baskets; beach grass in the technique of close twining with false-embroidery decoration; left to right: H 5" (12.7 cm), 4¾" (12.1 cm), 4½" (11.4 cm). Many Aleut baskets are so finely twined they feel almost like woven cloth. The false-embroidery technique may have been borrowed from the Alaskan Tlingit.

B. Tlingit (Alaska); c.1880; basket; twined spruce root fibers with native-dyed bear grass false-embroidery decoration; H 6¾" (17.2 cm).

A

B

A

B

C

D

A. Karok (Salmon Mountains region, Northern California); 1900–10; lidded basket; redwood root, bear grass, and maidenhair fern; H 6 1/4" (15.9 cm). Despite their geometric appearance, the bold designs of the baskets of the Karok and their Northern California neighbors are taken from natural models.

B. Karok (Northern California); 1880–1900; woman's cap; twined bear grass, redwood root, and hazel splints, with native dyes; H 3 1/2" (8.9 cm).

C. Hupa (Northern California); 1900–10; winnowing tray for grass seeds; H 20 1/4" (51.5 cm). Hupa basketry geometric designs represent the markings of rattlesnakes and sturgeons, swallow tails, grizzly paws, frogs, and other life forms.

D. Western Mono (central California); cradle; basketry; 1880–90; L 21 1/2" (54.6 cm).

A. Pomo (north-central California); c.1900; bowl; basketry, coiled and stitched in the weave the Pomo call *tsai,* with human, bird, and geometric designs, and embellished with clamshell beads and the remnants of quail topknot feathers; D 7" (17.8 cm); Peabody Museum of Natural History, Yale University.

B. Pomo (Northern California); c.1890; bowl; basketry decorated with two rows of linked human figures; Peabody Museum of Natural History, Yale University. The linked figures may represent dancers, the idea of friendship, or, metaphorically, members of the same lineage. Pomo women are generally considered the best native American coiled-basket makers.

C. Pomo (Northern California); c.1890; tray ("treasure basket"); basketry with allover mosaic of green, yellow, red, and blue feathers, clamshell beads, and abalone shell danglers; D 81/2" (21.6 cm). This type of feather basket displays the technical mastery and artistic sensibility of Pomo women basket weavers at their finest. Here the weaver inserted feathers of different colors under the stitches during the construction of the basket.

D. Pomo (Northern California); 1890–1910; treasure basket; bright yellow hummingbird feathers, meadowlark plumage, native clamshell, blue and white glass trade beads, and abalone shell disks; L 10" (25.4 cm); Newark Museum.

E. Yokut (Northern California); late nineteenth century; twined basketry bowl; D 121/4" (31.1 cm).

F. Yokut (Northern California); 1890–1900; bowl; finely twined basketry with classic black-and-red diamondback rattlesnake design; D 83/8" (21.3 cm).

A

A. Nez Percé (Idaho);
1890–1910; flat wallet; twined
corn husk and Indian hemp, with
wool yarn ornamentation in the
false-embroidery technique; 22 x
17½" (56 x 44.5 cm). The most
conspicuous woven object of the
Nez Percé and some of their
Plateau neighbors was the
flexible, flat, decorated wallet,
used for storage and transport.
Each side has a different
geometric design. Ownership of
the different designs may have
been vested in individual
weavers or their families,
although they could be
transferred to others as gifts or
inherited.

B. Washo (Lake Tahoe region of
California and Nevada); c.1910;
bowl; basketry; D 11½"
(29.2 cm.); coll. Nevada State
Museum. There were many great
Washo basket weavers, but the
most famous and desired work
was produced by the great
Datsolalee, between 1895 and
1925. Her own explanation for
these designs, which she used
also on other baskets, was "Rainy
weather in month succeeds by
clear sky after the storm".

B

159

BASKETRY
West

A. Mono (Great Basin, California); 1890–1900; bowl; basketry with black and red diamond designs; D 9 3/4" (24.8 cm).

B. Yokut (Northern California); 1880–90; gambling tray; basketry, with two bands in the classic black-and-red rattlesnake pattern; 23 3/4" (60.3 cm). Flexible trays like this one hid pairs of hardwood sticks whose position the players had to guess.

C. Washo (Lake Tahoe region); c.1900; bowl; basketry; D 12 1/4" (30.5 cm). This bowl illustrates a system of design organization that is common to central California basket weavers: setting figures alternately on the two sides of an axis.

A

B

C

D

E

F

D. Mono-Tulare (central California); c.1890; friendship or marital basket; black and red human figures and feather decoration; D 5" (12.7 cm).

E. Mission Indian (Southern California); 1860–70; food bowl; basketry with cascading lightning or rattlesnake design; D 10 1/2" (26.7 cm). "Mission Indian" is the collective name applied to diverse native peoples of Southern California who, in the late 1700s, came under the tutelage—often with tragic consequences—of the Franciscan missions established by Father Junipero Serra.

F. Chumash (Santa Barbara County, Southern California); c.1850; bowl; basketry with allover checkerboard design; D 9" (22.8 cm); Channing Dale Throckmorton Gallery, Santa Fe. Few of the beautiful baskets made by the Chumash, once a numerous and talented people inhabiting much of Southern California, have survived.

A

B

C

D

E

F

BASKETRY
Southwest

A. Pima (Arizona); c.1920; basket; lizard designs; D 13 1/4" (33.7 cm).

B. Pima (Arizona); 1890–1900; basket; variants of the *tasita,* or swastika, design; D 12 1/2" (31.8 cm). Nineteenth- and early-twentieth-century Pima basket weavers generally employed geometric forms representing vegetation, celestial bodies, and phenomena of the natural environment. The swastika symbolized the sun moving across the sky.

C. Pima (Arizona); 1890–1910; basket; figures of horses and people; H 11 1/2" (29.2 cm). Just as animals and other naturalistic motifs became more popular as a result of the advent of tourism, the Pima basket weavers responded to non-Indian demands for practicality with untraditional flat-bottomed shapes resembling wastepaper baskets.

D. Pima (Arizona); 1890–1900; bowl; basketry with whirling sun design; D 18" (45.7 cm).

E. Papago (southern Arizona); c.1910; storage *olla;* basketry with geometric designs of devil's claw; H 24 1/2" (62.2 cm).

F. Paiute (southern Nevada); 1880–90; bottle; basketry waterproofed inside and out with pine pitch; H 11 3/4" (29.8 cm). Several Southwestern desert peoples, including the Navajo, Ute, and Paiute, used waterproofed basket bottles of this shape, with flat or conical bottoms, to carry their precious drinking water. Long scorned by collectors as "ethnographic", these ingenious containers have recently gained in appreciation.

BASKETRY
Southwest

A. Apache (Arizona); c.1895; shallow bowl; basketry; W 11 3/4" (29.9 cm). Apache women were justly famed as the greatest of the Southwestern basket weavers.

B. Apache (Arizona); 1890–1900; jar; basketry decorated with male and female human figures and horses; H 13 1/2" (34.3 cm). The large *ollas,* some as high as three feet, are the most famous and desired of all Apache baskets. Many were made for sale to whites, but others served the Apache themselves for the storage of seeds and other foodstuffs.

C. Apache (Arizona); c.1890; storage jar with large mouth; basketry with geometric designs; H 17 1/2" (44.5 cm). Considering its purely abstract designs, it is probable that this storage basket was made for home use rather than for the tourist trade.

D. Apache (Arizona); 1885–90; bowl; basketry; D 24" (61 cm). Richly decorated with human figures and geometric forms, this large, exceptionally fine shallow basket is typical of those used for food offerings in the all-important Apache girls' puberty rite, a communal celebration in which the maiden is temporarily transformed into White Painted Woman, the personification of the holy earth—wife of the Sun and divine Mother of the culture hero. In these rituals, basket trays like this one were heaped with gifts for the girl, including ceremonial foods, tobacco, and sacred pollen, the symbol of fertility and plenty.

A

C

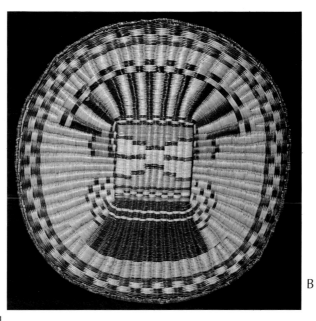

A. Hopi (Second Mesa, Arizona); 1900–1910; plaque; coiled basketry; D 19" (48.3 cm). Decorated with geometric directional and kachina designs, coiled basketry trays or plaques like this, heaped with sacred corn meal and other foods, are used in the ceremonial dances and kachina rites. They also accompany the dead. On Second Mesa no man could hope to be admitted into the company of the ancestors unless he carried such a tray.

B. Hopi (Third Mesa, Arizona); c.1900; meal tray; wickerwork decorated with kachina design; D 13" (33 cm); Fowler Museum of Cultural History, University of California at Los Angeles.

C. Hopi (Second Mesa, Arizona); c.1910; basket; coiled, with Crow Mother kachina design; H 83/4" (22.3 cm).

D. Navajo (Arizona); 1890–1900; "wedding basket"; D 147/8" (37.8 cm). Because the design originated with supernatural instruction, these ceremonial baskets were usually made for the Navajo by Ute and other Indian neighbors. The stepped triangles represent the mountains that encircle the world. The opening in the circular design, which during ritual must always face east, serves as entry and exit for the supernatural participants in the ritual. During construction, the weaver is required always to end the rim coil in a direct line with the spirit path. While they are popularly known as wedding baskets, their connection with weddings is not close.

A. Navajo (Arizona); Late Classic, 1870–80; wearing blanket (*serape*); wool; 49 x 29" (124.5 x 73.7 cm). This wearing blanket and the one in B are superb examples of Late Classic Navajo weaving, mixing commercial and raveled red, white, dark brown, and yellowish wool yarns, including Saxony and bayeta, and indigo, cochineal, and aniline dyes.*

B. Navajo (Arizona); Late Classic, 1870–75; child's or woman's wearing blanket; wool; 51 x 30 1/2" (77.5 x 129.6 cm).*

C. Navajo (Arizona/New Mexico); Late Classic Third Phase, 1875–85; Moki (Hopi) style of "chief's blanket" (*serape*); wool yarns in red, white, blue, dark brown, and black; 67 1/2 x 48" (171.5 x 121.9 cm). Of

mixed homespun, raveled red bayeta, Saxony and Germantown yarns, and natural and aniline dyes, this type of finely woven wearing blanket was in great demand among Plains Indian peoples. There is no legitimate reason for the popular, but inaccurate, term "chief's blanket".

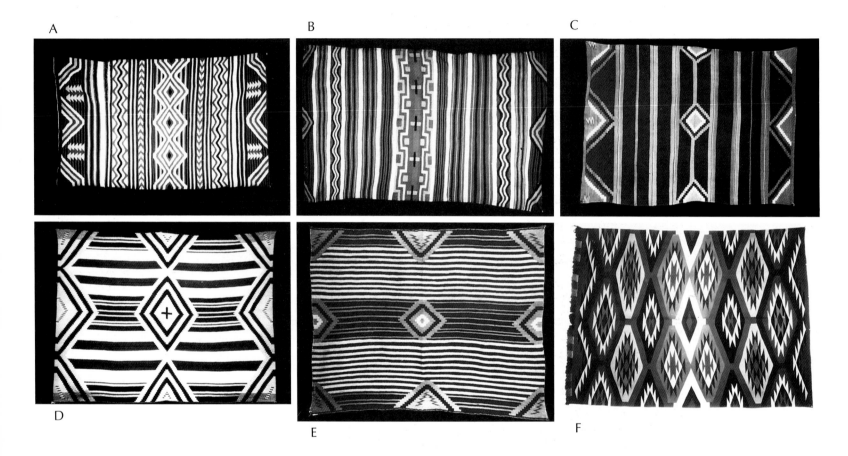

D. Navajo (Arizona/New Mexico); Late Classic Third Phase, 1875–85; "chief's blanket"; mixed wool yarns, including black, white, and pink bayeta; 71 1/2 x 54" (181.6 x 137.1 cm).

E. Navajo (Arizona/New Mexico); Late Classic Third Phase, 1875–85; terraced-style "chief's blanket"; black, white, brown, indigo blue, and red bayeta wool yarns. Navajo

women wove baskets long before they began to weave fabric. It is believed that the terraced zigzag stripe used to create a terraced diamond shape derives from early decorated Navajo basketry.

F. Navajo (Arizona/New Mexico); 1880–90; *serape*-style blanket; Germantown wool yarn in white, red, green, black, and tan; 84 x 62" (213 x 157.5 cm).

A

B

C

TEXTILES
Southwest

A. Navajo (Arizona/New Mexico); c.1890; Germantown saddle blanket; red, maroon, white, tan, green, and black wool yarn; 29 x 243/4" (73.6 x 62.9 cm); coll. Rex and Bonnie Arrowsmith, Santa Fe.

B. Navajo (Arizona/New Mexico); 1890–1900; Germantown saddle blanket; red, white, black, brown, green, and yellow wool yarn; 291/2 x 25" (75 x 63.5 cm).

C. Hopi (Arizona); c.1870; *manta*; diagonal twill weave, white cotton with red bayeta inner borders and indigo blue outer borders in diamond twill. 47 x 39" (119.4 x 99 cm). Fine Classic women's shawls like this one were presented to Hopi girls following their kachina initiations, around ages eight and twelve. Adult women also received such garments later in life, for wearing on festive occasions. In contrast to Navajo weaving, a women's art, Pueblo weaving was traditionally done by men, and *mantas* such as this were usually woven by the grandfathers of the young recipients.

TEXTILES
Southwest

A. Navajo (Arizona); c.1925; sandpainting-style rug with ten pairs of *yei* (holy people); 90 x 72" (228.6 x 183 cm); coll. Tad Dale, Santa Fe. The use of Navajo sandpainting sacred designs dates to about 1900. Some Navajo were at first outraged by such commercialism, but collectors responded enthusiastically to the new designs, and economic needs won out over tradition. By the 1920s, tapestries and rugs inspired by sandpaintings were being made by a number of weavers.

B. Navajo (Arizona/New Mexico); c.1880; Germantown *serape*; wool yarn with synthetic red, burgundy, green, and dark purple dyes and white undyed yarn; 68 x 56" (172.7 x 142.2 cm).

A

166

B

OPPOSITE PAGE

Navajo (Arizona/New Mexico); 1925–30; tapestry; wool with Summer Thunder sandpainting design; 75 x 70" (190.5 x 177.8 cm); coll. America Hurrah, New York. Of the four Summer Thunders, one for each direction, the weaver here used only two—Black Thunder in the east and Blue Thunder in the west. Male lightning bolts and rain fall from the Thunder beings' wings and male lightning from the feet. Between the two Thunders are the four plants sacred to the Navajo—beans, maize, squash, and tobacco. The weaver has diverged from the real Summer Thunder sandpainting by encircling the design on three sides with the Rainbow Guardian.

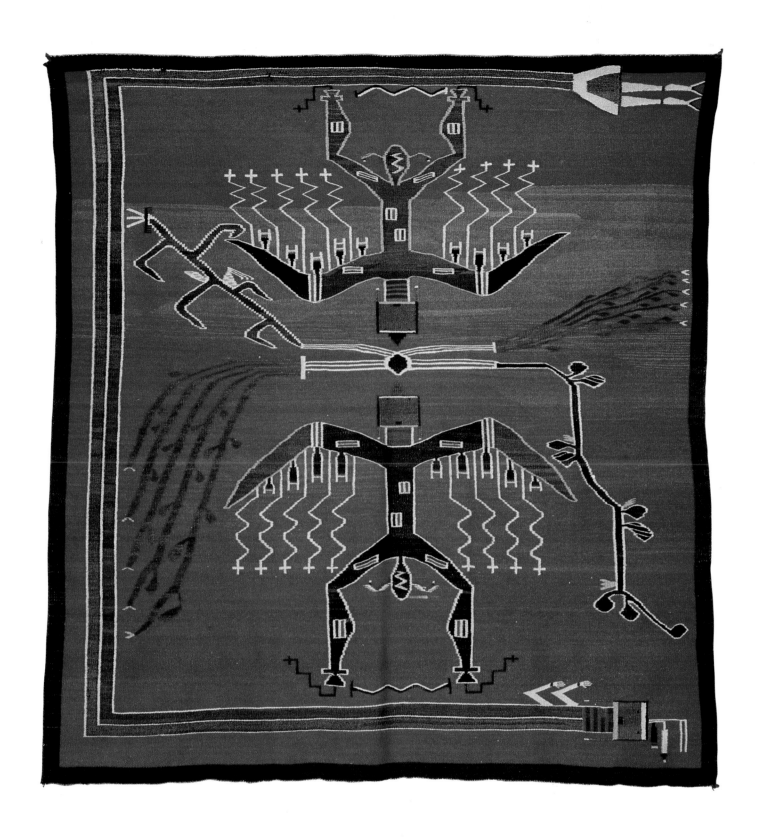

A. Navajo (Ganado, Arizona); c.1920; rug; natural light and dark brown and white wool yarns with red aniline dye center; 52 x 76" (132 x 193 cm).

B. Navajo (Two Grey Hills area, Arizona); c.1925; rug; undyed homespun yarns; 58 x 86 1/2" (147.3 x 219.8 cm). Fine rugs in the Two Grey Hills style, with natural wool colors and the characteristic wide border, were pioneered in the 1920s by two traders working with local weavers, and are still being produced. These rugs were based to some extent on Oriental rug designs, but the result is typically Navajo.

C. Navajo (Crystal area, Arizona); c.1900; rug; natural white and aniline-dyed red and black wool yarns; 77 1/2 x 51" (196.8 x 129.5 cm). This fine weaving has twenty-two weft threads and seven warp threads per inch (2.54 cm).

D. Navajo (Ganado area, Arizona); c.1940; rug; natural color wool yarns in browns, beige, gray, and ochre; 102 x 57 1/2" (259 x 146 cm).

A

B

C

D

Seminole (Everglades, Florida); 1920–30; man's "big shirt"; cotton cloth with patchwork and appliqué in red, orange, blue, white, gray, and yellow; L 48" (122 cm); coll. David and Steven Pickelner, Fort Collins, Colorado. The characteristic Seminole men's "big shirts" (often mistaken for women's dresses) have been traced to the influence of Scottish Highlander traders who married into this tribe in the eighteenth century. Belts were added in 1900, to be replaced by waistbands around 1920. In the 1930s, when Seminole men started taking jobs in the white community, traditional "big shirts" were shortened so they could be tucked into trousers.

TEXTILES
Northwest Coast

A. Tlingit (Alaska); c.1885; button blanket; symmetrical double-eagle design of mother-of-pearl buttons sewn on gray-black Hudson's Bay trade blanket bordered with red stroud; 67 x 51" (170 x 129.5 cm). Chilkat blankets are made entirely from indigenous materials—the wool of wild mountain goats, shredded cedar bark, and native dyes. In contrast, the famous Tlingit button blankets, likewise worn by nobles, were made entirely from trade goods. Thus, they represent one of the happier outcomes of the encounter between two cultures, the one contributing its ancient artistic conventions, the other its materials.

B. Chilkat Tlingit (Alaska); 1890–1900; blanket; dyed mountain goat wool on wool and cedar bark fiber warp, killer whale crest design; W 67" (170 cm); courtesy Sherwood's, Beverly Hills. Chilkat blankets, the most complex and abstract of all Northwest Coast art, are woven by women from designs painted on pattern boards by men. The design consists of three panels: a center panel with a frontal view of the wearer's crest animal and two side panels with abstracted profile views of the same creature.

A

B

Mesquakie (Fox) (Iowa);
1890–1910; sashes; finger-woven
wool yarn; L (top to bottom) 106"
(260 cm), 96" (243.8 cm), 88"
(223.5 cm).

TEXTILES
East

A. Huron (Quebec, Canada);
c.1910; sash; braided commercial
wool yarns and glass beads in
arrow pattern; L 100" (254 cm).
Braiding or finger-weaving with
native fibers predates European
contact, but the Woodlands
Indian women took advantage of
the availability of brightly dyed
commercial wool yarns and tiny
Bohemian glass beads to perfect
new techniques and designs.

B. Osage (Oklahoma); c.1920;
child's blanket; dark blue trade
cloth with machine-sewn
appliquéd satin ribbon designs
and red stroud hands; W 601/2"
(153.7 cm). Osage use of the
open human hand in design no
doubt derives from pre-Contact
times. It is a very ancient motif in
Southeastern ceremonial art,
particularly during the
Mississippian Period, which
climaxed between 1300 and
1600, when the ancestors of the
modern Osage made their homes
in what is now southern Illinois.
An open hand is a sign for peace
and generosity, and that is
probably its meaning on this and
similarly decorated Osage
ribbon-appliqué blankets.

A

B
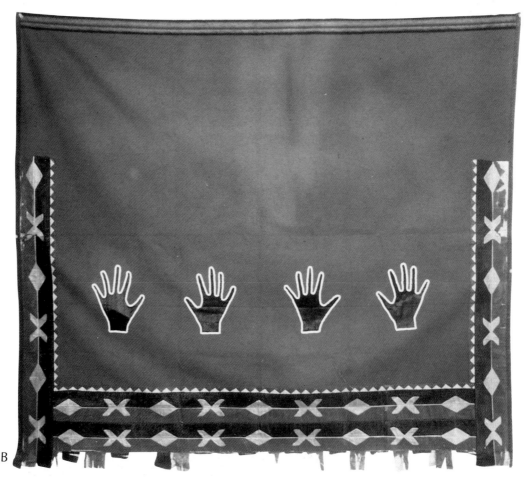

172

A

B

POTTERY
Prehistoric: East

A. Quapah (Arkansas); Late Mississippian Period, 1650–1750; bottle; shell-tempered terracotta with red and white cruciform symbol within a red bear-paw design; H 11½" (29.2 cm).

B. Quapah (Nodena area, Arkansas); Late Mississippian Period, 1650–1750; shell-tempered terracotta bowl with four red and white swirl designs; D 9" (22.8 cm). Cruciform and swastika swirl are among the most common symbols on painted pottery from the Mississippi Valley; both are generally interpreted as having solar meanings.

POTTERY
Prehistoric: East

A. Late Mississippian (Moundville, Black Warrior River, Alabama); 1300–1600; beaker; shell-tempered polished terracotta, black-smudged, or black-slipped, with engraved skull-and-bone motif (chalked to show design); H 41/2" (11.5 cm); Moundville State Monument Research Center, Alabama Museum of Natural History. The treatment of the skull with its upswept, pointed nose is reminiscent of Postclassic Mexican conventions.

B. Late Mississippian (Alabama); 1300–1600; owl effigy bottle; shell-tempered terracotta with buff slip and modeled and engraved designs; H 11" (28 cm); Peabody Museum of Natural History, Yale University.

C. Late Mississippian (Perry County, Missouri); 1300–1600; human effigy bottle; shell-tempered terracotta; H 101/4" (26 cm).

D. Caddoan (Arkansas); Late Mississippian Period, 1300–1500; seed jar; terracotta with gray slip and engraved spiral and crosshatched design; H 9" (22.8 cm).

A

B

C

A

B

A. Late Mississippian (Crittendon County, Arkansas); 1350–1550; bottle; terracotta with black slip and incised multiline spiral design; H 8 1/2" (21.6 cm).

B. Late Mississippian (Mississippi Valley); 1350–1550; wide-mouthed jar; terracotta with red slip and crosshatched sawtooth sun-circle design; H 8 3/4" (22.2 cm).

POTTERY
Prehistoric: Southwest

A. Hohokam (Gila River area, southern Arizona); c.50AD; platter; terracotta with red-on-buff continuous spiral design; D 11" (28 cm).

B. Mimbres, Mogollon Slipped Tradition (southwestern New Mexico); 1000–1250; bowl; terracotta decorated in black on white with a design of a pair of spotted bears and a pair of thunderbirds; D 10 1/2" (26.7 cm). This bowl, broken into numerous pieces when found, is somewhat unusual among Mimbres figural pottery in that it lacks the familiar kill-hole in the base.

C. Anasazi (Four-Mile Ruin area, Arizona); c.1300; bowl; terracotta with black, white, and red decoration; D 11 3/4" (29.8 cm). Four-Mile Ruin is a large village site on the southern edge of the Colorado Plateau; the ancient population were ancestors of the modern Hopi, and many of the designs developed at Four-Mile continued on into "historic" and recent Hopi pottery.

A

B

C

D

E

F

D. Mimbres, Mogollon Slipped Tradition (southwestern New Mexico); 1000–1250; bowl; terracotta with geometric black-on-white decoration and a large kill-hole in base; D 12 1/2" (31.8 cm).

E. Mimbres, Mogollon Slipped Tradition (southwestern New Mexico); 1000–1250; bowl; terracotta with black and white design of mountain lion and antelope figures; D 12" (30.5 cm).

F. Mimbres, Mogollon Slipped Tradition (southwestern New Mexico); 1000–1250; bowl; terracotta; decorated in black on white with geometric band encircling quail perforated by kill-hole; D 11" (28 cm). The purpose of the kill-hole is not well understood. One interpretation is that it released the essence of the bowl to allow it to join the spirit of its deceased owner.

POTTERY
Prehistoric: Southwest

Casas Grandes (northern Chihuahua, Mexico); 1100–1200; human effigy jar; terracotta with tan slip and red-and-black decoration; H 6¾" (17.2 cm). The relationship of the great northern Mexican trading center of Paquimé at Casas Grandes to Puebloan pottery traditions is unclear. Certainly there were trading relations, and Mimbres people may have migrated into what is now northern Chihuahua, merged with the Paquimé people, and, though losing their original cultural identity, influenced Casas Grandes with their own sophisticated pottery decoration traditions.

177

A. Anasazi (south-central New Mexico and Southwestern Colorado); 1125–1300; dipper and Mesa Verde handled terracotta mug; Tularosa terracotta with black-on-white decoration; dipper: L 10 1/4" (26 cm); mug: H 6" (15.2 cm). The dipper belongs to the Anasazi Mineral-Paint Tradition and dates to 1125-1520. The handled mug, dated 1200-1300, typical of Mesa Verde in southwestern Colorado, belongs to the Anasazi Vegetal-Paint Tradition. The division of Anasazi pottery into vegetal-paint and mineral-paint traditions dates back almost to the beginning of pottery in the region, the western Anasazi preferring a vegetal pigment, the eastern and central Anasazi a mineral paint.

A

B

C

D

B. Casas Grandes (northern Chihuahua, Mexico); 1300–1400; bowl; terracotta with tan slip and black and red geometric decoration; H 7 1/4" (18.4 cm).

C. Tularosa, Anasazi Mineral-Paint Tradition (south-central New Mexico); 1125–1250; *olla*; terracotta, black on white; H 13 1/2" (34.3 cm).

D. Tularosa, Anasazi Mineral-Paint Tradition (south-central New Mexico); 1125–1250; pitcher with effigy handle; terracotta; H 7" (17.8 cm).

A

B

C

D

F

POTTERY
Southwest

A. Hopi (Hano, First Mesa, Arizona); c.1905; jar; terracotta with red slip and polychrome decoration; old label on base, "Hopi Nampeyo, $4.50"; D 9" (22.8 cm). Inspired by the artistry of pre-Contact Hopi ceramics found at Sikyatki, Leah Nampeyo and other First Mesa potters revived high-quality Hopi work shortly before the turn of the century. Nampeyo, who made this jar, made the most famous and sought-after ceramics. Today, nearly a century later, a Nampeyo pot of this size and quality would bring one to two thousand times its original price.

B. Hopi (Second Mesa, Arizona); c.1930; water canteen; terracotta with polychrome Soyal kachina image; H 10" (25.4 cm).

C. Acoma (Acoma Pueblo, New Mexico); nineteenth century; canteen; terracotta with polychrome decoration; H 6 1/2" (16.5 cm). The form of water canteens, similar throughout the Pueblo Southwest, derived from its function: flat in back where it rests against the body, the globular shape maximizes the amount of liquid it can contain. The porous clay keeps the water cool through evaporation.

D. Acoma (Acoma Pueblo, New Mexico); c.1925; olla; terracotta with white slip and black-and-orange parrot and plant motif decoration; D 12" (30.5 cm).

E. Acoma (Acoma Pueblo, New Mexico); c.1900; olla; terracotta with white slip and abstract black-and-orange plant designs; D 12 1/2" (31.8 cm).

F. Zia (Zia Pueblo, New Mexico); c.1900; olla; terracotta with white slip and orange-and-black geometric and naturalistic plant designs; D 10 1/2" (26.7 cm).

179

POTTERY
Southwest

A. Acoma (Acoma Pueblo, New Mexico); pre-1910; *olla*; terracotta with scalloped rim and parrot and plant decoration in orange and black; D 12" (30.5 cm).

B. Santo Domingo (Santo Domingo Pueblo, New Mexico); c.1910; dough bowl; terracotta with cream slip and black geometric design, red-slipped interior; D 19¾" (49.5 cm).

A

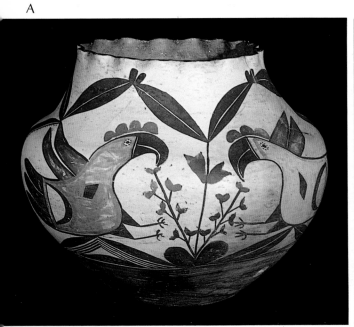

B

C

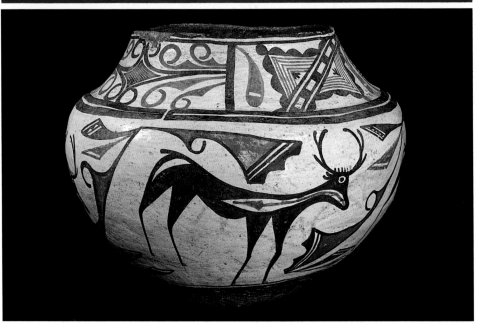

D

C. Zuni (Zuni Pueblo, New Mexico); early twentieth century; rain bowl; terracotta with white slip and stepped rain-cloud rim pattern and tadpole and horned toad designs in brown; D 13½" (34.3 cm); coll. Rex and Bonnie Arrowsmith, Santa Fe.

D. Zuni (Zuni Pueblo, New Mexico); c.1880; *olla*; terracotta with white slip and dark brown and red heart-line deer and abstract plant form decoration; H 9½" (24.1 cm); Smithsonian Institution. The Zuni call the heart line, which is found also in the arts of other American Indian peoples, the "entrance trail", because it leads to the source or breath of life.

A

POTTERY
Southwest

A. Maricopa (southern Arizona); 1900–1920; water canteen; terracotta with red slip and horse and rider in black; H 6 1/2" (16.5 cm). The highly stylized treatment of horse and rider is reminiscent of rock art, in which native artists of the early colonial period recorded their first impressions of mounted Spaniards.

B. Maricopa (southern Arizona); 1900–1920; *olla*; terracotta with highly polished red slip, black geometric decoration, and modeled human face; H 8" (20.3 cm). Maricopa pottery was made by women using the paddle-and-anvil method. Abstract decoration with black vegetal paint made from mesquite wood was often adapted from Hohokam prototypes. Early utilitarian Maricopa ware also had geometric designs painted in black on a red ground but did not have the highly polished surface of pottery intended for the tourist market.

B

181

A. Santa Clara (Santa Clara Pueblo, New Mexico); c.1900; double-spouted "wedding jar"; terracotta with polished iron oxide slip; H 13 1/4" (33.6 cm). Santa Clara was the center of polished black Pueblo ceramics in the nineteenth and early twentieth century and remains so, with several prominent families of traditional and innovative potters still active. The highly polished black surface is not due to smudging but to the fact that the red firing slip used by the Tewa potters contains ferric oxide. In an oxidizing atmosphere this yields a rich red surface, but when the same vessel is fired in an oxygen-reducing atmosphere, the red ferric oxide converts to magnetite, a black ferric oxide.

B. San Ildefonso (San Ildefonso Pueblo, New Mexico); 1926; vase; terracotta decorated in matte black on glossy black; H 13" (33 cm).

C. San Ildefonso (San Ildefonso Pueblo, New Mexico); 1925–35; platter; terracotta decorated in matte black on glossy black; D 12 1/4" (31.1 cm). This large plate, signed "Marie and Julian", is a good example of the technique of black matte on black decoration developed in the early 1920s by Maria Martinez and her husband, Julian.

D. San Ildefonso (San Ildefonso Pueblo, New Mexico); c.1910; *olla*; terracotta with cream slip and black and orange decoration; D 15 1/2" (39.4 cm). San Ildefonso pottery went into a decline in the mid-nineteenth century and by 1880 had virtually died out. It revived in response to demand from tourists and collectors. San Ildefonso is best known today for Maria Martinez' black-on-black ware, but her earliest pottery was the type of polychrome shown.

A

B

C

POTTERY
Southwest

Mojave (California/Arizona); 1890–1900; terracotta effigy jar; buff with red-and-white painted decoration; H 9 1/2" (24.1 cm); Natural History Museum of Los Angeles County. Although Mojave and Yuma potters produced charming effigy vessels such as this primarily for sale to tourists, the inspiration for combining a human effigy with a pottery vessel probably came from archaeological prototypes found in many places in the Southwest. Red-on-buff painted decoration likewise derives from earlier pottery, particularly that of the Hohokam.

JEWELRY

A. Zuni (New Mexico); c.1900; frog; turquoise mosaic on clamshell pendant, with black cannel coal inlay eyes; 5 1/4 x 4" (13.3 x 10.1 cm). This beautiful Zuni shell pendant rivals the best turquoise mosaic work of the ancient Southwest, even that of the Hohokam, from whom modern Pueblo peoples inherited this lapidary art. Frogs and shells are important rain symbols; green turquoise is valued for its relationship to plants, as the blue variety is for water.

B. Zuni (New Mexico); c.1940; Knifewing Dancer mosaic pin; finely polished blue and green turquoise, black cannel coal, white shell, and red spiny oyster shell in silver setting; H 3 1/2" (8.9 cm).

C. Zuni (New Mexico); c.1940; bracelets; turquoise and silver; left: H 3 1/8" (8 cm); right: 1 3/8" (3.5 cm); courtesy Millard Holbrook, Santa Fe.

D. Zuni (New Mexico); c.1970; necklace of sun god faces by William Zuni; mosaics of white shell, red oyster shell, black cannel coal, and turquoise set in silver; L 15" (38 cm).

A

B

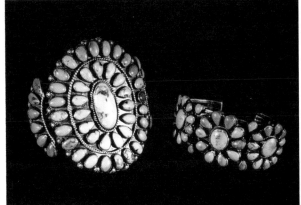

C

D

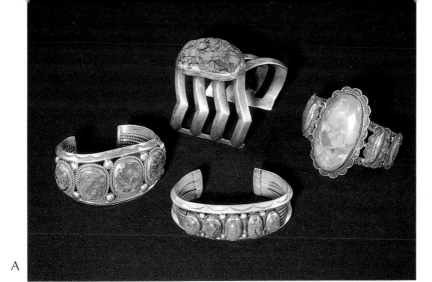

A

B

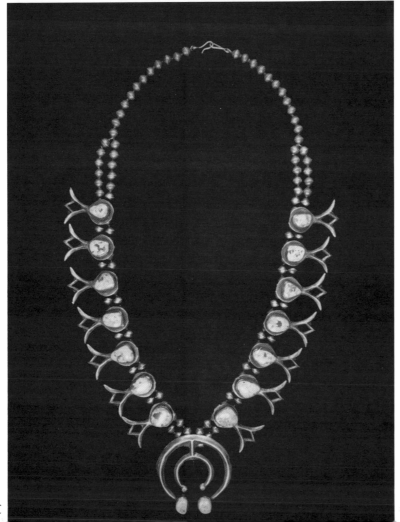

C

A. Navajo (Arizona/New Mexico); 1920–50; bracelets; silver and turquoise; left: H 2 1/2" (6.4 cm); front center: 1" (2.5 cm); right: 1 1/4" (3.2 cm); rear: 3" (7.6 cm). The earliest Navajo bracelets were all silver, with turquoise added later only to enhance the luster of the metal. In the early twentieth century silver was used increasingly to set off the beauty of the turquoise. The three bracelets in front date from the 1920s, that in back, an abstraction of Spider Grandmother, the old earth goddess and patron of weaving, from around 1950.

B. Navajo (Arizona/New Mexico); 1890–1910; wristguards (*ketöh*); silver and turquoise on leather; left: (1890) H 3 3/4" (9.5 cm); right: (1910) 4 1/2" (11.5 cm); courtesy Millard Holbrook, Santa Fe. In the days of bow and arrow the *ketöh* protected the wrist against the snapping bowstring. With the passage of the bow into history the *ketöh* lost its utilitarian role but was not abandoned; embellished with silver and turquoise, it became part of ceremonial apparel, not only for the Navajo but also for some of the Pueblo people, who traded for it from the Navajo.

C. Navajo (Arizona/New Mexico); 1950s; "squash blossom" necklace; sand-cast silver with polished blue turquoise nuggets; L 16" (40.6 cm). For this variant on the familiar squash blossom necklace, the silversmith replaced the hand-hammered flower petals with abstract sand-cast ones. The name "squash blossom" is a misnomer, because the flowers actually represent the pomegranate, which was introduced into Mexico by the Spanish. The Navajo, in turn, adopted the flower as a jewelry motif from Spanish/Moorish prototypes.

185

JEWELRY

A. Navajo (Arizona/New Mexico); 1900–24; concha belts; wrought silver on leather; left: buckle and seven conchas on narrow leather strap, L 41" (104.1 cm), conchas 4 x 33/8" (10.2 x 8.5 cm); center: buckle and six conchas separated by six spaces, or "butterflies", on narrow leather belt, L 411/2" (105.4 cm), conchas 31/2 x 3" (8.9 x 7.6 cm), spacers 13/4 x 11/2" (4.5 x 3.8 cm); right: buckle and seven conchas on full-width leather strap scalloped to accommodate concha shapes, L 40" (101.6 cm), conchas 4 x 37/8" (10.2 x 9.7 cm).

B. Navajo (Arizona/New Mexico); c.1935; tobacco flask; hammered and stamped coin silver with turquoise nugget; H 33/4" (9.5 cm); courtesy Ron Rakow, Los Angeles.

C. Santo Domingo (Santo Domingo Pueblo, New Mexico); c.1940; pendant; mosaic of cut turquoise, white shell, and jet on polished spiny oyster shell; H 33/8" (8.6 cm). This type of shell pendant is emblematic of the pueblo of Santo Domingo, most of whose population wears one on ceremonial occasions, such as the annual Corn Dance.

D. Pomo (Northern California); 1870–90; "Big Head" pendant; cut and polished abalone shell; H 57/8" (14.9 cm). In Pomo initiation and curing ceremonies, spirits of the six directions (the four cardinal points plus zenith and nadir) are impersonated by initiated members of the secret society with huge "Big Head" feather headdresses. But the true "Big Head", the one represented here in abalone, is Condor, god of the South.

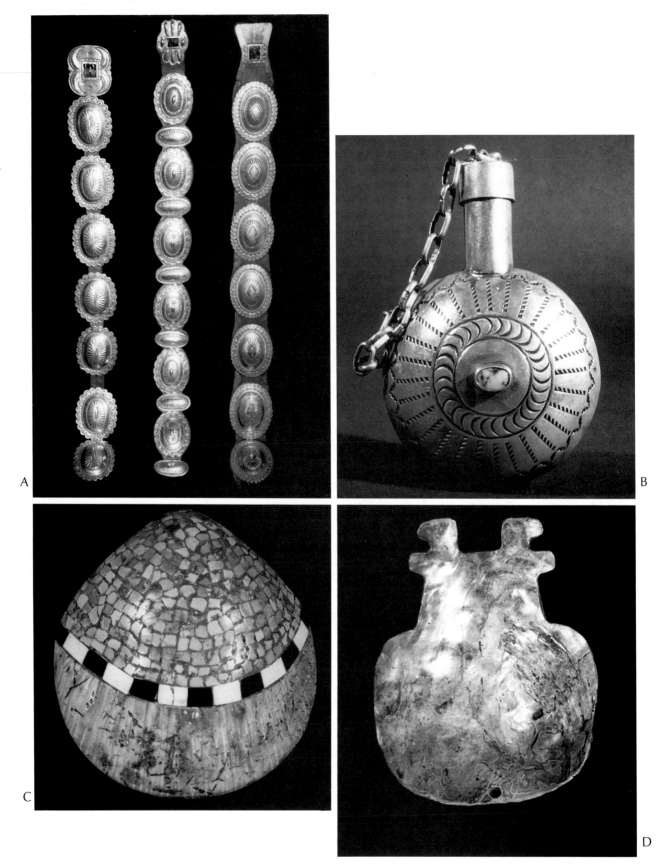

A

B

C

D

186

OPPOSITE PAGE

QUILL AND BEADWORK

Sioux (North Dakota); c.1890; child's dress; fringed buckskin with allover lazy-stitch beading; L 24" (61 cm); Museum of Natural History of Los Angeles County.

187

QUILL AND BEADWORK

A. and B. Sioux (Dakotas); late nineteenth century; man's vest; sinew-sewn buffalo hide fully beaded on front with geometric designs and American flags in dark blue, white, yellow, and red on blue ground with dark blue border, and on the back with four horses in dark blue, yellow, and red and a large blue-and-white thunderbird on a blue background; L 21 1/2" (54.6 cm).

A

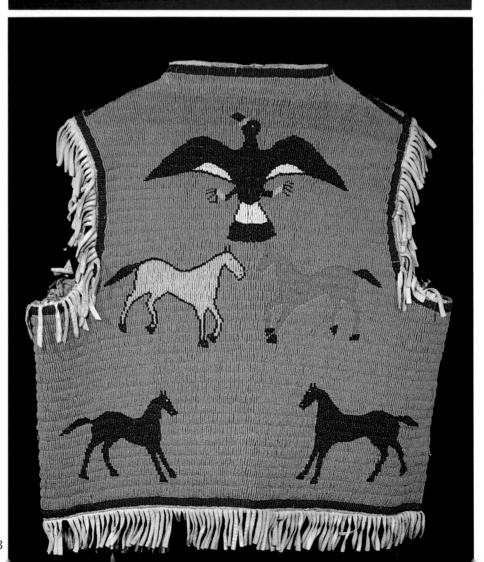

B

188

A. Blackfoot (Alberta, Canada); c.1870; boy's shirt; sinew-sewn tanned buckskin with painted and beaded striped decoration, tipi designs on sleeves, and fringes tipped with tin cones; L 35" (89 cm).

B. Hidatsa (Upper Missouri River); 1880–90; man's shirt; sinew-sewn buckskin with floral porcupine quill decoration, bands of dyed porcupine quill embroidery with triangular motifs in blue and pink on yellow, and long buckskin fringes; 61 x 36" (155 x 91.5 cm). An unusual feature is the absence of beadwork. In Reservation period clothing and other Plains Indian articles beadwork is usually used with the older-style quill embroidery.

A

B

189

QUILL AND BEADWORK

A. Sioux (Dakotas); c.1890; woman's dress; sinew-sewn buckskin with beaded yoke with geometric figures; including tipi symbols, in red, dark blue, green, yellow, and white on blue background, and fringes along the arms strung with glass trade beads; 41 x 40" (104 x 101.6 cm). This is a typical example of fine Plains women's buckskin clothing of the nineteenth century.

B. Assiniboin (Upper Missouri River); c.1880; man's war shirt; tanned buckskin cut poncho style with open sides, with traces of red, blue, and yellow pigment and white, red, blue, and metallic beadwork; 60 x 39" (152.4 x 99 cm).

A

B

190

A

B

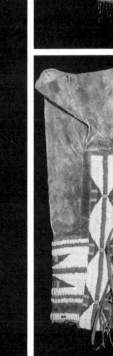

C

D

E

F

QUILL AND BEADWORK

A. Cree (Ontario/Quebec, Canada); 1830–50; hood; white, pink, and blue floral beadwork on black trade cloth; 19 x 21" (48.3 x 53.3 cm). This is a variant of a type of woman's hood common throughout the Canadian Maritime Provinces in the nineteenth century.

B. Winnebago (Wisconsin); 1890–95; bandolier bag; trade cloth with floral beadwork embroidery; L 42" (106.7 cm). The naturalistic floral style of beadwork is typical of Woodlands, Eastern Sioux, and other Great Lakes tribes. In earlier beadwork, flowers and plant life were conventionalized into geometric forms.

C. Kiowa (Oklahoma); 1880–90; woman's boots; sinew-sewn tanned buckskin stained with yellow ochre and embroidered with blue-and-white beadwork; H 19" (48.3 cm).

D. Cheyenne (Colorado); c.1880; man's leggings; blue-stained tanned buckskin with red, blue, and green bead embroidery on white beaded background; H 16½" (42 cm), coll. David and Steven Pickelner, Fort Collins, Colorado.

E. Sioux (Dakotas); 1880–90; moccasins; sinew-sewn buckskin with white, blue, maroon, green, and yellow geometric beadwork on uppers and sole; L 10" (25.4 cm).

F. Sioux (Dakotas); c.1900; moccasins; sinew-sewn rawhide soles and buckskin uppers with allover beadwork in white, green, blue, and red, with calico edging along cuff; L 10½" (26.7 cm).

191

QUILL AND BEADWORK

A. Flathead (Idaho); 1890–1900; baby carrier; sinew-sewn tanned buckskin on wood backing, with naturalistic floral beadwork in green, red, yellow, and blue on light blue beaded background; L 30" (76.2 cm).

B. Sioux (Dakotas); c.1880; cradle cover; sinew-sewn buckskin with beadwork embroidery in the Sioux lazy-stitch technique, with geometric designs on a white background on the sides and green beading with protective designs in white, red, and blue on the hood; L 23" (58.4 cm). Plains Indian women, like those of other native American peoples, lavished not only their love but an enormous amount of energy and creative talent on children. It was not uncommon for a newborn to receive splendidly beaded cradle covers from various female relatives.

C. Sioux (Dakotas); c.1880; cradle cover; sinew-sewn buckskin lined with trade cloth ticking and beaded in the lazy-stitch method; H 27" (68.6 cm).

D. Sioux (Dakotas); 1880–90; pipe bag; sinew-sewn tanned antelope buckskin with beadwork panel picturing a pronghorn antelope in dark green on white and a red quill-wrapped openwork rawhide panel decorated with tipi symbols; L (incl. fringe) 40" (101.6 cm); coll. Mark Zaplin, Santa Fe. Tobacco was sacred to Indian peoples, who smoked it only for ceremonial purposes. However, Indians readily sold pipe bags, as well as pipes, to collectors. During the Reservation period, the making of fine beaded pipe bags and pipes for the white market constituted one of the few sources of income for Indians deprived of their independent way of life.

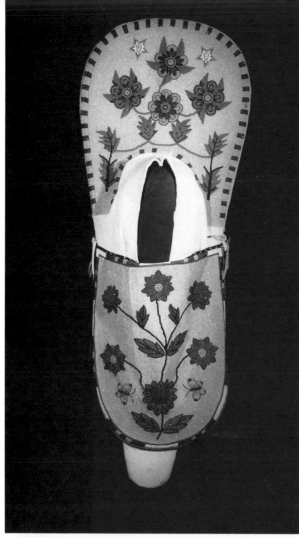

A

B

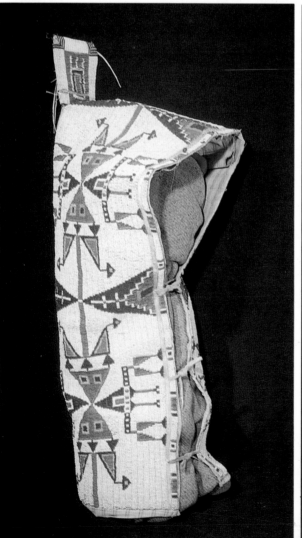

C

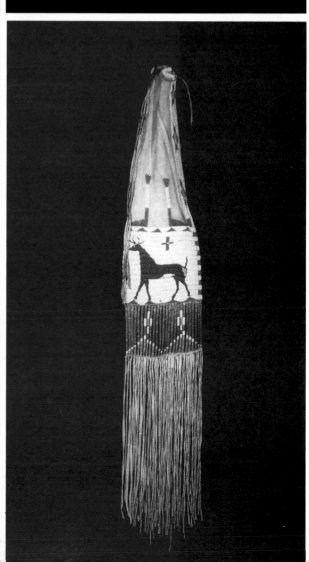

D

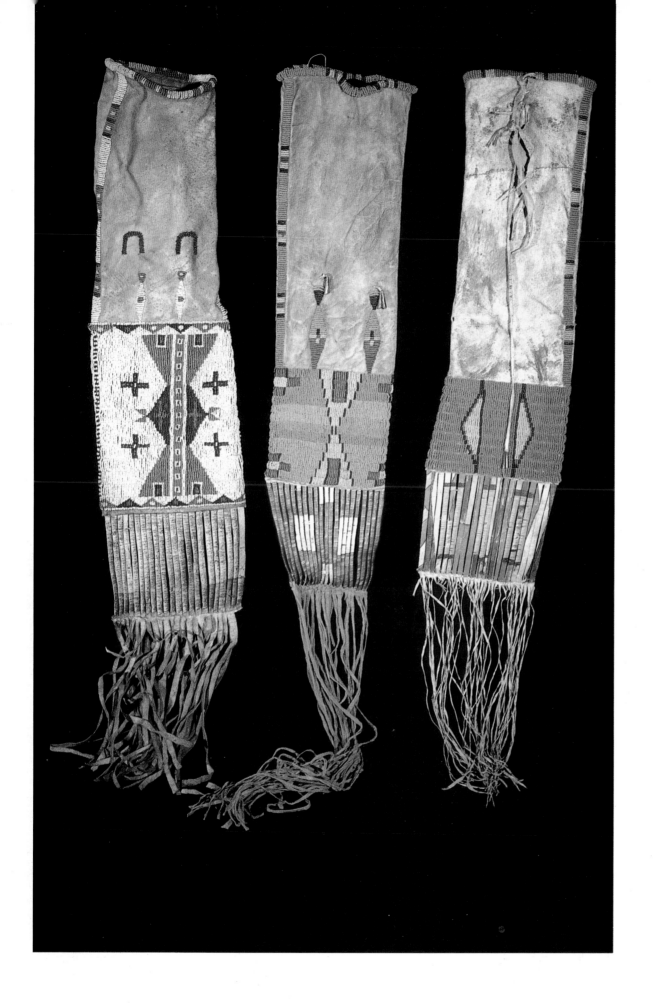

QUILL AND BEADWORK

Sioux and Arapaho (Dakotas and
Colorado); 1870s–1880s; pipe
bags; sinew-sewn buckskin with
beadwork panels, quill-wrapped
rawhide slat panels, and buckskin
fringes; left: Sioux, L (incl. fringe)
33" (83.8 cm); center: Arapaho,
391/2" (100.3 cm); right: Arapaho,
33" (83.8 cm).

QUILL AND BEADWORK

A. Dakota Sioux (North Dakota); 1875–1900; pipe bag and pipe; bag of sinew-sewn tanned buckskin with lazy-stitch beadwork, buckskin fringe on dyed porcupine quill–wrapped slat panel; pipe bowl of red pipestone (catlinite) with a flat, carved, and file-marked ash stem; bag: L (incl. fringe) 30" (76.2 cm); pipe: 20 1/2" (52 cm). The Sioux and other Plains Indians kept the pipe stems, considered male, and bowls, female, separated in bags such as this. Joining them for ceremonial use charged them with power.

B. Apache (Arizona); 1880–90; left: woman's strike-a-light pouch; dark blue, white, maroon, and green beadwork on army-issue leather, a German silver (nickel) button on the flap, and tin cone danglers and metal pendants on buckskin fringes; right: awl case; buckskin beaded with blue, white, and maroon seed beads, with tin cones on the flaps and long twisted buckskin strands ending in flat brass rings; pouch: L (excl. suspensions) 6 1/2" (16.5 cm); case: 8" (20.3 cm).

C. Plains Indian (Dakotas, Wyoming, and Colorado); nineteenth century; paint bags; sinew-sewn buckskin with beadwork; L 3 1/2" (9 cm) to 12" (30.5 cm); coll. David and Steven Pickelner, Fort Collins, Colorado.

A

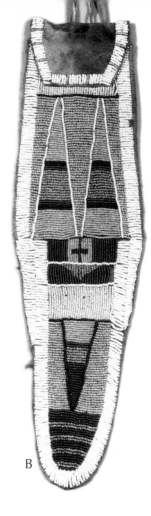

B

194

C

QUILL AND BEADWORK

A. Northeastern Woodlands (Hudson Valley or Connecticut); c.1760; pouch; smoked moose hide with dyed porcupine embroidery; H 9" (22.9 cm). New York State Museum.*

B. Nez Percé (Idaho); c.1870; Dreamer Society flat bag; beaded with floral designs in rose, orange, green, brown, and dark blue on a blue field and trimmed with white pony beads, buckskin carrying straps with white, green, blue, and maroon seed beads, buckskin danglers of bead-tipped dentalium shells; H 13½" (30.4 cm).

C. Micmac (Northern Maine); c.1850; birchbark boxes; geometric porcupine quill work in brown, blue, cream, and yellow; left: L 9¼" (23.5 cm); right: 10" (25.4 cm).

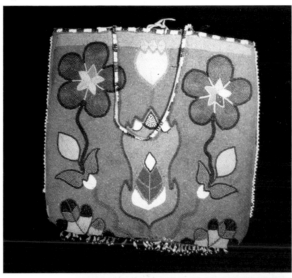

B

A

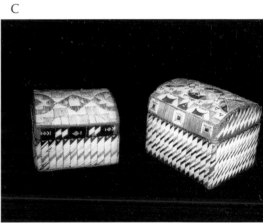

C

D

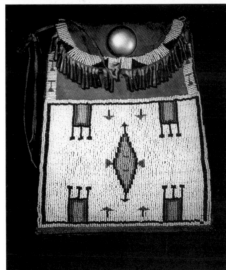

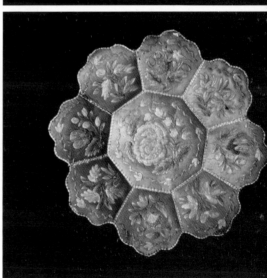

E

F

D. Micmac (northern Maine); 1825–40; chair seat; birchbark with geometric dyed porcupine quill work; W 15" (38 cm). The Micmac women carried the ancient art of quillwork to unequaled heights, eventually adapting it, as in this type of chair seat, for trade with the Europeans.

E. Apache (Arizona); 1880–90; dispatch case; military-issue leather with Southern Plains–style beadwork embroidery, with German silver (nickel) button and tin cone danglers; H 10¼" (26 cm).

F. Huron (northeastern Canada); c.1850; octagonal bowl; birch bark with moose hair embroidery; D 11¼" (28.6 cm); courtesy Tad Dale, Santa Fe. The use of dyed moose hair for embroidery on birch bark and trade cloth was peculiar to the Northeastern Woodlands, particularly the Iroquois of upstate New York and the Huron of Quebec.

QUILL AND BEADWORK

A. Mohegan (Connecticut); 1830–40; bandolier-style pouch; trade cloth with beadwork embroidery of stylized plant motifs; L 22" (56 cm). The beaded double C, or scroll, motifs and other design elements are reminiscent of birchbark decoration. They are thought to have been inspired by fiddlehead ferns when they first emerge from the ground in spring, which were to many Woodlands peoples symbols of new life.

B. Ojibwa (Chippewa) (Minnesota); 1850–70; bib; black trade cloth with human figure embroidered with white beads; H 8" (20.3 cm). The figure, with its heart line and joint marks on the arms and legs, is that of a *midé,* an initiated member of the shamanistic Grand Medicine Society, or *midéwiwin.*

C. Sioux (Dakotas); c.1880; pouch; sinew-sewn tanned buckskin with porcupine quill work and beadwork, with quill-wrapped fringe ending in horsehair tufts; 13 1/2 x 12" (34.3 x 30.5 cm). The side of this pouch is decorated with thirty-seven quilled horse tracks, presumably recording the number of horses its owner had captured in raids, while on the reverse eight bullet-wound symbols recorded the number of warriors he had killed or wounded.

D. Arapaho (Colorado); 1840–50; pouch; sinew-sewn buckskin with dyed porcupine quill work; D 5 3/4" (13.3 cm).

196

A

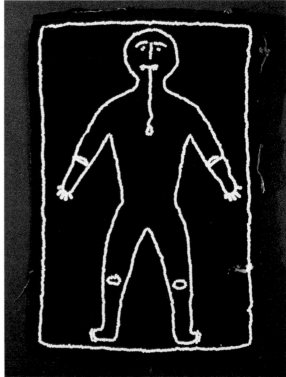

B

C

D

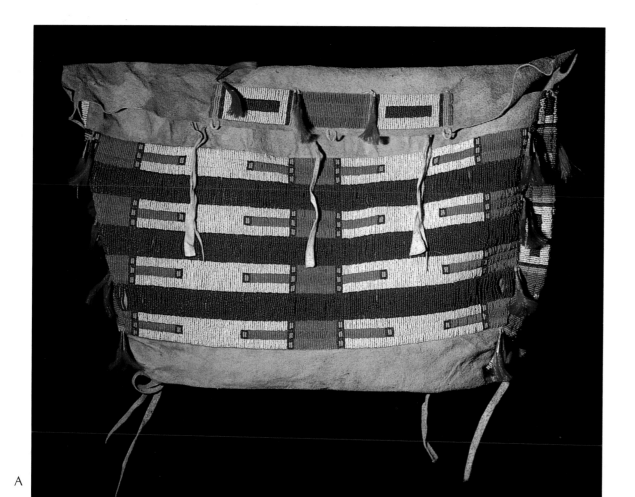

A

A. Cheyenne (Colorado/ Wyoming); 1870–80; "possible" bag; tanned elkhide with tin cone and dyed horsehair danglers; W 21" (53.3 cm). This curious name for these well-known Plains Indian saddle bags and tipi storage containers may have derived from a Sioux term translating as "a bag for every possible thing".

B. Dakota Sioux (Dakotas); 1875–85; women's saddle bags; tanned elkhide with designs in lazy-stitch green, blue, red, and yellow beadwork embroidery on white, and tin cone and red-dyed horsehair danglers; 13 x 21" (33 x 53.3 cm). The geometric design elements used by Sioux women had specific meanings, long since forgotten. The forked elements at top and bottom are thought to be clouds. The red diamond in the center probably stands for Turtle, the animal that in Sioux tradition regulated women's body functions.

B

PAINTING

A. Northwest Coast, possibly Bella Bella (British Columbia); 1860–80; storage box; red cedar with stylized painted crest design; H 17 1/4" (43.8 cm).

B. Tlingit (Alaska); 1880–90; drum; bear rawhide stretched over wooden hoop and painted with raven crest; D 16 1/2" (42 cm). This type of one-sided drum resembles those used by shamans in Siberia.

C. Ojibwa/Chippewa or Cree (Great Lakes or Ontario); 1870–80; two-sided shaman's drum; hide over wood frame with bell and beater inside, one side painted with red horizontal line, two dark blue human figures, and a bird, the other with blue rings, red dot, and blue band; D 15 1/2" (39.4 cm).

D. Arapaho or Cheyenne (Upper Missouri River); 1880–90; dance shield; red-stained buckskin cover over rawhide with dream or vision painting of black buffalo and thunderbird encircled by green serpent; D 11 1/2" (29.2 cm).

E. Hopi (Second Mesa, Arizona); 1920s Women's Society dance shield; painted with kachina dancer and rain cloud design; D 19" (48.3 cm).

F. Sioux (Dakotas); 1880–90; shield cover; buckskin stained with yellow ochre and painted with scene of battle; D 19 1/2" (49.5 cm); Witte Museum, San Antonio.

G. Sioux (Dakotas); 1870–80; drum; rawhide stained with blue, painted with buffalo head with spirit breath lines issuing from the muzzle and flanked by two medicine drums connected to the Upperworld with morning stars and comets; D 17 1/2" (44.5 cm).

198

B

A

C

D

E

F

G

PAINTING

A

A. Bannock-Shoshone (Wyoming); 1895–1900; detail of buffalo hide painting; full hide, L 73" (185.5 cm); Channing Dale Throckmorton Gallery, Santa Fe. This painting of a buffalo hunt is by the well-known Shoshone artist Chief Washakie. Two centuries ago the number of buffalo in North America was probably about sixty million. By the time Chief Washakie was painting his memories of life in the old days, the great shaggy beast, once the mainstay of life on the Plains, was practically extinct.*

B. Bannock-Shoshone (Wyoming); c.1898; detail of painting of the Shoshone Wolf Dance by Chief Washakie; on muslin; 42 x 351/2" (106.7 x 89 cm); figures, left: H 9" (22.8 cm); right: 111/2" (29.2 cm); Natural History Museum of Los Angeles County.*

B

PAINTING

Crow (Montana); 1880–90; dance shield cover; cloth, buckskin, and feathers, painted with native and commercial paints; D 16 1/2" (42 cm). Collectors should be aware that laws intended to protect endangered species have placed severe restrictions with penalties on selling the feathers of eagles and certain other birds. These apply even to works of native American art created long before the law was passed.

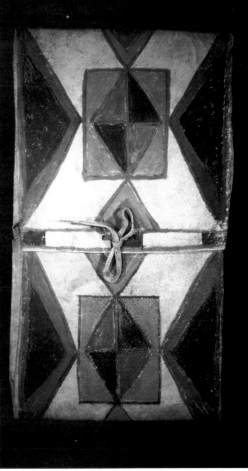

PAINTING

A. Tlingit (Alaska); 1875–90; chief's or shaman's drum; hide stretched over red cedar hoop, with conventionalized split bear design in black and red native paints arranged in the form of a "copper"; D 241/2" (62.3 cm). Drums are used by shamans to summon spirit helpers and ancestors and to help project the shaman's soul into the Otherworld. Coppers, shield-shaped emblems of beaten sheet copper engraved and/or painted with crest images, were the most valuable of the chief's possessions, and were sometimes used as gifts of enormous prestige at potlatches.

B. Crow (Montana); 1900–10; matched pair of parfleches; tobacco plant designs in green and yellow; 26" (66 cm). All the Plains peoples used the parfleche (from the French *parer,* to ward off, and *flèche,* arrow), but each tribe had its own style of decoration. It almost always consisted of traditional geometric forms and colors that, like other apparently abstract symbols in Plains women's art, had specific meanings that are no longer remembered (see C). The use of tobacco plants here suggests that these parfleches were for the storage of tobacco, and thus perhaps pertained to the important Crow Tobacco Society, whose members were charged with caring for the tobacco gardens.

C. Northern Plains; 1890s; painted parfleche with geometric designs in green, blue, yellow, and red; L 271/2" (67 cm).

A

B

C

SCULPTURE
Eskimo

A. Eskimo (St. Lawrence Island, Alaska); 300 BC–30 AD; schematized Okvik (Old Bering Sea culture) figure of a woman; fossil mammoth or walrus ivory with fine-line incising; H 7½" (19 cm). The Okvik tradition, which takes its name from an archaeological site on Punuk Island, off the eastern end of St. Lawrence Island, is the most ancient of the Northern Maritime Eskimo cultures.

B. Bering Sea Eskimo (Alaska); 1850–80; amulet or tool in the form of a double-headed figure; walrus ivory; H 3½" (9 cm); Peabody Museum of Natural History, Yale University.

C. Eskimo (Bering Sea); c. 1840; female figure; walrus ivory; H 7½" (19 cm); Museum of Anthropology and Ethnology, St. Petersburg.

D. Bering Sea Eskimo (Alaska); 1850–80; spear guard amulets; walrus ivory; H 2" (5 cm); Peabody Museum of Natural History, Yale University. The powerful *tunghat* spirit and others who decide which animals, and how many, are to become available to the Eskimo are often depicted in Eskimo art with pierced hands, symbolizing their practice of allowing the sea creatures to slip through their fingers to thus ensure their continued abundance. Pierced-hand symbolism to enhance hunting luck and abundance was used on many articles of ceremonial and everyday life.

202

A

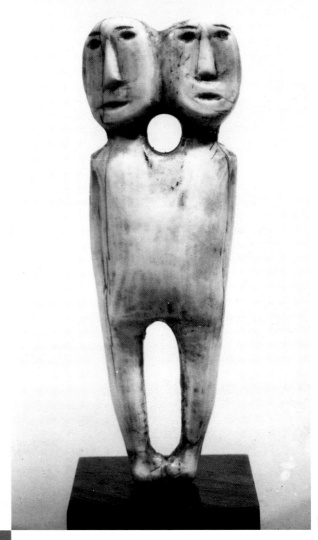

B

C

D

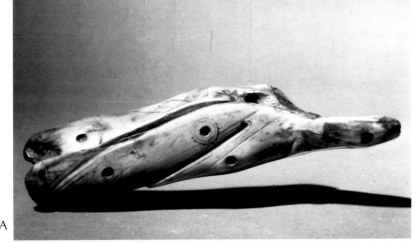

A

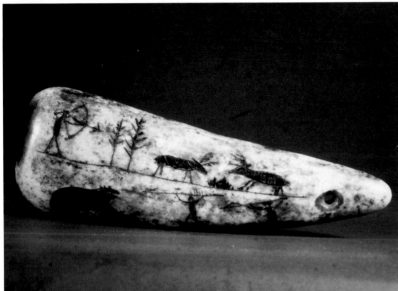

B

C

SCULPTURE
Eskimo

A. Eskimo (St. Lawrence Island, Alaska); c.300BC–30AD; harpoon socket; fossil ivory engraved in the Old Bering Sea II style; L 7 1/4" (18.4 cm). This style shares many features with the earlier Okvik tradition and has approximately the same distribution. Okvik, too, used circles, but in the Old Bering Sea II style the circles became larger and embellished with small thorn-like points or spurs.

B. Eskimo (Alaska); 1860–80; hunter's charm; fossil ivory with blackened engraving of caribou hunt; L 3 1/2" (9 cm); coll. Millard Holbrook, Santa Fe.

C. Eskimo (Alaska); 1860–80; shaman's transformation charm representing polar bear with human features and walrus tusks; driftwood and ivory; L 5 1/2" (14 cm). Simultaneity and qualitative equivalence of different life forms are characteristic of much Eskimo art and myth, as they are also of the arts and oral traditions of their Northwest Coast neighbors. What differentiates them is only their outer appearance, not their inner essence. That remains constant, whether the individual takes on the form of a polar bear, human being, walrus, caribou, or any other phenomenon in the natural world.

SCULPTURE
Northwest

A. Yurok/Karok (Northern California); 1870–80; acorn mush hospitality ladles; carved horn; L 5 3/8" to 8 1/4" (13.6 to 21 cm). As a token of a host's respect, good manners, and artistic taste, each guest was given a special carved spoon of wood or horn with which to eat.

B. Nootka (Vancouver Island, British Columbia); 1850–70; otter effigy feast bowl; cedar; L 15" (38 cm). Beautifully carved wooden animal bowls were used all along the Northwest Coast, especially for the highly valued fish oil that was drunk at the potlatches and other ceremonials.

C. Nootka (Vancouver Island, British Columbia); c.1850; war club; whalebone with incised design and eagle head handle; L 20 3/4" (52.7 cm). The engraving on this club shows stylistic influences from the north, but the basic form and material are characteristically Nootka.

D. Nootka (British Columbia); eighteenth century; ceremonial comb with a human face or mask in high relief; wood. This piece was at one time in the collection of James Thomas Hooper. For the collector, "Hooper Collection" and high quality are virtually synonymous.

E. Coast Salish (western Washington State); 1880–90; shaman's spirit puppet; wood with jointed legs and pull string and traces of red and black face paint; H 16" (40.7 cm). Salish carvers commonly depicted supernatural beings as large-headed and blocky, with little attention to detail. For curing and other rituals, shamans made their articulated puppets, which personified their spirit helpers, speak through ventriloquism.

F. Kwakiutl (British Columbia); c.1900; model totem pole; polychromed yellow cedar; H 34 1/2" (87.6 cm). This piece was made by the famous Kwakiutl carver Charlie James.

SCULPTURE
Northwest

A. Salish (Vancouver Island, British Columbia); c.1820; large spindle whorl; wood with relief carving of cosmological motifs; D 85/8" (20.3 cm). The central motif is two stacked figures, human above, toad below, in the birth-giving position. Salish mythology connects Toad with Moon, and Moon in turn with women and the feminine crafts of spinning and weaving. The two birds are ravens with Sun and Moon disks.*

B. Haida (Vancouver Island, British Columbia); 1880–85; box; carved and painted bent cedar with a bear on the front and human faces on the sides; W 121/2" (30.5 cm); New York State Museum. This is a miniature version of the famous Northwest Coast bentwood storage chests that were made in many sizes and widely traded among the native peoples of the coast. The vertical boxes were usually only painted with crest designs, while horizontal ones were more often carved in low relief, in addition to the painting.*

C. Tanaina (Northern Athapascan) (Upper Yukon, Alaska); c.1880; woman's knife; metal blade set into red-stained wood carved in the form of a bird's profile; L 63/4" (17.2 cm).

A

B

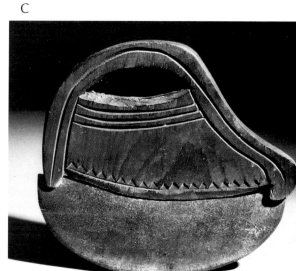

C

D

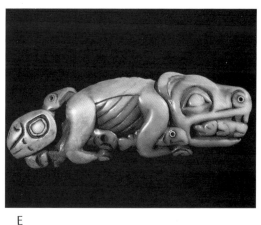

E

F

D. Tlingit (Alaska); c.1850; shaman's killer whale amulet; partially fossilized bone; L 23/4" (7 cm).

E. Tlingit (Alaska); c.1870; shaman's amulet of bear, bird, and fish spirit helpers; ivory; L 43/4" (12 cm).

F. Tlingit (Alaska); c.1750; spear thrower (atlatl); stone-carved wood; L 143/4" (37.5 cm). The underside of this weapon, which functioned as an extension of the throwing arm, is richly decorated with the crest animal imagery familiar from totem poles and other Tlingit art forms. The raised hole provides a fingerhold; the flat reverse side is grooved to support the spear.

SCULPTURE
Northwest

A. Tsimshian (British Columbia); 1860–70; two-faced shaman's rattle with toad or frog entering the mouth on the reverse side and emerging on the front; wood; H 11 3/4" (29.8 cm). Toads and frogs figure prominently in Northwest Coast iconography as sources of supernatural power (see also B).

B. Tlingit (Alaska); c.1880; knife with wooden handle carved with stacked crest figures, including, second from top, the toad or frog; H 10 1/4" (26 cm); Sheldon Jackson Collection, The Art Museum, Princeton University.

C. Tlingit (Alaska); c.1880; left, complete halibut hook; carved wood with iron barb; right, decorated front section of a halibut hook; left: H 10 1/2" (26.7 cm); right: 10 5/8" (27 cm); New York State Museum. These fishing tools are almost always carved with mythological motifs relating to shamanism. The octopus, which figures prominently in shamanic imagery, is a favorite subject for halibut hooks, as is the otter. The original owner of the beautiful little sculpture at left was probably the very shaman depicted on it, with his animal guardian watching over him and a pair of otters climbing down his legs.

D. Tlingit (Alaska); 1750–80; club with bear's head at top; caribou or elk antler with engraved eagle design and abalone and jet inlay; H 18" (45.7 cm). This club, like similar ones used by the Athapascan Tanaina Indians of the Upper Yukon, formerly had an inset stone blade.*

206

A

B

C

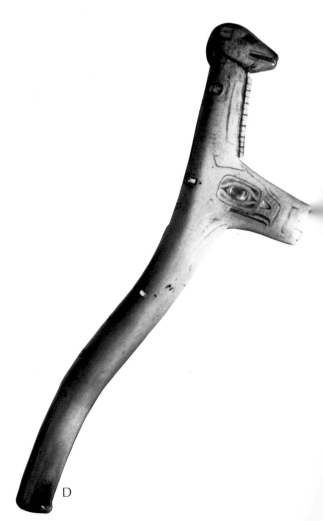

D

A

B

SCULPTURE
Northwest

A. Tlingit (Alaska); pre-1880; Frog Clan hat; wood with three woven fiber potlatch rings; D 16 3/4" (42.5 cm); The Art Museum, Princeton University. Each of the rings atop a chief's clan hat stands for one of the gift-giving feasts known as potlatches. Chiefs sponsored these periodic giveaways—a practice common to many native Americans—at important points in the life cycle, such as marriage, birth, naming, etc. Sometimes the giveaways were so prodigious that the host was totally impoverished. However, guests were honor-bound to reciprocate in kind.*

B. Tlingit (Alaska); 1880–90; shaman's amulet carved and engraved in the form of a killer whale; abalone shell; L 3 3/4" (9.5 cm).

207

SCULPTURE
Southwest

A. Mojave (Southern California); 1890–1900; mother-and-child doll; polychromed terracotta with trade bead jewelry, cloth skirt, and wool yarn sash; H 8 1/2" (21.5 cm); Natural History Museum of Los Angles County. Yuma and Mojave dolls have similarities—red-on-buff body paint, as well as similar bead jewelry—but Mojave dolls are distinguished by their prominent noses, while Yuma dolls have small noses and hair tucked into a depression on top of the head.

B. Mojave (Southern California); 1890–1900; doll; buff terracotta with red paint on body and face and black-and-white eyes, human hair, bead jewelry, skirt of raveled red yarn with black yarn sash; H 7" (17.8 cm); Natural History Museum of Los Angeles County.

Plains and East

C. Penobscot or Iroquois (Northeastern Woodlands); c.1850; crooked knife, steel blade made from an old file, wire fastening, and carved wood handle ending in an unusual large human face; L 8 1/4" (21 cm). Crooked knives are found all over the northern forest belt, but it was among the Penobscot and Iroquois that they were transformed into real works of art. The term "crooked knife" refers to the fact that the handle is at an angle to the blade.*

D. Iroquois (upper New York State); c.1840; club; wood with traces of red paint; L 22" (56 cm); New York State Museum.

A

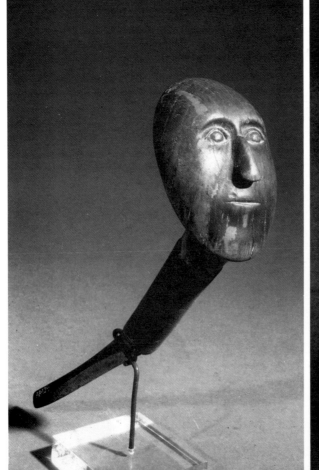

C

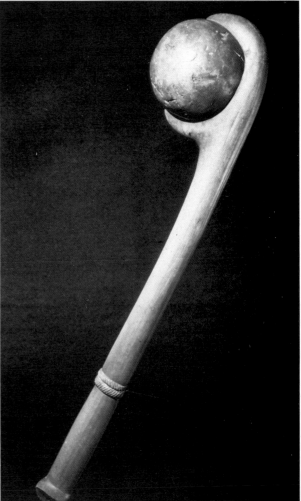

B

D

SCULPTURE
Plains and East

A. Sioux (Dakotas); c.1875; flute stop in form of bird with human head; Minnesota catlinite; L 2 3/8" (6 cm).

B. Crow (Montana): c.1880; love charm; cut from an old parfleche in the form of an elk, decorated with blue and yellow paint, and bearing on the reverse a small portion of the painted parfleche pattern; L 7 1/4" (18.5 cm).

C. Eastern Sioux (Great Lakes region); 1850–70; miniature sculpture of an Indian seated with knees drawn up; catlinite; L 3 7/8" (9.8 cm).

D. Ojibwa (Minnesota); 1880–1900; duck decoys; wicker; left: H 9 3/4" (24.8 cm); center: 5" (12.7 cm); right: 10" (25.4 cm).

E. Wampanoag or Massachuset (Massachusetts); c.1630; miniature animal effigy bowl; stone-carved burlwood, with two otter-like animals as handles on the ends; L 6 1/4" (15.9 cm). The high prices of wooden bowls of comparable age and perfection as this one (note the lead-inlay repair of an old split in the rim) stem from both their remarkable beauty and their great rarity.*

F. Potawotami (Michigan); 1870–80; wooden horse medicine bundle fetish with black-painted head, red body, and red wool halter; L 5 5/8" (14.4 cm).

G. Chippewa/Ojibwa (Minnesota); 1850–70; crooked knife; steel blade made from an old file with two-piece carved wood horse-and-rider handle; L 12 3/4" (32.5 cm).*

H. Passamaquoddy or Penobscot (Maine); 1830–50; crooked knife with the end of the wooden handle sculpted into a nude human figure; L 9" (22.9 cm). The handles of most Woodlands crooked knives are wood wrapped with steel or copper wire or, less frequently, a leather thong, to help secure the blade.

SCULPTURE
Pipes

A. Kwakiutl (British Columbia); 1880–90; killer whale effigy tobacco pipe; wood with metal chimney, shell teeth, and copper buttons in the eyes; L 6 1/2" (16.5 cm). The hole in the whale's dorsal fin is a common convention in both Northwest Coast and Eskimo art (see 202D).

B. Haida (Queen Charlotte Islands, British Columbia); c.1840; nonfunctional "panel pipe"; argillite with a central architectural motif and white people in various activities, including a copulating couple; L 10" (25.5 cm). Argillite, a shale that is easily worked when it comes out of the ground but hardens quickly on exposure to air, is found only in the Queen Charlotte Islands. Its use for carving dates back to the early nineteenth century, when the Haida carvers started making pipes for sale to sailors and traders. The long, thin panel pipes were often inspired by shipboard scenes, with an architectural feature, such as a ship's cabin or a house.

A

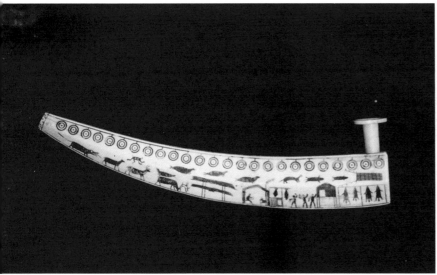

C

C. Eskimo (St. Lawrence Island, Alaska); 1870–80; souvenir pipe with detachable bowl engraved on both sides with scenes of a wolf and a human hunter stalking caribou, various sea and land animals, and village life; walrus ivory; L 13 3/4" (35 cm). Very few such pipes show evidence of native use, as they were mainly made for sale to Europeans interested in carved and engraved ivory. The Eskimos had long decorated their drill bows and carrying handles in the same illustrative style, and in the nineteenth century they transferred their designs to these popular pipes.

D. Tlingit (Alaska); c.1860; smoking pipe; wood with carving of bear copulating with a human female, with inset brass chimney; L 4 3/4" (12 cm). The mating of bear and human is part of the Northwest Coast Bear Mother myth.

210

A

SCULPTURE
Pipes

A. Haida (Queen Charlotte Islands, British Columbia); 1870–80; pipe; wood with carving of Raven opening a clamshell; H 4 3/4" (12 cm); Übersee-Museum, Bremen. The theme of this pipe is the Haida myth in which Raven, in opening a clam, found in it the first human beings and was thus responsible for the original peopling of the world.

B. Tlingit (Alaska); 1870–80; smoking pipe; oak, depicting a mythic bear pulling on a fishing net, with chimney made from a Russian brass bell with sheet metal inset; L 6 7/8" (17.5 cm).

B

211

SCULPTURE
Pipes

A. Sioux (Dakotas); c.1870; boy's pipe; catlinite with lead inlay; L 4" (10.2 cm). As early as the eighteenth century Indian pipe makers developed the technique of decorating catlinite and steatite pipe bowls with metal inlays.

B. Sioux (Dakotas); 1880–90; presentation pipe; catlinite bowl with lead chimney carved in the form of a tomahawk blade and an ash stem of the openwork "puzzle" type decorated with reliefs of buffalo, turtle, elk, and mountain sheep; L 20" (50.8 cm). Two or three pipe makers are known to be responsible for innovative animal effigy pipe stems of this type, made for presentation to admired Indian chiefs and a few whites who had proven their friendship for Indian people. They were not souvenir pipes, however, but made for ceremonial smoking.

C. Eastern Sioux (Minnesota); 1875–85; pipe with catlinite bowl in form of an eagle claw holding an egg, with spiraling ash stem; bowl, H 6½" (15.2 cm). The beautiful pipes in this style were inspired not by indigenous symbolism but by meerschaum pipes imported from Europe.

A

B

C

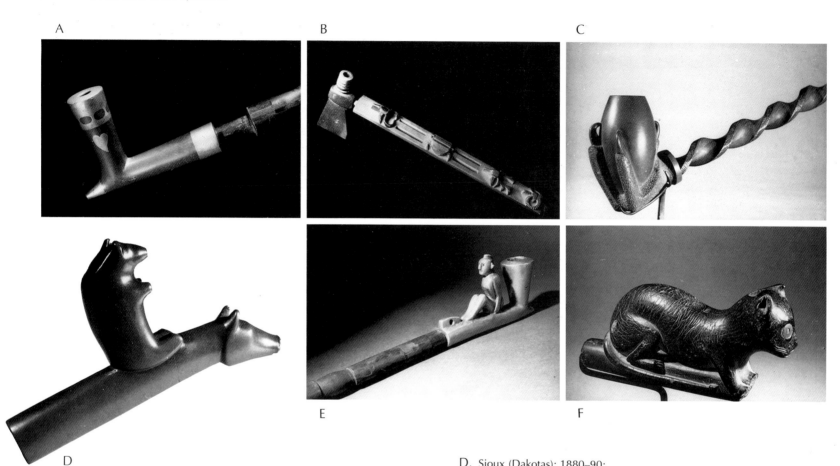

D

E

F

D. Sioux (Dakotas); 1880–90; pipe with bowl of a bear riding a horse; catlinite; L 5⅞" (15.2 cm). Though made for sale rather than personal use, this pipestone sculpture nevertheless employs traditional themes.

E. Ojibwa or Sauk and Fox (Minnesota or Wisconsin); c.1830; pipe with bowl of lead and tin alloy with seated human figure facing the smoker; L 5³⁄₁₆" (13.2 cm).

F. Ojibwa (Great Lakes region); 1790–1800; panther effigy pipe with bowl of black steatite, with copper disk inlays in the eyes; L 5½" (14 cm).

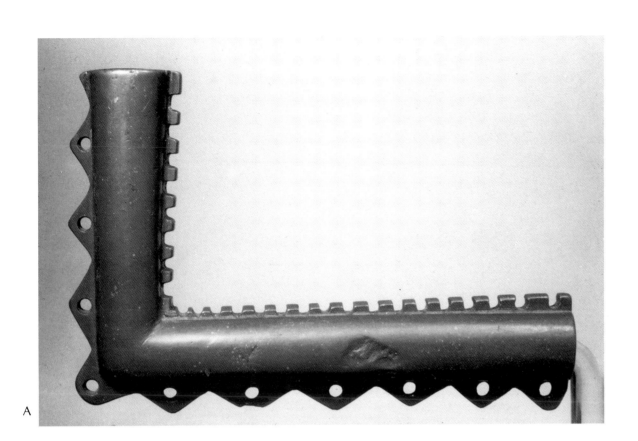

A

SCULPTURE
Pipes

A. Iroquois (Northeastern Woodlands); c.1840; pipe; catlinite bowl of the elbow type with lacy edge; L 53/16" (13.2 cm). With southwestern Minnesota and a small deposit in the Southwest the only known sources of catlinite, the raw material for this Iroquois pipe is a long way from home. However, archaeology shows the Iroquois to have been trading for the precious red pipestone as early as the 1600s.

B. Ojibwa (Great Lakes region); 1750–80; human effigy pipe; wood with lead inlays; L 51/2" (14 cm). Humans or animals facing the smoker on American Indian effigy pipes are believed to represent the owner's spirit helper.

B

213

A. Ojibwa (Great Lakes region); 1820–30; tobacco pipe; black steatite with channel inlays of lead and catlinite; on the prominent fin two seated men are playing the hand guessing game still popular with many Indian peoples; L 53/4" (14.6 cm).

B. Ojibwa (Great Lakes region); 1820–30; disk-type tobacco pipe; light-colored stone with lead, black steatite, and catlinite inlays; L 41/8" (10.5 cm).

B

A

C

D

C. Iroquois (Hudson Valley, upstate New York); 1650–80; tobacco pipe; terracotta; L 43/4" (12 cm).

D. Iroquois (Hudson Valley, upstate New York); 1650–80; tobacco pipe with owl effigy bowl; terracotta; L 43/4" (12 cm). Effigy pipes of this style are found in Iroquois sites dating to the time of first contact with Europeans.

SCULPTURE
Masks

Eskimo (Alaska); c.1885;
composite seal spirit mask; wood
with attachments of wooden fish,
polar bear, and birds; H 30 1/2"
(77.5 cm); Southwest Museum,
Los Angeles.*

SCULPTURE
Masks

A. Eskimo (Northern Alaska); c.1880; whale cult gorget; painted wood with sinew and baleen; W 18 1/2" (47 cm); Smithsonian Institution. Breast gorgets like this one were worn by whalers as they danced house to house to celebrate the end of the whaling season and invite guests to whale-meat feasts. Images of whales, bears, and whaling boats decorate the flat wings projecting from the central mask. The black band across the eyes, known as the "whaleman's mark", proclaims status and pride.

B. Eskimo (Kuskokwim River, Alaska); 1890–1910; dance mask representing an otter; wood with blue and white paint; H 20 1/2" (52 cm). The hinged door, which the dancer can open and close by means of a string, reveals the otter's human essence or soul. The downturned mouth reveals it to be female. Masks like this were not worn but held in front of the face by the participants in the dance drama. Other composite masks were suspended from the ceiling.

C. Eskimo (Alaska); c.1885; bird spirit mask; wood with polychrome decoration; H 11 1/2" (29.2 cm); Southwest Museum, Los Angeles. In Eskimo convention the down-turned mouth is female and hence identifies the spirit essence of the bird portrayed by this mask as female.

D. Nootka (Nootka Sound, British Columbia); c.1750; mask; cedar with traces of red and black paint and human hair; H 10 1/2" (26.7 cm).

E. Bella Coola (British Columbia); c.1880; mask; wood, with bulging eyes and bared teeth; H 8 3/4" (24.8 cm). This mask, lacking eyeholes, was not worn on the face but carried by a performer in a ritual.

A

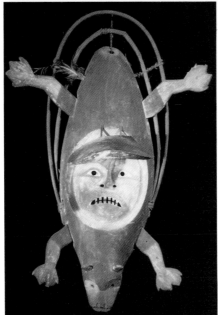

B

D

C

E

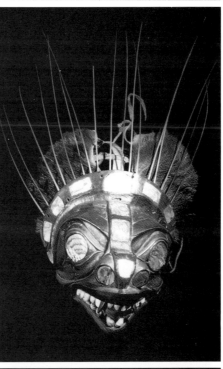

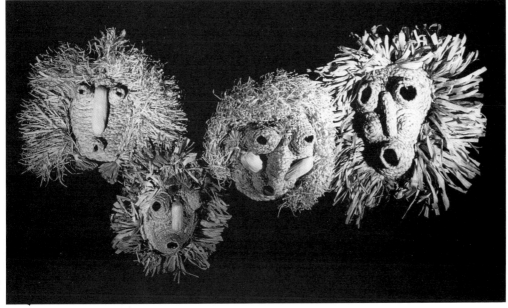

A

B

C

D

E

SCULPTURE
Masks

A. Tlingit (Sitka, Alaska); 1840–70; shaman's mask of the Moon Spirit with naturalistic human features; wood stained blue and red; H 9 1/2" (24.1 cm); Princeton University Museum of Natural History. In Tlingit masks, the ruling spirits of the moon and sun, other celestial bodies, and phenomena of the natural landscape were given the physical attributes of human beings, often, as here, with great sensitivity and beauty.*

B. Tlingit (Alaska); c.1880; Raven mask with long movable lower beak; wood; H 9" (22.8 cm).

C. Haida (Queen Charlotte Islands, British Columbia); 1870–80; portrait mask of a woman with red bird crest designs painted on the forehead, cheeks, and chin; wood; H 8 3/4" (22.3 cm); Princeton University Museum of Natural History.

D. Tlingit (Alaska); 1830–50; headdress frontlet; painted wood, native copper fangs, animal teeth, abalone inlays, sea lion bristles, and bear fur; H 12 1/4" (31.1 cm). This represents the sea spirit Gonaqadet, which brought good luck to those it favored and misfortune and death to others.

E. Iroquois (upstate New York); 1930–50; Husk Face masks; braided cornhusk; left to right, H 14" (35.5 cm), 11 1/2" (29.2 cm), 11" (28 cm), 17" (43 cm). The Husk Face Society masks, braided of dried cornhusk by Iroquois women, are the female counterparts to the wooden "False Faces" (see 218A) but can be worn by both men and women. They represent vegetation spirits who visit homes to treat people for various illnesses, and in the seasonal ceremonies help the members of the False Face Society drive out disease, bad luck, and evil spirits.

SCULPTURE
Masks

A. Iroquois (Grand River, Ontario, Canada); c.1920; False Face Society crooked-mouth mask; basswood, with horsehair mane, and painted black with red eyebrows and lips; H 12" (30.5 cm); New York State Museum. This is a classic portrait of the great mask spirit Gagóhsa, "Face". In Iroquois origin mythology, during a contest to determine who was the more powerful, the Creator summoned a mountain to rush up behind Gagóhsa. Hearing the whooshing sound, Gagóhsa turned around, and the impact broke his nose and distorted his mouth.

B. Cherokee (Big Cove, North Carolina); 1935–40; mask of a Rattlesnake Warrior from the Cherokee Booger Dance; buckeye wood; H 11 1/2" (29.2 cm).

C. Navajo (New Mexico/ Arizona); 1930–40; yei mask; blue and yellow painted buckskin with sheep's wool hair and projecting bamboo snout; H 14" (35.5 cm). Yeis are spirit beings who are personified by masked dancers in the Nightway, which is both an elaborate curing ceremony and the initiation ceremony for Navajo boys and girls. It lasts nine days. Elaborate sandpaintings are made during the last four, and the climax, the dramatization of an elaborate origin myth, comes on the ninth.

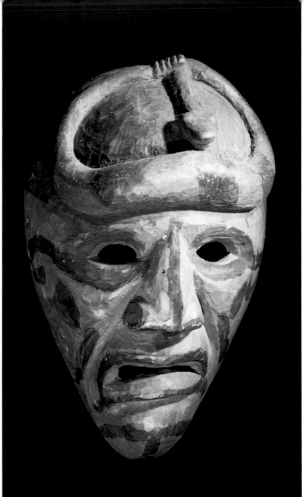

B

A

C

A

SCULPTURE
Masks

A. Hopi (Second Mesa, Arizona); c.1950; Kachina plaza dance case mask; painted hide, wood, fabric, and animal fur; H 11 1/2" (29.2 cm). This mask belongs to Novantsi-tsiloaqua, He-who-strips-you, one of the Wawash, or Runners. These are masked dancers who entertain the audience at the masked plaza dances. The Runners challenge people to contests; if He-who-strips-you wins the match, he tears off the loser's clothes.

B. Zuni (New Mexico); c.1920; Koyemshi, or "Mudhead", kachina case mask; mud-colored cloth; H 18" (45.7 cm). The Koyemshi, who seem to be witless clowns charged with entertaining the audience at the ceremonials, trace their origin back to an act of primordial incest between a brother and sister that resulted in the birth of ten children, one normal, the other nine the original Koyemshi. The horn of this mask identifies it as that of Koyemshi Apithlashi-wanni, who is supposed to inspire awe as Bow Priest of the company of the Koyemshi, but in fact acts the complete coward, afraid of everything.

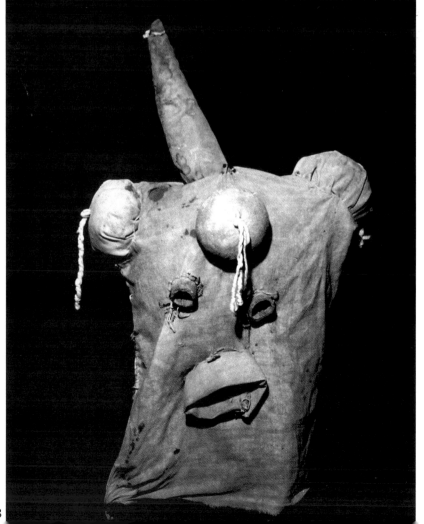

B

219

SCULPTURE
Kachinas

A. Zuni (New Mexico); c.1950; Mudhead jumping-jack kachina; painted cottonwood root, with movable arms and legs; H 5" (12.7 cm). Both the Zuni and the Hopi made jumping-jack kachinas for sale.

B. Hopi (Second Mesa, Arizona); c.1910; kachina "doll" representing Tasaf kachina, also called Navajo kachina; painted cottonwood root; H 8³/4" (22.3 cm). Tasaf or Navajo *kachin-tihu* (the Hopi term for kachina "doll") is a very popular kachina, appearing in several ceremonies.

C. Hopi (Hopi Mesas, Arizona); c.1950; kachina "doll" representing the kachina spirit called Kuwan Heheya; cottonwood root, with green wool ruff, green and yellow case mask with red, blue, and yellow rain cloud symbols on both cheeks, red and yellow painted body, and white kilt; H 11¹/4" (28.5 cm). Kuwan Heheya (Colorful Heheya) appears in the Powamu, or Bean Festival, as companion to the so-called Ogre kachinas on their collecting rounds. On First Mesa, Kuwan Heheya also accompanies the female kachina spirits called *kachin manas* during the Niman, the farewell ceremony for the kachinas in July.

B

A

C

220

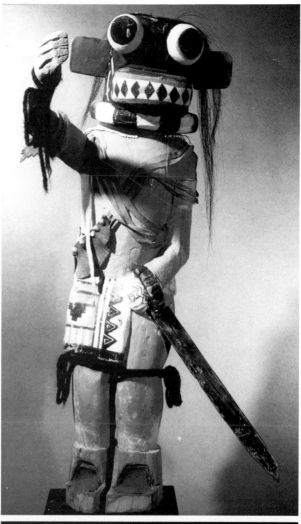

A

B

C

D

SCULPTURE
Kachinas

A. Hopi (Arizona); 1920–30; a pair of Koyalas, or Hano Clown kachinas; cottonwood root painted with black and white stripes; H 10½" (26.7 cm); coll. Rex and Bonnie Arrowsmith, Santa Fe. The Koyalas are better known as Koshares, their name among the Rio Grande Pueblos. Indian people regard them not merely as figures of fun and irreverence, referring to them respectfully as the fathers of all the kachinas.

B. Hopi (Second Mesa, Arizona); c.1935; Chaveyo kachina; cottonwood; with pink body, black goggle-eyed case mask with projecting sawtoothed snout and prominent red ears, a black-and-white collar, and a sword in one hand; H 21" (53.3 cm).

C. Hopi (Third Mesa, Arizona); c.1939; kachina "doll" representing Masau'u kachina; cottonwood; H 13¼" (33.6 cm). Masau'u kachina is an aspect of Masau'u, the aged earth and fire god whom some Hopis regard as the most important of their deities. The skull-like mask with its goggle eyes, reminiscent of the ancient Mexican god Tlaloc, and the protruding teeth suggest the death aspect of Masau'u. But he also has a feminine aspect, evident in his off-the-shoulder woman's dress of rabbit fur and the cotton *manta,* and in the basketry food tray he holds in the manner of the women offering food in the ceremonials. This example was carved by the Hopi carver William Quotskuyva of Oraibi.

D. Hopi (Arizona); c.1935; kachina "doll" representing one of the Waka kachinas dressed in a long white carved cloak and a case mask with a pair of multicolored horns with feather bundles projecting from its sides; cottonwood root; H 10" (25.5 cm); coll. Millard Holbrook, Santa Fe.

A. Hopi (First Mesa, Arizona); 1925–35; Ahülani kachina "doll"; cottonwood root; H 8 1/2" (21.6 cm); coll. Rex and Bonnie Arrowsmith, Santa Fe. Ahülani is the Winter Solstice kachina of First Mesa, who in odd-numbered years, i.e., those in which the snake dance is performed, appears in mid-December as the first of all the kachinas. Accompanied by two *kachin-manas,* female kachinas, he opens the kivas, and it is only when he has completed his rounds that the kachina season can commence.

B. Zuni (New Mexico); c.1930; Shalako kachina; cottonwood root, wool, horsehair, animal fur, cloth, and bead ornaments; H 16 1/2" (42 cm). Of all the Zuni spirit beings, the giant Shalako kachinas are the best-known. They are the messengers of the gods, and their journey to the village of Zuni reenacts the ancient migration tradition. Their full meaning is highly complex and only barely understood by outsiders; suffice it to say that they bring to the people all the good things in life. The Shalako ritual in December is the high point of the Zuni ceremonial year, so important to Zuni identity that it draws back the pueblo Zuni living elsewhere.

C. Zuni (New Mexico); 1925–30; kachina "doll" representing two of the six warrior-guardians known as Salamopia; cottonwood root with movable arms and cotton kilts; H approx. 6" (15.3 cm). The Salamopia, who embody youth, beauty, and strength, are warriors and runners of great speed. They guard the kachinas, search the four corners of the world for seeds, punish transgressions, and never appear in summer, because they are also dangerous spirits whose breath can bring on the wind.

A

E

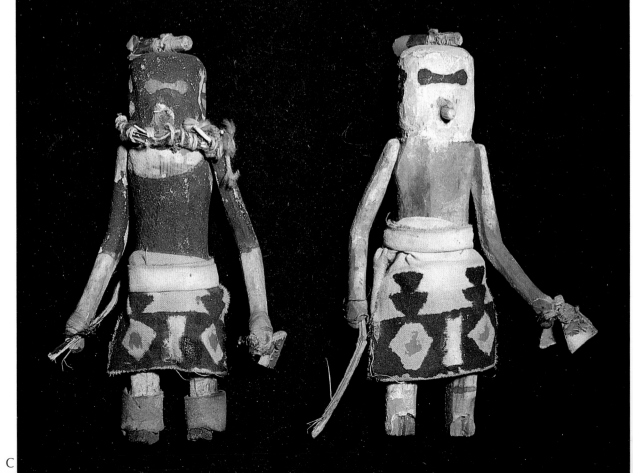

C

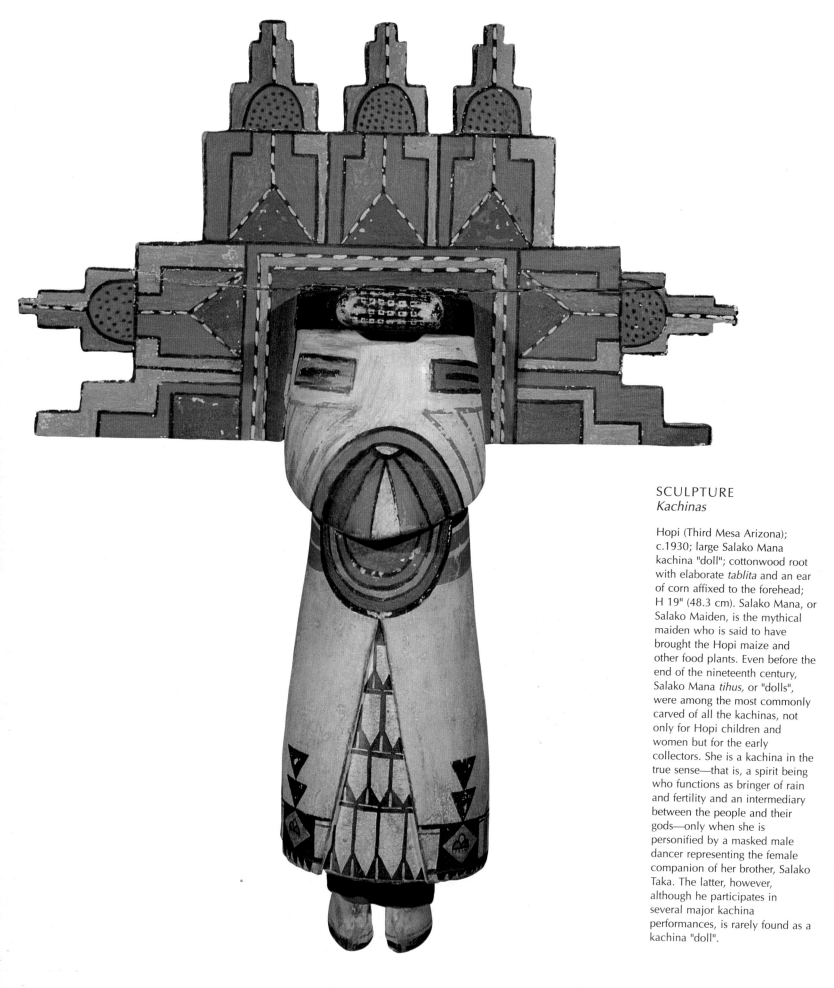

SCULPTURE
Kachinas

Hopi (Third Mesa Arizona); c.1930; large Salako Mana kachina "doll"; cottonwood root with elaborate *tablita* and an ear of corn affixed to the forehead; H 19" (48.3 cm). Salako Mana, or Salako Maiden, is the mythical maiden who is said to have brought the Hopi maize and other food plants. Even before the end of the nineteenth century, Salako Mana *tihus*, or "dolls", were among the most commonly carved of all the kachinas, not only for Hopi children and women but for the early collectors. She is a kachina in the true sense—that is, a spirit being who functions as bringer of rain and fertility and an intermediary between the people and their gods—only when she is personified by a masked male dancer representing the female companion of her brother, Salako Taka. The latter, however, although he participates in several major kachina performances, is rarely found as a kachina "doll".

223

SCULPTURE
Kachinas

A. Hopi (Third Mesa, Arizona);
c.1939; kachina "doll"
representing the Hopi god Ahöla;
cottonwood root with fur ruff,
wool yarn, and feathers; H 13"
(33 cm). Ahöla is not actually a
kachina but a god; in fact, he has
a close relationship with the sun
god and is sometimes characterized as such. He also overlaps
with the germinator god Alosaka
(see B) in that he too helps
activate the corn and other
plants. His distinctive mask
appears in ancient rock art in the
Southwest, and he is thus one of
the oldest identifiable Hopi
deities.

B. Hopi (Third Mesa, Arizona);
1920–30; kachina dance wands;
pine slats painted with the figure
of the horned germinator god
Alosaka atop clouds with rain
falling from them on an ear of
corn; left: H 201/4" (51.5 cm);
right: 221/4" (56.5 cm). These
wands, called *mánayawi,* are
always made in pairs and are
carried by women dancers in the
Butterfly Dance and other
ceremonial or social dances.

C. Hopi (Second Mesa, Arizona);
c.1950; representation of Palhik
Mana, Butterfly Kachina Girl,
grinding corn; cottonwood; H 19"
(48.3 cm). Palhik Mana is often
confused with Salako Mana, the
female companion of the Hopi
Salako, and, in fact, both the
mask and the *tablita* are often
identical.

D. Hopi (Third Mesa, Arizona);
c.1940–43; kachina "doll" based
on Mickey Mouse; cottonwood
root; H 121/8" (30.8 cm).
Surprisingly, the Mickey Mouse
kachina is not a curiosity made
for the tourist market but a
traditional Mouse kachina a Hopi
carver modeled on the popular
Disney cartoon character after
seeing *Mickey Mouse Goes to
War,* a government propaganda
film made during World War II.
Mice figure in Hopi mythology as
powerful curers, especially of
emotional ills.*

A

B

C

D

Appendix

MUSEUMS

A selected list of institutions with collections of Pre-Columbian and/or American Indian art

N.B. Some of the museums listed have collections that are not on permanent exhibit. These may usually be seen by special request. It should be noted also that the collections vary significantly in size and subject emphasis. Inquiry prior to visits is recommended.

PRE-COLUMBIAN AND AMERICAN INDIAN ART

AUSTRIA
Museum für Völkerkunde. Neue Hofburg, Heldenplatz, Vienna 1014.

DENMARK
Nationalmuseet. Frederiksholms Kanal 12, Copenhagen 1220.

FRANCE
Musée de l'Homme. 17 Place du Trocadero, 75116 Paris.

GERMANY
Hamburgisches Museum für Völkerkunde. Binderstrasse 14, Hamburg 2000.
Linden-Museum. Hegelplatz 1, Stuttgart 7000.
Museum für Völkerkunde. Arnimallee 23-27, Berlin-Dahlem 1000.
Staatliches Museum für Völkerkunde. Maximilianstrasse 42, Munich 8000.
Städtisches Reiss-Museum. Zeughaus C 5, Mannheim 6800.

GREAT BRITAIN
Horniman Museum. London Road, Forest Hill, London SE23 3PQ.
Museum of Mankind. 6 Burlington Gardens, London WIX 2EX.
University Museum of Archaeology and Anthropology. Downing Street, Cambridge CB2 3OZ.

SWEDEN
Folkens Museum. Djurgardsbrunnsv. 34, Stockholm 115 27. (Formerly Etnografiska Museet.)

SWITZERLAND
Musée de Ethnographie. 65 Boulevard Carl Vogt, Geneva 1205.
Völkerkundemuseum der Universität Zürich. Pelikanstrasse 40, Zürich 8001.

UNITED STATES
California
Phoebe Apperson Hearst Museum of Anthropology. University of California, 103 Kroeber Hall, Berkeley 94720. (Formerly Robert H. Lowie Museum.)

Los Angeles County Museum of Art. 5095 Wilshire Boulevard, Los Angeles 90036.
Museum of Cultural History. University of California, Los Angeles 90024.
Museum of Man. 1350 El Prado, San Diego 92101.

Colorado
Anthropology Museum. University of Colorado, Boulder 80309.
Denver Art Museum. 100 West 14th Avenue Parkway, Denver 80204.
Denver Museum of Natural History. City Park, Denver 80205.
Taylor Museum. Colorado Springs Fine Arts Center, 30 West Dale Street, Colorado Springs 80903.

Connecticut
Peabody Museum of Natural History. Yale University, New Haven 06511.

Florida
Lowe Art Museum. University of Miami, Coral Gables 33146.

Illinois
Field Museum of Natural History. Roosevelt Road at Lake Shore Drive, Chicago 60605.

Indiana
Snite Museum. University of Notre Dame, Notre Dame 46556.

Massachusetts
Peabody Museum. 11 Divinity Avenue, Cambridge 02138.

Michigan
Detroit Institute of Arts. 5200 Woodward Avenue, Detroit 48202-9959.

Minnesota
Minnesota Institute of the Arts. 2400 Third Avenue South, Minneapolis 55404.

New Jersey
The Art Museum, Princeton University. Princeton 08544.

New York
American Museum of Natural History. Central Park West and 79th Street, New York City 10024.

Brooklyn Museum. Eastern Parkway at Washington Avenue, Brooklyn 11238.
Metropolitan Museum of Art. Fifth Avenue at 82nd Street, New York City 10028.
National Museum of the American Indian. Broadway at 155th Street, New York City 10032.

Pennsylvania
University Museum. University of Pennsylvania, 33rd and Spruce Streets, Philadelphia 19104.

Virginia
Bayly Art Museum. University of Virginia, Charlottesville.

Washington, D.C.
National Museum of Natural History. Smithsonian Institution, 10th Street and Constitution Avenue, N.W., 20560.

PRE-COLUMBIAN ART

BELGIUM
Musées Royaux d'Art et d'Histoire. Avenue J. F. Kennedy, 1040 Brussels.

CANADA
Gardiner Museum of Ceramic Art. 111 Queen's Park, Toronto, Ontario M56 2C7.

COLOMBIA
Museo del Oro. Banco de la Republica, Calle 16, No. 5-41, Bogota.

GERMANY
Hamburgisches Müseum für Völkerkunde & Vorgeschichte. Binderstrasse 14, 2 Hamburg 13.

ITALY
Museo Preistorico Etnografico Luigi Pigorini. Via Lincoln 1, 00187, Rome.

MEXICO
Museo de Antropologia. Universidad de Veracruz, Jalapa, Veracruz.
Museo Nacional de Antropologia. Paseo de la Reforma y Gandhi 11550, Mexico D.F.

Museo Regional de Antropologia. Avenida Carlos Pellicer 511, Villahermosa, Tabasco.

Museo Regional de Antropologia y Historia. Guadalajara, Jalisco.

Museo Regional de Antropologia y Historia. Calle Mexico 91 Norte, Tepic, Nayarit.

Museo Regional de Oaxaca. Calles de Gurrion y Alcala, Oaxaca.

NETHERLANDS

Rijksmuseum voor Volkenkunde. Steensraat 1, Leyden 3213 BT.

PERU

Brüning Museo Arqueologia. Calle 2 de Mayo 48, Lambayeque.

Museo Arqueologia Rafael Larco Herrero. Avenida Bolivar 1515, Lima.

Museo Nacional de Antropologia y Arqueologia. Plaza Bolivar 21, Lima.

SPAIN

Museo de las Américas. Avenida de los Reyes Catolicos, Ciudad Universitaria, Madrid 3.

Museo Etnologic. Paseo de Santa Madrona, Parque de Montjuic, 08004, Barcelona.

SWITZERLAND

Musée Barbier-Mueller. 10, Rue Jean-Calvin, Geneva CH-1204.

Museum für Völkerkunde. Augustinergasse 2, Basel 4001.

UNITED STATES

California

Natural History Museum of Los Angeles County. 900 Exposition Boulevard, Los Angeles 90007.

Illinois

Art Institute of Chicago. Michigan Avenue at Adams Street, Chicago 60603.

Iowa

University of Iowa Art Museum. 150 North Riverside Drive, Iowa City 52242.

Ohio

Columbus Art Museum. 480 East Broad Street, Columbus 43215.

Texas

Dallas Museum of Art. 1717 North Harwood, Dallas 75201.

Washington, D.C.

Dumbarton Oaks. 1703 32nd Street, N.W., 20007.

AMERICAN INDIAN ART

CANADA

Glenbow-Alberta Institute. 130 Ninth Avenue Southeast, Calgary, Alberta.

McCord Museum of Canadian History. 690 Sherbrooke Street West, Montreal, Quebec H3A 1E9.

Museum of Anthropology. University of British Columbia, 6393 N.W. Marine Drive, Vancouver, British Columbia V6T 1W5.

National Museum of Man. National Museums of Canada, Ottawa, Ontario.

Royal Ontario Museum. 100 Queen's Park, Toronto, Ontario M5S 2C6.

FINLAND

Suomen Kansallismuseo. Mannerheimintie 34, Helsinki 00130.

GREAT BRITAIN

Pitt Rivers Museum. University of Oxford, South Parks Road, Oxford OXI 3PP.

Royal Museum of Scotland. Chambers Street, Edinburgh EH1 1JF.

RUSSIA

Musei Antropologi i Etnografi. St.Petersburg.

SWITZERLAND

Bernisches Historisches Museum. Helvetiaplatz 5, Bern 3000.

Indianer Museum der Stadt. Schulehaus, Feldstrasse, Zürich 8004.

Musée de Ethnographie. Rue St. Nicolas, Neuchâtel 2006.

UNITED STATES

Alaska

Alaska State Museum. 395 Whittier Street, Juneau 99801-1718.

Sheldon Jackson Museum. 104 College Drive, Sitka 99835.

Arizona

Arizona State Museum. University of Arizona, Tucson 85721.

Heard Museum. 22 East Monte Vista Road, Phoenix 85004.

Museum of Northern Arizona. Fort Valley Road, Route 4, Box 720, Flagstaff 86001.

California

California State Indian Museum. 2618 K Street, Sacramento 85816.

Natural History Museum. California Academy of Sciences, Golden Gate Park, San Francisco 94100.

Southwest Museum. 234 Museum Drive, Los Angeles 90065.

Indiana

Eiteljorg Museum. 500 West Washington Street, Indianapolis 46204.

New Hampshire

Hood Museum of Art. Dartmouth College, Wheelock Street, Hanover 03755.

New Jersey

Montclair Art Museum. 3 South Mountain Avenue, Montclair 07042.

Newark Museum. 49 Washington Street, Newark 07101.

New Mexico

Museum of American Indian Arts. 1369 Cerillos Road, Santa Fe 87501.

Museum of Anthropology. Old Santa Fe Trail, Santa Fe 87501.

Millicent A. Rogers Museum. Churchill Road, Taos 87571.

School of American Research. P.O. Box 2188, Santa Fe 87501.

Wheelwright Museum of the American Indian. 704 Camino Lejo, Santa Fe 87502.

North Dakota

State Historical Society Museum of North Dakota. North Dakota Heritage Center, 612 East Boulevard Avenue, Bismarck 58505.

Ohio

Cincinnati Art Museum. Eden Park, Cincinnati 45202.

Oklahoma

Gilcrease Museum. 1400 North 25th West Avenue, Tulsa 74127.

Philbrook Museum of Art. 2727 South Rockford Road, Tulsa 74152.

Oregon

Portland Art Museum. 1219 Southwest Park Avenue, Portland 97205.

Rhode Island

Haffenreffer Museum of Anthropology. Brown University, Mount Hope Grant, Bristol 02809.

Texas

San Antonio Museum of Art. 200 West Jones Avenue, San Antonio 78215.

Witte Museum of History & Natural Science. 3801 Broadway, San Antonio 78209.

Washington

Thomas Burke Memorial Washington State Museum. University of Washington, Seattle 98195.

Wisconsin

Elvehjem Museum of Art. 800 University Avenue, Madison 53706.

Wyoming

Buffalo Bill Historical Center. 720 Sheridan Avenue, Cody 82414.

DEALERS

A selected list of dealers who sell Pre-Columbian and American Indian art

NB. These lists were compiled solely for the information of readers. The inclusion of a dealer's name does not constitute an endorsement by the author, editor, or publisher, nor is any responsibility accepted for the outcome of any transactions between readers and dealers listed, or for the inclusion or omission of any dealer's name. Note also that most of the dealers listed have galleries open to the public, but some deal privately by appointment only.

PRE-COLUMBIAN ART

BELGIUM
Lin and Émile Deletaille. 12 Rue Watteau, 1000 Brussels. Tel.: 322-5129773

FRANCE
Galerie Artes des Amériques. 42 Rue de Seine, 75006 Paris. Tel.: 1-46631831
Galerie Mermoz. 9 Rue du Cirque, 75008 Paris. Tel.: 1-42258480

GERMANY
Galeria Peruana, Ulrich Hoffmann. Schwabstrasse 82, D-7000 Stuttgart 1. Tel.: 07-11-6363184

ITALY
Dr. Giorgio Ceccini. Via del Loretino Settignano, 50135 Florence. Tel.: 39-55-697
Mazzoleni Art. 20121 Milano, via G. Morone 6. Tel.: 39-2795026

SPAIN
Frederico Benthem. Diputacion 304-4, 2A, 08009 Barcelona. Tel.: 93-318-4723

UNITED STATES
California
Al Stendahl Gallery. 7055 Hillside Boulevard, Hollywood 90068. Tel.: (213) 876-7740
Stuart Gallery. 748 North La Cienega Boulevard, Los Angeles 90069. Tel.: (310) 652-7422

New York
Ancient Art of the New World. 42 East 76th Street, New York City 10021. Tel.: (212) 737-3761
David Bernstein Fine Arts. 737 Park Avenue, New York City 10021. Tel.: (212) 794-0389
Fine Arts of Ancient Lands Inc. 12 East 86th Street, New York City 10028. Tel.: (212) 249-7442
Harmer Rooke Gallery. 3 East 57th Street, New York City 10022. Tel.: (212) 751-1900

The Lands Beyond. 1218 Lexington Avenue, New York City 10028. Tel.: (212) 249-6275
Merrin Gallery. 724 Fifth Avenue, New York City 10019. Tel.: (212) 757-2884

AMERICAN INDIAN ART

UNITED STATES
Arizona
Arrowsmith's. P.O. Box 2078, Prescott 86302. Tel.: (602) 445-7196
Michael J. Bradford. P.O. Box 174, Cottonwood 86326. Tel.: (602) 646-5596
Cameron Trading Post. P.O. Box 339, Cameron 85020. Tel.: 1 (800) 338-7385
Gallery 10. 7045 Third Avenue, Scottsdale 85251. Tel.: (602) 994-0405
Peter Hester, Fourth World Native Art. Box 1442, Camp Verde 86332. Tel.: (602) 567-9481
Michael Higgins and Paul Shepard, Primitive Arts. 3026 East Broadway, Tucson 85711. Tel.: (602) 326-4852
John C. Hill. 6990 East Main Street, Scottsdale 85251. Tel.: (602) 946-2910
Margaret Kilgore Gallery. 6961 Fifth Avenue, Scottsdale 85251. Tel.: (602) 990-2890
Richard Rosenthal, Morning Star Traders Inc. 2020 East Speedway, Tucson 85719. Tel.: (602) 881-2112

California
Amerind Art. 1304 12th Street, Santa Monica 90401. Tel.: (213) 395-5678
Caskey-Lees. P.O. Box 1637, Topanga 90290. Tel.: (213) 455-2886
Philip Garaway, Native American Art Gallery. 215 Windward Avenue, Venice 90291. Tel.: (213) 392-8465
Michael Haskell. 19 West Ortega, Santa Barbara 93101. Tel.: (805) 962-9653
Sandra Horn. 736 Alta Vista, Mill Valley 94941. Tel.: (415) 388-2245

James Jeter. P.O. Box 682, Summerland 93067. Tel.: (805) 969-6746
Lauris and Jim Phillips, Fairmont Trading Company. P.O. Box 689, South Pasadena 91030. Tel.: (818) 796-3609
Sherwoods Spirit of America. 325 North Beverly Drive, Beverly Hills 90210. Tel.: (213) 274-6700
Gary Spratt. Box 182, Rutherford 94573. Tel.: (707) 963-4022
Len and Toni Wood, Indian Territory. 305 North Coast Highway, Laguna Beach 92851. Tel.: (714) 497-5747

Colorado
James H. Collins. P.O. Box 9174, Aspen 81612. Tel.: (303) 923-3190
David Cook, Fine American Art Ltd. 1601 17th Street, Denver 80202. Tel.: (303) 623-8181
Hozho' Gallery. 311 5th Street, Crested Butte 81224. Tel.: (303) 349-7350
Robert W. Musser. P.O. Box 4659, Boulder 80306. Tel.: (303) 447-9548
David and Steve Pickelner, Benzav Trading Company. P.O. Box 911, Fort Collins 80522. Tel.: (303) 482-6397
George Shaw. 525 East Cooper, Aspen 81611. Tel.: (303) 925-2873
Neal R. Smith. 2353 East Third Avenue, Denver 80206. Tel.: (303) 399-3119
Martha Hopkins Struever. 1777 Larimer Street, #2108, Denver 80202. Tel.: (303) 298-1707
Mark Winter, American Renaissance. P.O. Box 1570, Pagosa Springs 81147. Tel.: (303) 264-5533

Connecticut
Guthman Americana. P.O. Box 392, Westport 06881. Tel.: (203) 259-9763

Florida
Jennifer and H. Bruce Greene, Hogan Gallery Inc. P.O. Box 7901, Naples 33941-7901. Tel.: (813) 455-1752

Idaho
Pawel Raczka. P.O. Box 647, Sun Valley 83353. Tel.: (208) 726-4817

Illinois

Alan Edison, American West Gallery. 2110 North Halstead Street, Chicago 60614. Tel.: (312) 871-0400

Louisiana

Merrill B. Domas. 824 Chartres, New Orleans 70116. Tel.: (504) 586-0479

Massachusetts

Robert Bauver. 69 South Pleasant Street, Amherst 01002. Tel.: (413) 256-8388

Hurst Gallery. 53 Mount Auburn Street, Cambridge 02138. Tel.: (617) 491-6888

Gregory Quevillon. Box 306, South Dennis 02060. Tel.: (508) 362-8744

Marc Rudick, Visions Ltd. 370 Great Pond Road, North Andover 01845. Tel.: (508) 975-4448

Alan Silberburg, Nashoba Trading Company. P.O. Box 1190, Littleton 01450. Tel.: (508)-486-8250

Michigan

Richard Pohrt, Jr. 340 Brookside Drive, Ann Arbor 48105. Tel.: (313) 769-3942

New Jersey

James D. Hart, Jr. 6554 Irving Avenue, Pennsauken 08109. Tel.: (609) 663-1466

New Mexico

Adobe Gallery. 413 Romero N.W., Albuquerque 87104. Tel.: (505) 243-8485

Joshua Baer. 116½ East Palace Avenue, Santa Fe 87501. Tel.: (505) 988-8944

Canfield. 414 Canyon Road, Santa Fe 87501. Tel.: (505) 988-4199

W. E. Channing. 53 Old Santa Fe Trail, Santa Fe 87501. Tel.: (505) 984-2133

Dewey Galleries Ltd. 74 East San Francisco Street, Santa Fe 87501. Tel.: (505) 982-8632

Rick Dillingham. 607 Old Santa Fe Trail, Santa Fe 87504. Tel.: (505) 983-3447

Economos Works of Art. 500 Canyon Road, Santa Fe 87501. Tel.: (505) 982-6347

H. Jay Evetts and Robert Vanderberg. P.O. Box 2783, Corrales 87048. Tel.: (505) 897-4029

Larry Frank, Art Quest. P.O. Box 292, Arroyo Hondo 87513. Tel.: (505) 776-2281

Robert Gallegos. P.O. Box 247, Albuquerque 87103. Tel.: (505) 255-6740

Gallery 10. 225 Canyon Road, Santa Fe 87501. Tel.: (505) 983-9707

Mary Hunt Kahlenberg, Textile Arts Inc. 1571 Canyon Road, Santa Fe 87501. Tel.: (505) 983-9780

Kania/Ferrin Gallery. 662 Canyon Road, Santa Fe 87501. Tel.: (505) 982-8767

Alan Kessler. 305 Camino Cerrito, Santa Fe 87501. Tel.: (505) 986-1017

Benson Lanford and Robert Gilmore. 924 Paseo de Peralta, #1, Santa Fe 87501. Tel.: (505) 989-9115

Morning Star Gallery. 513 Canyon Road, Santa Fe 87501. Tel.: (505) 982-8187

Robert F. Nichols. 419 Canyon Road, Santa Fe 87501. Tel.: (505) 982-2145

James Reid. 114 East Palace Avenue, Santa Fe 87501. Tel.: (505) 988-1147

Christopher Selser. P.O. Box 9328, Santa Fe 87504. Tel.: (505) 984-1481

Bob Ward. P.O. Box 179, Santa Fe 87501. Tel.: (505) 983-2656

New York

Alexander Acevedo, Alexander Gallery. 996 Madison Avenue, New York City 10021. Tel.: (212) 472-1836

America Hurrah Antiques. 766 Madison Avenue, New York City 10021. Tel.: (212) 535-1930

Trotta Bono. P.O. Box 34, Shrub Oak 10588. Tel.: (914) 528-6604

Eleanor Tulman Hancock. 202 Riverside Drive, New York City 10025. Tel.: (212) 866-5267

Jeffrey R. Meyers. 222 East 81st Street, New York City 10028. Tel.: (212) 472-0115

Ron Nasser Inc. 50 East 78th Street, New York City 10021. Tel.: (212) 242-4338

Scott Rodolitz, Graven Images. P.O. Box P, Woodmere 11598. Tel.: (516) 374-3364

Paul Steinhacker. 151 East 71st Street, New York City 10021. Tel.: (212) 879-1245.

Pennsylvania

Marcy Burns, Southwest Indian Arts. P.O. Box 181, Glenside 19038. Tel.: (215) 576-1559

Crown and Eagle Antiques. P.O. Box 181, Route 202, New Hope 18938. Tel.: (215) 794-7972

Texas

Jan Duggan. P.O. Box 9075-243, Houston 77290. Tel.: (713) 440-9120

Michael J. McKissick, Waterbird Traders. 3420 Greenville Avenue, Dallas 75206. Tel.: (214) 821-4606

Washington

Bruce Boyd. P.O. Box 20252, Seattle 98012. Tel.: (206) 322-8516

AUCTIONS

A selected list of galleries and auctioneers holding Pre-Columbian or American Indian art auctions

N.B. These lists were compiled solely for the information of readers. The inclusion of a name does not constitute an endorsement by the author, editor, or publisher, nor is any responsibility accepted for the outcome of any transactions between readers and any party listed, or for the inclusion or omission of any name.

PRE-COLUMBIAN ART

The following auction houses regularly hold specialized Pre-Columbian sales:

Harmer Rooke Galleries. 3 East 57th Street, New York, N.Y. 10022.
Tel.: (212) 751-1900
Sotheby's, New York. 1334 York Avenue, New York, N.Y. 10021.
Tel.: (212) 606-7000

Other auction houses and auctioneers occasionally hold specialized Pre-Columbian sales or include Pre-Columbian items in general sales of tribal and ancient art. Among these are the following:

Ader Tajan. 12 Rue Favart, 75002 Paris, France. Tel.: 1-42618007
Bonhams. Montpelier Street, Knightsbridge, London SW7 1HH, England.
Tel.: 071-584-9161
Christie, Manson & Woods. 8 King Street, St. James's, London SW1Y 6QT, England. Tel.: 071-839-9060

Guy Loudmer. 45 Rue Lafayette, 75009 Paris, France. Tel.: 1-488989
Sotheby's. 34-35 New Bond Street, London W1A 2AA, England.
Tel.: 071-493-8080

AMERICAN INDIAN ART

CANADA
D. and J. Ritchie. 429 Richmond Street East, Toronto, Ontario M5A 1R1.
Waddington's. 189 Queen Street East, Toronto, Ontario M5A 1S2.

UNITED STATES
California
Don Bennett. P.O. Box 283, Agoura 91301.
Butterfield and Butterfield. 220 San Bruno Avenue, San Francisco 94103.
R. G. Munn. 8243 La Mesa Boulevard, La Mesa 92041.

Illinois
Dunning's. 755 Church Road, Elgin 60123.

Massachusetts
Willis Henry. 22 Main Street, Marshfield 02050.
Skinners. Route 117, Bolton 01740.

Montana
Doug Allard. P.O. Box 460, St. Ignatius 59865.

New Mexico
W. E. Channing. 53 Old Santa Fe Trail, Santa Fe 87501.

New York
Sotheby's. 1334 York Avenue, New York City 10021.

Ohio
Garth's Auctions. P.O. Box 369, Delaware 43015.
Old Barn Auction. 10040 S.R. 224 W., Findlay 45840.

Washington
Dennis Eros. P.O. Box 186, Ocean Park 98640.

BOOK SOURCES

A selected list of specialized booksellers

PRE-COLUMBIAN AND AMERICAN INDIAN ART

Louis Collins Books. 1211 East Denny Way, Seattle, Wash. 98122.
Tel.: (206) 323-3999
Ethnographic Arts Publications. 1040 Erica Road, Mill Valley, Calif. 94941.
Tel.: (415) 383-2998

Bob Fein Books. 150 Fifth Avenue, New York, N.Y. 10011.
Tel.: (212) 807-0489
Michael Graves-Johnston. P.O. Box 532, 54 Stockwell Park Road, London SW9 0DR, England. Tel.: 071-274-2069
Harmer Johnson Books. 21 East 65th Street, New York, N.Y. 10021.
Tel.: (212) 535-9118
O.A.N. 15 West 39th Street, New York, N.Y. 10018-3806. Tel.: (212) 840-8844

PRE-COLUMBIAN ART

Arte Primitivo. 3 East 65th Street, Suite 2B, New York, N.Y. 10021.
Tel.: (212) 570-0393
Flo Silver Books. 8442 Oakwood Court North, Indianapolis, Ind. 46260.
Tel.: (317) 255-5118

GLOSSARY

Atlantean. Pertaining to, and having the strength of, the mythical demigod Atlas, particularly referring to the traditional figure supporting the world on his shoulders.

bannerstone. A pierced stone ornament, usually of elegant geometric form; probably worn as a ceremonial pendant by prehistoric North American Indians.

bayeta. An early Navajo raveled yarn combining indigenous handspun yarn with commercial products.

birdstone. A stone abstracted bird form found in central North America, the use and origins of which are uncertain.

bow guard. A leather strap worn by Navajo men around their wrists to protect them from the snap of the bowstring.

catlinite. A soft red slate mined at Pipestone, Minnesota, primarily for use in carving pipe bowls. It was named for the American painter George Catlin, one of the first non-Indians to see the quarries. Catlinite is also called "pipestone".

celt. An axe-form of stone or metal.

concha. The Spanish word for "shell", referring here to shell-like silver ornaments on Navajo and Zuni belts.

crooked knife. Knife with carved wooden handle and curved blade made from discarded curved file. Blades were later manufactured in England for trade and used with the handle mounted at an angle to the blade. These are still referred to as "crooked knives", although the blade may be straight.

eyedazzler. A type of Navajo blanket made during the 1890s using vividly dyed commercial yarns woven into colorful, jagged terrace patterns and zigzag designs.

false embroidery. In twined basketry, a decorative technique in which a weft of contrasting color is wrapped around the two outer wefts and remains invisible on the inside of the basket.

false face. The masked ceremonies of the Iroquois to exorcise evil spirits and drive away diseases, and the masks used.

finger weaving. The technique of weaving without the use of loom, heddle, bobbin, or shuttle.

fire cloud. An irregular discoloration on a terracotta vessel's surface, usually caused by burning fuel coming into direct contact with the vessel during firing.

Germantown. Navajo blankets woven of commercial woolen yarn dyed with brightly colored aniline and other synthetic dyes, originally made in Germantown, Pennsylvania.

glyph. A painted or carved pictorial image representing an idea, name, number, word, or sound. Seen in Mesoamerican art on stelae, painted vases, architectural features, and carved stone and terracotta objects.

gorget. A pendant, usually crescentic, worn at the throat.

hacha. An axe-like stone, usually with a sculpted head, associated with the ball game and possibly a court marker.

incensario. A vessel used for the burning of ceremonial incense.

kill-hole. An intentional hole made in the center of many Prehistoric pottery bowls, particularly in the Southwest, probably for a ritual purpose.

kiva. In a pueblo dwelling or community building, a room used for religious ceremonial purposes.

knapping. The chipping of stone.

lazy stitch. A method of stitching beadwork to hide for covering large surfaces. The lazy stitch produces transverse strings of beads in a series of loose bands unconnected to the surface.

lost wax. A method of making metal castings in which a heat-resistant mold is formed around a wax model of an object and then heated so that the wax melts away through openings in the mold, leaving a cavity into which molten metal is poured. When the metal cools and hardens, the mold is removed and the metal object's surface is finished.

manta. A small blanket woven wider than long, and worn over the shoulder.

metate. A stone corn-grinding table, common throughout the ancient Americas.

midden. A refuse heap.

necropolis. A cemetery.

olla. The Spanish term usually applied to a wide-mouthed, medium-size to large terracotta water storage vessel.

palma. A tall, thin angular stone that was attached to the top of the yoke in the ball game.

parfleche. A folded or sewn rawhide container, usually elaborately painted on the outer surfaces.

pectoral. An ornament worn on the breast.

plumbate. A specific lead-glazed pottery unique to the Postclassic period in Mexico and Guatemala.

pony bead. A type of glass bead more than three times the size of a seed bead, brought from Europe by traders early in the nineteenth century and used by Indians to replace quillwork. The diameter of pony beads is usually about 1/8" (3.1mm).

"pretty lady". A miniature terracotta figure of a young, attractive woman from the Preclassic cultures in Mexico's central highlands.

repoussage. Decoration or raised relief created by hammering on the reverse side of thin metal.

serape. A woolen blanket or shawl, often brightly colored, worn as an outer garment in Spanish-American areas.

shaman. A practitioner of medicine in Indian societies who uses powers derived from direct contact with spiritual sources for curing and other beneficial rites.

slip. A clay solution of creamy consistency, generally combined with color pigments, used for coating or decorating pottery. The slip is applied before firing.

stele. An upright stone slab or pillar bearing an inscription or design, and serving as a monument or marker.

stirrup spout. On terracotta vessels, a combined spout and handle having the shape of a stirrup. The body of the vessel forms the step and the inverted U-shaped handle the arch, from the top of which the spout projects.

stroud. A woolen trade cloth from England, generally red or blue, named after the town in which it originated. It was introduced in the early 19th century.

talud tablero. A feature of Teotihuácan architecture. The *talud* is a sloping buttress surmounted by a rectangular horizontal element called a *tablero.*

yei. A Navajo spirit being. *Yeis,* or Holy People, are impersonated by masked dancers, and depicted in weaving and painting.

yoke. A U-shaped object worn around the waist as protection when playing the Mesoamerican ball game. Known examples are made of stone, but the actual protector was probably made of wood.

BIBLIOGRAPHY

PRE-COLUMBIAN ART

Mesoamerica

GENERAL

Anton, Ferdinand. *Ancient Mexican Art.* London: Thames and Hudson, 1969.

Berjonneau, Gerald, Émile Deletaille, and Jean-Louis Sonnery. *Rediscovered Masterpieces of Mesoamerica: Mexico-Guatemala-Honduras.* Boulogne: Éditions Arts 135, 1985.

Bernal, Ignacio. *Museo Nacional de Antropologia de Mexico.* Mexico City: Daimon, 1977.

Boone, Elizabeth H., ed. *Falsifications and Misreconstructions of Pre-Columbian Art.* Washington, D.C.: Dumbarton Oaks, 1982.

Coe, Michael D. *Mexico.* New York: Frederick A. Praeger, 1962.

Covarrubias, Miguel. *Indian Art of Mexico and Central America.* New York: Knopf, 1957.

Dockstader, Frederick J. *Indian Art in Middle America: Pre-Columbian and Contemporary Arts and Crafts of Mexico, Central America and the Caribbean.* Greenwich, Conn.: New York Graphic Society, 1964.

Easby, Elizabeth K. *Ancient Art of Latin America from the Collection of Jay C. Leff.* New York: Brooklyn Museum, 1966.

Easby, Elizabeth K., and John F. Scott. *Before Cortes: Sculpture of Middle America.* New York: Metropolitan Museum of Art/New York Graphic Society, 1970.

Emmerich, André. *Art Before Columbus: The Art of Ancient Mexico.* New York: Simon and Schuster, 1963.

Furst, Jill Leslie and Peter T. *Pre-Columbian Art of Mexico.* New York: Abbeville Press, 1980.

Furst, Peter T., and Debra Gabrielson. *The Ninth Level: Funerary Art from Ancient Mesoamerica.* Iowa City: University of Iowa Museum of Art, 1978.

Keleman, Pal. *Medieval American Art.* New York: Dover, 1969.

Kubler, George. *The Louise and Walter Arensberg Collection: Pre-Columbian Sculpture.* Philadelphia: Philadelphia Museum of Art, 1954.

————, ed. *Pre-Columbian Art of Mexico and Central America.* New Haven: Yale University Art Gallery, 1986.

Lothrop, Samuel K. *Treasures of Ancient America.* Geneva: Éditions d'Art Albert Skira, 1964.

Lothrop, Samuel K., et al. *Essays in Pre-Columbian Art and Archaeology.* Cambridge: Harvard University Press, 1964.

Lothrop, Samuel K., W. F. Foshag, and Joy Mahler. *Pre-Columbian Art: Robert Woods Bliss Collection.* New York: Garden City Books, 1957.

Nicholson, Irene. *Mexican and Central American Mythology.* London: Paul Hamlyn, 1967.

Nicholson, Henry B., and Alana Cordy-Collins. *Pre-Columbian Art from the Land Collection.* San Francisco: California Academy of Sciences, 1979.

Parsons, Lee A. *Pre-Columbian Art: The Morton D. May and Saint Louis Art Museum Collections.* New York: Harper and Row, 1980.

Parsons, Lee A., et al. *The Face of Ancient America: The Wally and Brenda Zollman Collection of Precolumbian Art.* Indianapolis: Indianapolis Museum of Art in cooperation with Indiana University Press, 1988.

Paz, Octavio, et al. *Art Millénaire des Amériques de la Découverte à l'Admiration, 1492–1992.* Geneva: Musée Barbier-Mueller, 1992.

Peterson, Jeanette Favrot, and Judith Strupp Green. *Precolumbian Flora and Fauna: Continuity of Plant and Animal Themes in Mesoamerican Art.* San Diego: Mingei International Museum, 1990.

Taube, Karl. *The Albers Collection of Pre-Columbian Art.* New York: Hudson Hills Press, 1988.

Vasquez, Pedro Ramirez, et al. *The National Museum of Anthropology, Mexico: Art, Architecture, Archaeology, Ethnography.* New York: Harry N. Abrams in association with Helvetica Press, 1968.

Von Winning, Hasso. *Pre-Columbian Art of Mexico and Central America.* New York: Harry N. Abrams, 1968.

Weaver, Murial Porter. *The Aztecs, Maya, and Their Predecessors.* New York: Seminar Press, 1972.

VARIOUS CULTURAL AREAS

Bernal, Ignacio. *The Olmec World.* Berkeley and Los Angeles: University of California Press, 1969.

Bocs, Frank H. *The Ceramic Sculpture of Ancient Oaxaca.* New York: A. S. Barnes, 1966.

Caso, Alfonso, and Ignacio Bernal. *Urnas de Oaxaca.* Instituto Nacional de Antropologia e Historia, Memorias 2, Mexico, D.F., 1952.

Coe, Michael D. *The Jaguar's Children: Pre-Classic Central Mexico.* Museum of Primitive Art, New York. Greenwich, Conn.: New York Graphic Society, 1965.

————. *America's First Civilization.* New York: American Heritage Publishing, 1968.

Frierman, Jay D., ed. *The Natalie Wood Collection of Pre-Columbian Ceramics from Chupicuaro, Guanajuato, Mexico, at UCLA.* Los Angeles: University of California, 1969.

Gallagher, Jacki. *Companions of the Dead: Ceramic Tomb Sculpture from Ancient West Mexico.* Los Angeles: Museum of Cultural History, University of California, 1983.

Gay, Carlo T. E. *Mezcala Stone Sculpture: The Human Figure.* New York: Museum of Primitive Art, 1967.

————*Xochipala: The Beginnings of Olmec Art.* Princeton, N.J.: Art Museum, Princeton University, 1972.

————*Mezcala Architecture in Miniature.* Brussels: Palais des Académies, 1984.

Gay, Carlo, and Frances Pratt. *Mezcala: Ancient Stone Sculpture From Guerrero, Mexico.* Geneva: Balsas Publications, 1992.

Hammer, Olga, ed. *Ancient Art of Veracruz.* Los Angeles: Ethnic Arts Council, 1971.

Kan, Michael, Clement Meighan, and H. B. Nicholson. *Sculpture of Ancient West Mexico: Nayarit, Jalisco, Colima: The Proctor Stafford Collection.* Albuquerque: Los Angeles County Museum of Art with University of New Mexico Press, 1989.

Montreal Museum of Fine Arts. *Man-Eaters and Pretty Ladies: Early Art in Central Mexico, from the Gulf to the Pacific, 1500 B.C. to 500 A.D.* Montreal, 1971.

Nicholson, H. B., and Eloise G. Keber. *Art of Aztec Mexico.* Washington, D.C.: National Gallery of Art, 1983.

Paddock, John, ed. *Ancient Oaxaca.* Stanford, Calif.: Stanford University Press, 1966.

Pasztory, Esther. *Aztec Art.* New York: Harry N. Abrams, 1983.

Stierlin, Henri. *Art of the Aztecs.* New York: Rizzoli, 1982.

Wicke, Charles R. *Olmec: An Early Art Style of Precolumbian Mexico.* Tucson: University of Arizona Press, 1971.

MAYA

Anton, Ferdinand. *Art of the Maya.* New York: G. P. Putnam's Sons, 1970.

Clancy, Flora S., et al. *Maya: Treasures of an Ancient Civilization.* New York: Harry N. Abrams in association with the Albuquerque Museum, 1985.

Coe, Michael D. *The Maya Scribe and His World.* New York: Grolier Club, 1973.

———. *Classic Maya Pottery at Dumbarton Oaks.* Washington, D.C.: Dumbarton Oaks, 1975.

———. *The Lords of the Underworld.* Princeton, N.J.: Princeton University Press, 1978.

———. *The Maya.* New York: Thames and Hudson, 1980.

Coggins, Clemency C. *Cenote of Sacrifice: Maya Treasures from the Sacred Well at Chichen Itza.* Austin: University of Texas Press, 1984.

Digby, Adrian. *Maya Jades.* London: British Museum, 1972.

Hammond, Norman. *Ancient Maya Civilization.* New Brunswick, N.J.: Rutgers University Press, 1982.

Morley, Sylvanus. *The Ancient Maya.* Stanford, Calif.: Stanford University Press, 1983.

Proskouriakoff, Tatiana. *Jades from the Cenote of Sacrifice, Chichen Itza, Yucatan.* Memoirs of the Peabody Museum of Archaeology and Ethnology, Vol. 10, No. 1. Cambridge: Harvard University, 1974.

Réunion des Musées Nationaux. *Arts Mayas du Guatemala.* Paris: Ministère d'État Affaires Culturelles, 1968.

Robicsek, Francis. *Copan: Home of the Mayan Gods.* New York: Museum of the American Indian, Heye Foundation, 1972.

———. *The Smoking Gods: Tobacco in Maya Art, History, and Religion.* Norman: University of Oklahoma Press, 1978.

Robicsek, Francis, and D. F. Hales. *The Maya Book of the Dead: The Ceramic Codex.* Charlottesville, Va.: University of Virginia Art Museum, 1981.

Schele, Linda, and Mary Ellen Miller. *The Blood of Kings: Dynasty and Ritual in Maya Art.* Fort Worth: Kimbell Art Museum, 1986.

Stierlin, Henri. *Art of the Maya.* New York: Rizzoli, 1981.

Thompson, J. Eric S. *The Rise and Fall of Maya Civilization.* Norman: University of Oklahoma Press, 1954.

———. *Maya Hieroglyphic Writing: An Introduction.* Norman: University of Oklahoma Press, 1960.

Tozzer, Alfred M. *Chichen Itza and Its Cenote of Sacrifice.* Memoirs of the Peabody Museum of Archaeology and Ethnology, Vols. 11 (text) and 12 (plates). Cambridge: Harvard University, 1957.

Central America

COSTA RICA/PANAMA

Abel-Vidor, Suzanne, et al. *Between Continents/Between Seas: Precolumbian Art of Costa Rica.* New York: Harry N. Abrams in association with the Detroit Institute of Arts, 1981.

Easby, Elizabeth Kennedy. *Pre-Columbian Jade from Costa Rica.* New York: André Emmerich Inc., 1968.

Lothrop, Samuel K. *The Pottery of Costa Rica and Nicaragua.* 2 vols. Contributions from the Museum of the American Indian, Heye Foundation, New York, 1926.

———. *Cocle: An Archaeological Study of Central Panama.* 2 vols. Memoirs of the Peabody Museum of Archaeology and Ethnology, Harvard University, Cambridge, Mass., 1937–1942.

Mason, J. Alden. *Costa Rican Stonework: The Minor C. Keith Collection.* New York: American Museum of Natural History, 1945.

Stone, Doris Z. *Precolumbian Man in Costa Rica.* Cambridge, Mass.: Peabody Museum Press, 1977.

South America

COLOMBIA/ECUADOR

Fondation de l'Hermitage. *Equateur: La Terre et l'Or.* Lausanne, 1991.

Labbe, Armand J. *Colombia Before Columbus: The People, Culture, and Ceramic Art of Prehistoric Colombia.* New York: Rizzoli, 1986.

Lathrap, Donald W., et al. *Ancient Ecuador: Culture, Clay and Creativity 3000–300 B.C.* Chicago: Field Museum of Natural History, 1975.

Meggers, Betty J. *Ecuador.* New York: Praeger, 1966.

Reichel-Domatoff. *Colombia.* London: Thames and Hudson, 1965.

PERU

Bennett, Wendell C. *Ancient Arts of the Andes.* New York: Museum of Modern Art, 1954.

Benson, Elizabeth F. *The Mochica: A Culture of Peru.* New York: Praeger Publishers, 1972.

Bushnell, G.H.S. *Peru.* London: Thames and Hudson, 1956.

Clifford, Paul A., et al. *Art of the Andes: Pre-Columbian Sculptured and Painted Ceramics from the Arthur M. Sackler Collections.* Washington, D.C.: Arthur M. Sackler Foundation and the AMS Foundation for the Arts, Sciences and Humanities, 1983.

de Lavalle, Jose Antonio. *Arte y Tesoros del Peru. Arte Precolombino.* Lima: Banco de Credito del Peru en la Cultura, 1979.

———. *Arte y Tesoros del Peru. Culturas Precolombinas: Huari.* Lima: Banco de Credito del Peru en la Cultura, 1984.

———. *Arte y Tesoros del Peru. Culturas Precolombinas: Lambayeque.* Lima: Banco de Credito del Peru en la Cultura, 1989.

———, ed. *Arte y Tesoros del Peru. Culturas Precolombinas: Chavin Formativo.* Lima: Banco de Credito del Peru en la Cultura, 1981.

———. *Arte y Tesoros del Peru. Culturas Precolombinas: Chancay.* Lima: Banco de Credito del Peru en la Cultura, 1982.

———. *Arts y Tesoros del Peru. Culturas Precolombinas: Nazca.* Lima: Banco de Credito del Peru en la Cultura, 1986.

———. *Arte y Tesoros del Peru. Culturas Precolombinas: Chimu.* Lima: Banco de Credito del Peru en la Cultura, 1988.

D'Harcourt, Raoul. *Textiles of Ancient Peru and Their Techniques.* Seattle: University of Washington Press, 1962.

Dockstader, Frederick J. *Indian Art in South America: Pre-Columbian and Contemporary Arts and Crafts.* Greenwich, Conn.: New York Graphic Society, 1967.

Donnan, Christopher B. *Moche Art of Peru.* Los Angeles: Museum of Cultural History, University of California, 1978.

Ferdinand, Anton. *Ancient Peruvian Textiles.* London: Thames and Hudson, 1987.

Thomas Gibson Fine Art. *Feather Masterpieces of the Ancient Andean World.* London, 1990.

Industria Textil Piura. *Coleccion Art Textil del Peru.* Lima, 1988.

Jones, Julie. *Art of Empire: The Inca of Peru.* Museum of Primitive Art, New York. Greenwich, Conn.: New York Graphic Society, 1964.

King, Mary Elizabeth. *Ancient Peruvian Textiles from the Collection of the Textile Museum, Washington, D.C.* Museum of Primitive Art, New York. Greenwich, Conn.: New York Graphic Society, 1965.

Lapiner, Alan. *Pre-Columbian Art of South America.* New York: Harry N. Abrams, 1976.

Rowe, John Howland. *Chavin Art: An Inquiry into Its Form and Meaning.* Museum of Primitive Art, New York: University Publishers, 1962.

Sawyer, Alan R. *Ancient Peruvian Ceramics: The Nathan Cummings Collection.* New York: Metropolitan Museum of Art, 1966.

––––––. *Mastercraftsmen of Ancient Peru.* New York: Solomon R. Guggenheim Foundation, 1968.

Stierlin, Henri. *Art of the Incas.* New York: Rizzoli, 1984.

Von Hagen, Victor W. *The Desert Kingdoms of Peru.* London: Weidenfeld and Nicolson, 1965.

Wasserman–San Blas, B. J. *Ceramicas del Antiguo Peru.* Buenos Aires: Casa Jacobo Peuser, 1938.

Gold and Silver

Bray, Warwick. *The Gold of El Dorado.* London: Royal Academy, 1978.

Center for Inter-American Relations and the American Federation of Arts. *El Dorado: The Gold of Ancient Colombia. From El Museo del Oro, Banco de la Republica, Bogota, Colombia.* New York, 1974.

Emmerich, André. *Sweat of the Sun and Tears of the Moon.* Seattle: University of Washington Press, 1965.

Foundation de l'Hermitage. *L'Or du Peru.* Lausanne, 1988.

Furst, Peter T. *Gold Before Columbus.* Los Angeles: Los Angeles County Museum, 1964.

Gallo, Miguel Mujica. *The Gold of Peru.* Recklinghausen, Germany: Aurel Bongers, 1959.

Metropolitan Museum of Art. *The Art of Precolumbian Gold: The Jan Mitchell Collection.* New York, 1985.

Museum of Primitive Art. *Pre-Columbian Gold Sculpture.* New York, 1958.

Perez de Barradas, Jose. *Orfebreria Prehispanica de Colombia: Estilo Calima.* Banco de la Republica, Museo del Oro, Bogota. Madrid: Talleres Graficos "Jura", 1954.

––––––. *Orfebreria Prehispanica de Colombia: Estilos Tolima y Muisca.* Banco de la Republica, Museo del Oro, Bogota. Madrid: Talleres Graficos "Jura", 1958.

––––––. *Orfebreria Prehispanica de Colombia: Estilos Quimbaya y Otros.* Banco de la Republica, Museo del Oro, Bogota. Madrid: Talleres Graficos "Jura", 1966.

Tushingham, A. D. *Gold for the Gods.* Toronto: Royal Ontario Museum, 1976.

Wardwell, Allen. *The Gold of Ancient America.* Greenwich, Conn.: New York Graphic Society, 1968.

AMERICAN INDIAN AND ESKIMO ART

General

Arts Council of Great Britain. *Sacred Circles: Two Thousand Years of North American Indian Art.* London, 1977.

Benndorf, Helga, and Arthur Speyer. *Indianer Nordamerikas 1760–1860 Aus der Sammlung Speyer.* Offenbach am Main: Deutsches Ledermuseum, Deutsches Schuhmuseum, 1968.

Coe, Ralph T. *Lost and Found Traditions: Native American Art 1965–1985.* New York: University of Washington Press in association with the American Federation of Arts, 1986.

Conn, Richard. *Native American Art in the Denver Art Museum.* Denver: Denver Art Museum, 1979.

Dockstader, Frederick J. *Indian Art in America.* Greenwich, Conn.: New York Graphic Society, n.d.

Fane, Diana, Ira Jacknis, and Lisa M. Breen. *Objects of Myth and Memory: American Indian Art at The Brooklyn Museum.* New York: Brooklyn Museum, 1991.

Feder, Norman. *American Indian Art.* New York: Harry N. Abrams, 1969.

Feest, Christian F. *Indianer Nordamerikas.* Vienna: Museum für Völkerkunde, 1968.

Flint Institute of Arts. *The American Indian, The American Flag.* Flint, Mich., 1975.

Furst, Peter T., and Jill L. Furst. *North American Indian Art.* New York: Rizzoli, 1982.

Glenbow Museum. *The Spirit Sings: Artistic Traditions of Canada's First Peoples.* Toronto: Glenbow-Alberta Institute and McClelland and Stewart, 1987.

Haberland, Wolfgang. *The Art of North America.* New York: Crown, 1964.

Heard Museum. *Fred Harvey Fine Arts Collection.* Phoenix, 1976.

King, J.C.H. *Smoking Pipes of the North American Indian.* London: British Museum, 1977.

Lenz, Mary Jane. *The Stuff of Dreams: Native American Dolls.* New York: Museum of the American Indian, 1986.

Maurer, Evan M. *The Native American Heritage: A Survey of North American Indian Art.* Chicago: Art Institute of Chicago, 1977.

Orchard, William C. *The Technique of Porcupine Quill Decoration Among the Indians of North America.* Contributions from the Museum of the American Indian, Heye Foundation, Vol. 4, No. 1. New York: Museum of the American Indian, 1971.

––––––. *Beads and Beadwork of the American Indians.* Contributions from the Museum of the American Indian, Heye Foundation, Vol. 11. New York: Museum of the American Indian, 1975.

Peabody Museum. *Hall of the North American Indian: Change and Continuity.* Cambridge, Mass.: Peabody Museum Press, 1990.

Philbrook Art Center. *Native American Art at Philbrook.* Tulsa: Philbrook Art Center, 1980.

Rautenstrauch-Joest-Museum der Stadt Köln. *Indianer Nordamerikas Schatze des Museum of the American Indian–Heye Foundation–New York.* Cologne, 1969.

Roosevelt, Anna Curtius, and James G. E. Smith, eds. *The Ancestors: Native Artisans of the Americas.* New York: Museum of the American Indian, 1979.

Thompson, Judy. *The North American Indian Collection. A Catalogue.* Bern: Bern Historical Museum, 1977.

Wade, Edwin L., Carol Haralson, and Rennard Strickland. *As in a Vision: Masterworks of American Indian Art.* Norman: University of Oklahoma Press and Philbrook Art Center, 1983.

Walker Art Center. *American Indian Art: Form and Tradition.* Minneapolis: Walker Art Center, 1972.

Eskimo and Northwest Coast

Collins, Henry B., et al. *The Far North: 2000 Years of American Eskimo and Indian Art.* National Gallery of Art, Washington, D.C.: Indiana University Press, 1973.

Duff, Wilson. *Images; Stone B.C.: Thirty Centuries of Northwest Coast Indian Sculpture.* Seattle: University of Washington Press, 1975.

Duncan, Kate C. *Northern Athapaskan Art: A Beadwork Tradition.* Seattle: University of Washington Press, 1989.

Fitzhugh, William W., and Aron Crowell. *Crossroads of Continents: Cultures of Siberia and Alaska.* Washington, D.C.: Smithsonian Institution Press, 1988.

Fitzhugh, William W., and Susan A. Kaplan. *Inua: Spirit World of the Bering Sea Eskimo.* Washington, D.C.: Smithsonian Institution Press, 1982.

Hawthorn, Audrey. *Kwakiutl Art.* Seattle: University of Washington Press, 1979.

Holm, William. *Spirit and Ancestor: A Century of Northwest Coast Indian Art at the Burke Museum.* Seattle: University of Washington Press, 1987.

Holm, William, and William Reid. *Form and Freedom.* Houston: Rice University Press, 1975.

Jonaitis, Aldona. *Art of the Northern Tlingit.* Seattle: University of Washington Press, 1986.

———. *From the Land of the Totem Poles: The Northwest Coast Indian Art Collection at the American Museum of Natural History.* Seattle: American Museum of Natural History and University of Washington Press, 1988.

———, ed. *Chiefly Feasts: The Enduring Kwakiutl Potlatch.* Seattle: American Museum of Natural History and University of Washington Press, 1991.

Kaplan, Susan A., and Kristin J. Barsness. *Raven's Journey: The World of Alaska's Native People.* Philadelphia: University Museum, 1986.

King, J.C.H. *Artificial Curiosities from the Northwest Coast of America: Native American Artefacts in the British Museum Collected on the Third Voyage of Captain James Cook and Acquired through Sir Joseph Banks.* London: British Museum, 1981.

Ray, Dorothy Jean. *Eskimo Art: Tradition and Innovation in North Alaska.* Seattle: University of Washington Press, 1977.

———. *Aleut and Eskimo Art: Tradition and Innovation in South Alaska.* Seattle: University of Washington Press, 1981.

Sheehan, Carol. *Pipes That Won't Smoke; Coal That Won't Burn; Haida Sculpture in Argillite.* Calgary, Alberta: Glenbow Museum, 1981.

Varjola, Pirjo. *The Etholen Collection: The Ethnographic Alaskan Collection of Adolf Etholen and His Contemporaries in the National Museum of Finland.* Helsinki: National Board of Antiquities of Finland, 1990.

Wardwell, Allen. *Ancient Eskimo Ivories of the Bering Strait.* New York: Hudson Hills Press in association with the American Federation of Arts, 1986.

Wright, Robin K. *A Time of Gathering: Native Heritage in Washington State.* Seattle: Burke Museum/University of Washington Press, 1991.

Plains

Conn, Richard. *A Persistent Vision: Art of the Reservation Days. The L.D. and Ruth Bax Collection of the Denver Art Museum.* Denver: Denver Art Museum, 1986.

Ewers, John C. *Plains Indian Sculpture: A Traditional Art from America's Heartland.* Washington, D.C.: Smithsonian Institution Press, 1986.

Feder, Norman. *Art of the Eastern Plains Indians: The Nathan Sturges Jarvis Collection.* New York: Brooklyn Museum, 1964.

Hail, Barbara A. *Hau, Kola!: The Plains Indian Collection of the Haffenreffer Museum of Anthropology.* Bristol, R.I.: Haffenreffer Museum of Anthropology, Brown University, 1980.

Hartmann, Horst. *Die Plains- und Prarieindianer Nordamerikas.* Berlin: Museum für Völkerkunde, 1973.

Mails, Thomas E. *The Mystic Warriors of the Plains.* New York: Doubleday, 1972.

———. *Dog Soldiers, Bear Men and Buffalo Women: A Study of the Societies and Cults of the Plains Indians.* Englewood Cliffs, N.J.: Prentice-Hall, 1973.

Minneapolis Institute of Arts. *I Wear the Morning Star: An Exhibition of American Indian Ghost Dance Objects.* Minneapolis: Minneapolis Institute of Arts, 1976.

Petersen, Karen Daniels. *Plains Indian Art from Fort Marion.* Norman: University of Oklahoma Press, 1971.

Southwest Museum. *Akicita: Early Plains and Woodlands Indian Art from the Collection of Alexander Acevedo.* Los Angeles, 1983.

Walton, Ann T., John C. Ewers, and Royal B. Hassrick. *After the Buffalo Were Gone: The Louis Warren Hill, Sr., Collection of Indian Art.* St. Paul: Northwest Area Foundation, 1985.

Wildschut, William, and John C. Ewers. *Crow Indian Beadwork: A Descriptive and Historical Study.* Contributions from the Museum of the American Indian, Heye Foundation, Vol. 16. New York: Museum of the American Indian, 1959.

Southwest

GENERAL

Ferg, Alan, ed. *Western Apache Material Culture: The Goodwin and Guenther Collections.* Tucson: University of Arizona Press, 1987.

Washburn, Dorothy K., ed. *The Elkus Collection: Southwestern Indian Art.* San Francisco: California Academy of Sciences, 1984.

Whiteford, Andrew Hunter, Stewart Peckham, et al. *I Am Here: Two Thousand Years of Southwest Indian Arts and Culture.* Santa Fe: Museum of New Mexico Press, 1989.

Wright, Barton. *Pueblo Shields from the Fred Harvey Fine Arts Collection.* Flagstaff, Ariz.: Northland Press, 1976.

BASKETRY

Bates, Craig D., and Martha J. Lee. *Tradition and Innovation: A Basket History of the Indians of the Yosemite–Mono Lake Area.* Yosemite National Park, Calif.: Yosemite Association, 1990.

Fields, Virginia. *The Hover Collection of Karuk Baskets.* Eureka, Calif.: Clarke Memorial Museum, 1985.

Lopez, Raul A., and Christopher L. Moser, eds. *Rods, Bundles & Stitches: A Century of Southern California Indian Basketry.* Riverside, Calif.: Riverside Museum Press, 1981.

Moser, Christopher L. *Native American Basketry of Central California.* Riverside, Calif.: Riverside Museum Press, 1986.

———. *American Indian Basketry of Northern California.* Riverside, Calif.: Riverside Museum Press, 1990.

Tanner, Clara Lee. *Apache Indian Baskets.* Tucson: University of Arizona Press, 1982.

———. *Indian Baskets of the Southwest.* Tucson: University of Arizona Press, 1983.

Turnbaugh, Sarah Peabody, and William A. Turnbaugh. *Indian Baskets.* West Chester, Pa.: Schiffer Publishing, 1986.

Whiteford, Andrew Hunter. *Southwestern Indian Baskets: Their History and Their Makers.* Santa Fe: School of American Research Press, 1988.

JEWELRY

Bedinger, Marjorie. *Indian Silver: Navajo and Pueblo Jewelers.* Albuquerque: University of New Mexico Press, 1973.

Frank, Larry, and Millard J. Holbrook. *Indian Silver Jewelry of the Southwest, 1868–1930.* New York: New York Graphic Society, 1978.

Lincoln, Louise, ed. *Southwest Indian Silver from the Doneghy Collection.* Austin: University of Texas Press, 1982.

Schiffer, Nancy. *Jewelry by Southwest American Indians: Evolving Designs.* West Chester, Pa.: Schiffer Publishing, 1990.

Sotheby Parke Bernet and Harmer Johnson. *The C. G. Wallace Collection of American Indian Art.* New York: 1976.

Turnbaugh, William A., and Sarah Peabody Turnbaugh. *Indian Jewelry of the American Southwest.* West Chester, Pa.: Schiffer Publishing, 1988.

Wright, Barton. *Hallmarks of the Southwest.* West Chester, Pa.: Schiffer Publishing, 1989.

Wright, Margaret Nickelson. *Hopi Silver.* Flagstaff, Ariz.: Northland Press, 1982.

KACHINAS

Bassman, Theda. *Hopi Kachina Dolls and Their Carvers.* West Chester, Pa.: Schiffer Publishing, 1991.

Colton, Harold. *Hopi Kachina Dolls, with a Key to Their Identification.* Albuquerque: University of New Mexico Press, 1949.

Dockstader, Frederick J. *The Kachina and the White Man: The Influences of White Culture on the Hopi Kachina Cult.* Albuquerque:

University of New Mexico Press, 1985.

Haberland, Wolfgang. *Kachina-Figuren der Pueblo-Indianer Nordamerikas aus der Studiensammlung Horst Antes.* Karlsruhe: Badisches Landesmuseum, 1980.

Hartmann, Horst. *Kachina-Figuren der Hopi Indianer.* Berlin: Museum für Völkderkunde, 1978.

Wright, Barton. *Hopi Kachinas: The Complete Guide to Collecting Kachina Dolls.* Flagstaff, Ariz.: Northland Press, 1977.

————. *Kachinas of the Zuni.* Flagstaff, Ariz.: Northland Press with the Southwest Museum, 1985.

POTTERY

Allen, Laura Graves. *Contemporary Hopi Pottery.* Flagstaff: Museum of Northern Arizona, 1984.

Batkin, Jonathan. *Pottery of the Pueblos of New Mexico, 1700–1940.* Colorado Springs: Colorado Springs Fine Arts Center, 1987.

Brody, J. J. *Beauty from the Earth: Pueblo Indian Pottery from the University Museum of Archaeology and Anthropology.* Philadelphia: University Museum of Archaeology and Anthropology, 1990.

Brody, J. J., and Steven A. LeBlanc, eds. *Mimbres Pottery: Ancient Art of the American Southwest.* New York: Hudson Hills Press, 1983.

Dittert, Alfred E., Jr., and Fred Plog. *Generations in Clay: Pueblo Pottery of the American Southwest.* Flagstaff, Ariz.: Northland Press, 1980.

Frank, Larry, and Francis H. Harlow. *Historic Pottery of the Pueblo Indians, 1600–1880.* Boston: New York Graphic Society, 1974.

Harlow, Francis H. *Matte-paint Pottery of the Tews, Keres and Zuni Pueblos.* Santa Fe: Museum of New Mexico Press, 1973.

————. *Modern Pueblo Pottery, 1880–1960.* Flagstaff, Ariz.: Northland Press, 1977.

————. *Two Hundred Years of Historic Pueblo Pottery: The Gallegos Collection.* Santa Fe: Morning Star Gallery, 1990.

LeFree, Betty. *Santa Clara Pottery Today.* Albuquerque: University of New Mexico Press, 1975.

Lister, Robert H., and Florence C. Lister. *Anasazi Pottery: Ten Centuries of Prehistoric Ceramic Art in the Four Corners Country of the Southwestern United States.* Albuquerque: Maxwell Museum of Anthropology and

University of New Mexico Press, 1978.

Maxwell Museum of Anthropology. *Seven Families in Pueblo Pottery.* Albuquerque: University of New Mexico Press, 1974.

Peckham, Stewart. *From This Earth: The Ancient Art of Pueblo Pottery.* Santa Fe: Museum of New Mexico Press, 1990.

Rodee, Marian, and James Ostler. *Zuni Pottery.* West Chester, Pa.: Schiffer Publishing, 1986.

Spivey, Richard L. *Maria.* Flagstaff, Ariz.: Northland Press, 1979.

WEAVING

Berlant, Anthony, and Mary Hunt Kahlenberg. *Walk in Beauty.* Boston: New York Graphic Society, 1977.

Blomberg, Nancy J. *Navajo Textiles: The William Randolph Hearst Collection.* Tucson: University of Arizona Press, 1988.

Campbell, Tyrone, and Joel and Kate Kopp. *Navajo Pictorial Weaving 1880–1950: Folk Art Images of Native Americans.* New York: Dutton Studio Books, 1991.

Fisher, Nora. *Spanish Textile Tradition of New Mexico and Colorado.* Santa Fe: Museum of New Mexico Press, 1979.

James, H. L. *Rugs and Posts: The Story of Navajo Weaving and Indian Trading.* West Chester, Pa.: Schiffer Publishing, 1988.

Jeter, James, and Paula Marie Juelke. *The Saltillo Serape.* Santa Barbara, Calif.: Santa Barbara Museum of Art, 1978.

Kahlenberg, Mary Hunt. *The Navajo Blanket.* New York: Praeger Publishers in association with the Los Angeles County Museum of Art, 1972.

Kaufman, Alice, and Christopher Selser. *The Navajo Weaving Tradition: 1650 to the Present.* New York: E. P. Dutton, 1985.

Kent, Kate Peck. *Pueblo Indian Textiles: A Living Tradition.* Santa Fe: School of American Research Press, 1983.

————. *Navajo Weaving: Three Centuries of Change.* Santa Fe: School of American Research Press, 1985.

Mera, H. P. *Spanish-American Blanketry.* Santa Fe: School of American Research Press, 1987.

Mera, H. P., and Joe Ben Wheat. *The Alfred I. Barton Collection of Southwestern Textiles.* Coral Gables, Fla.: Lowe Art Museum, 1978.

Rodee, Marian E. *Weaving of the Southwest.* West Chester, Pa.: Schiffer Publishing, 1987.

Northeast

Brasser, Ted J. *"Bo'jou, Neejee!": Profiles of Canadian Indian Art.* Ottawa: National Museum of Man, 1976.

Fenton, William N. *The False Faces of the Iroquois.* Norman: University of Oklahoma Press, 1987.

Flint Institute of Arts. *The Art of the Great Lakes Indians.* Flint, Mich., 1973.

King, J.C.H. *Thunderbird and Lightning: Indian Life in Northeastern North America 1600–1900.* London: British Museum, 1982.

Penney, David W., ed. *Great Lakes Indian Art.* Detroit: Wayne State University Press and the Detroit Institute of Arts, 1989.

Phillips, Ruth B. *Patterns of Power: The Jasper Grant Collection and Great Lakes Indian Art of the Early Nineteenth Century.* Kleinburg, Ontario: McMichael Canadian Collection, 1984.

Torrence, Gaylord, and Robert Hobbs. *Art of the Red Earth People: The Mesquakie of Iowa.* Iowa City: University of Iowa Museum of Art, 1989.

Eastern Prehistoric

Brose, David S., James A. Brown, and David W. Penney. *Ancient Art of the American Woodland Indians.* New York: Harry N. Abrams in association with the Detroit Institute of Arts, 1985.

Burnett, E. K., and Forrest E. Clements. *The Spiro Mound Collection in the Museum* and *Historical Sketch of the Spiro Mound.* Contributions from the Museum of the American Indian, Heye Foundation, Vol. 14. New York: Museum of the American Indian, 1945.

Dickens, Roy S., Jr. *Of Sky and Earth: Art of the Early Southeastern Indians.* Atlanta: High Museum of Art, 1982.

Fundaburk, Emma Lila, and Mary Douglass Fundaburk Foreman, eds. *Sun Circles and Human Hands, The Southeastern Indians—Art and Industries.* Luverne, Ala., 1957.

Hathcock, Roy. *The Quapaw and Their Pottery.* Camden, Ark.: Hurley Press, 1983.

————. *Ancient Indian Pottery of the Mississippi River Valley.* Marceline, Miss.: Walsworth Publishing Company, 1988.

Knoblock, Byron W. *Bannerstones of the North American Indian.* LaGrange, Ill., 1939.

Townsend, Earl G. *Birdstones of the North American Indian.* Indianapolis, 1959.

Index

239